URBAN REFUGEES AND DIGITAL TECHNOLOGY

MCGILL-QUEEN'S REFUGEE AND FORCED MIGRATION STUDIES

Series editors: Megan Bradley and James Milner

Forced migration is a local, national, regional, and global challenge with profound political and social implications. Understanding the causes and consequences of, and possible responses to, forced migration requires careful analysis from a range of disciplinary perspectives, as well as interdisciplinary dialogue.

The purpose of the McGill-Queen's Refugee and Forced Migration Studies series is to advance in-depth examination of diverse forms, dimensions, and experiences of displacement, including in the context of conflict and violence, repression and persecution, and disasters and environmental change. The series will explore responses to refugees, internal displacement, and other forms of forced migration to illuminate the dynamics surrounding forced migration in global, national, and local contexts, including Canada, the perspectives of displaced individuals and communities, and the connections to broader patterns of human mobility. Featuring research from fields including politics, international relations, law, anthropology, sociology, geography, and history, the series highlights new and critical areas of enquiry within the field, especially conversations across disciplines and from the perspective of researchers in the global South, where the majority of forced migration unfolds. The series benefits from an international advisory board made up of leading scholars in refugee and forced migration studies.

7 Finding Safe Harbour
Supporting the Integration of Refugee Youth
Emily Pelley

8 Documenting Displacement
Questioning Methodological Boundaries in Forced Migration Research
Edited by Katarzyna Grabska and Christina R. Clark-Kazak

9 Voluntary and Forced Migration in Latin America
Law and Policy Reforms
Edited by Natalia Caicedo Camacho and Luisa Feline Freier

10 The Right to Research
Historical Narratives by Refugee and Global South Researchers
Edited by Kate Reed and Marcia C. Schenck

11 Kingdom of Barracks
Polish Displaced Persons in Allied-Occupied Germany and Austria
Katarzyna Nowak

12 Urban Refugees and Digital Technology
Reshaping Social, Political, and Economic Networks
Charles Martin-Shields

Urban Refugees and Digital Technology

Reshaping Social, Political, and Economic Networks

CHARLES MARTIN-SHIELDS

McGill-Queen's University Press
Montreal & Kingston • London • Chicago

© McGill-Queen's University Press 2024

ISBN 978-0-2280-2051-6 (cloth)
ISBN 978-0-2280-2052-3 (paper)
ISBN 978-0-2280-2053-0 (ePDF)
ISBN 978-0-2280-2054-7 (ePUB)
ISBN 978-0-2280-2055-4 (OA)

Legal deposit first quarter 2024
Bibliothèque nationale du Québec

Printed in Canada on acid-free paper that is 100% ancient forest free (100% post-consumer recycled), processed chlorine free

McGill-Queen's University Press in Montreal is on land which long served as a site of meeting and exchange amongst Indigenous Peoples, including the Haudenosaunee and Anishinabeg nations. In Kingston it is situated on the territory of the Haudenosaunee and Anishinaabek. We acknowledge and thank the diverse Indigenous Peoples whose footsteps have marked these territories on which peoples of the world now gather.

Library and Archives Canada Cataloguing in Publication

Title: Urban refugees and digital technology : reshaping social, political, and economic networks / Charles Martin-Shields.
Names: Martin-Shields, Charles P., author.
Series: McGill-Queen's refugee and forced migration studies ; 12.
Description: Series statement: McGill-Queen's refugee and forced migration studies ; 12 | Includes bibliographical references and index.
Identifiers: Canadiana (print) 20230529763 | Canadiana (ebook) 20230529895 | ISBN 9780228020516 (cloth) | ISBN 9780228020523 (paper) | ISBN 9780228020530 (ePDF) | ISBN 9780228020547 (ePUB) | ISBN 9780228020554 (OA)
Subjects: LCSH: Refugees—Colombia—Bogotá—Case studies. | LCSH: Refugees—Kenya—Nairobi—Case studies. | LCSH: Refugees—Malaysia—Kuala Lumpur—Case studies. | LCSH: Technology—Social aspects—Colombia—Bogotá—Case studies. | LCSH: Technology—Social aspects—Kenya—Nairobi—Case studies. | LCSH: Technology—Social aspects—Malaysia—Kuala Lumpur—Case studies.
Classification: LCC HV640 .M35 2024 | DDC 305.9/06914—dc23

This book was typeset by True to Type in 10½/13 Sabon

Contents

Tables and Figures   vii
Preface   ix
Acknowledgments   xv

PART ONE   CONCEPTUALIZING TECHNOLOGY AND URBAN DISPLACEMENT IN THEORY AND HISTORY

1 Urban Refugees in a Digital World   3
2 The Urban Context: Where Displacement and Digitalization Meet   25
3 Technological Change, New Displacement Patterns, and Urbanization   44
4 Digitalization and Urban Administration: Evolutions of Surveillance   65

PART TWO   CONTEMPORARY CASE STUDIES AND THE DIGITAL FUTURE OF URBAN DISPLACEMENT

5 Methods in the Contemporary Context: Case Studies and Data Collection   85
6 Bogotá: ICT Access in the Neighbourhood   99
7 Kuala Lumpur: Time, Distance, and Legal Exclusion   120
8 Nairobi: Shifting Politics in a Digital Metropolis   141
9 Digitalization and Urban Displacement: Future Scenarios   160
10 The Future: Digitalization, Displacement, and New Urban Societies   181

Notes   191
References   195
Index   213

Tables and Figures

TABLES

5.1 Comparative factors between cities   90
6.1 Mobile download and upload speeds using 3G roaming services across neighbourhoods in Bogotá   107

FIGURES

2.1 Scenarios for digital technological change and urban migration in developing countries   38
6.1 Fixed broadband versus mobile cellular subscriptions per 100 inhabitants in Colombia   105
6.2 Percentage of population accessing the internet by gender in Colombia   106
6.3 Approximations of where data were collected in Bogotá   111
7.1 Fixed broadband vs mobile cellular subscriptions per 100 inhabitants in Malaysia   127
7.2 Approximations of where data were collected in Kuala Lumpur   131
8.1 Fixed broadband versus mobile cellular subscriptions per 100 inhabitants in Kenya   148

Preface

Understanding the relationship between technology, urban displacement, and the development arc of host cities is going to be a critical endeavour as we move into a world that is becoming more and more mobile and urban. The primary goal of this book is to show how digital technological change is influencing how urban refugees arrive in and affect the development of cities like Bogotá, Kuala Lumpur, and Nairobi. To that end, the history of urban displacement will help put into perspective how technology and urban demographic change have taken place in response to each other over time. To understand how urbanization, technology, and displacement shaped metropolises like London and New York, as well as cities in the American Steel Belt, I draw on the history of the Industrial Revolution, the Great Migration from Europe to the United States, and the Great Migration of Black Americans from the southern states to the northern cities. Many urban refugees in today's middle-income countries are moving between cities and countries with varying levels of "legality," just as, in the past, many urban displaced people were seeking economic opportunity and simultaneously fleeing famine, political exclusion, and war. Like the urban refugees and displaced people whose contemporary stories this book captures, urban displaced people in previous centuries may have arrived with formal identity documentation and suitcases, or with nothing.

Cities present the context in which technological change, administrative oversight, and urban displacement come together. Just as technological and administrative change affected urbanization and the growth of cities like Manchester and New York City, digitalization as an economic, political, and social phenomenon will create path dependencies that will serve and shape how wealth, power, and identity manifest themselves in rapidly growing metropolises in the Global South. Urban displacement and technological change have an entwined history, and the twenty-first century presents an opportunity to evaluate how cities like Bogotá, Kuala Lumpur, and Nairobi will grow economically, socially, and physically in the digital era. Using historical analysis and new empirical data, this book lays out new theoretical directions for understanding how the growth trajectories of metropolises in the Global South will converge and diverge from those of their legacy peers in Europe and North America.

This book started out asking a far narrower question – do urban refugees in developing countries use digital technologies to meet their economic, social, and political needs? My colleague Constantin Ruhe, a professor at Goethe University Frankfurt, and I were discussing how to research this topic in 2017 when he shared an anecdote with me about how internet access is distributed in urban spaces. He described to me how, during the peak of the Syrian refugee crisis, he could see the entrance to the local MediaMarkt, a German electronics chain store, from his apartment in Konstanz, Germany. He noticed that on Sunday mornings, large numbers of refugees would gather in front of that store, which seemed strange to him, since it was closed and there are nicer places in Konstanz to gather socially. As he observed this, he noticed that everyone had a phone out – they were using the public wifi, which stayed on during the weekends, to talk to their loved ones at home. This anecdote was surprisingly affecting; it seems that urban spaces have all kinds of idiosyncratic attributes that can be used in ways planners and policy-makers had not thought of. Indeed, the banality of a MediaMarkt entrance juxtaposed with the intimacy of hearing a family member's voice was to me a perfect example of urban refugees' adaptation to the digital urban landscape. As I thought about this more, questions arose: How does being a refugee in a city affect access to and use of digital technology? Does digital technology make cities of arrival more economically, socially, and politically legible to migrants? At a macro level, how will increasing digitalization change the development trajectories of cities of refugee arrival?

Refugees' adaptation to cities' idiosyncratic features often comes about because of political hostility toward asylum seekers. Municipalities and national governments have the capacity to provide access to digital services for refugees, but many do not. There are examples of cities that provide digital services to refugees, like Wellington, New

Zealand; some are even in the United States. However, where there is a lack of services, including access to the internet, it is often by design – to create a "hostile environment," as the United Kingdom's Home Office has done with regard to migrants and asylum seekers. That is why it is important to bear in mind that when refugees find innovative ways to use the digital environment around them, it is often not a "good news" story. Too often, it is a reflection of what people are forced to do where the politics of exclusion predominate. At a micro level, it is good that people can stay in regular contact with loved ones using tools like WhatsApp, Facebook, and SMS text messages. At a macro level, it reflects a failure of politics that the most vulnerable among us have to stand outside a chain store hoping to tap its wifi so that they can log onto these apps.

I was motivated to write this book by the dichotomy between the promise of technology and the realities of politics, and what this means for urban development in the low- and middle-income countries of the Global South. The urban refugees who were interviewed and surveyed were mostly poor and often lived in vulnerable circumstances. International organizations, NGOs, and technologists who support urban refugees have worked hard to integrate the promise of digital technology into their work. However, the relationship between technological change and demographic change is infused with the prevailing political realities regarding who is a "good" refugee or migrant. As a migrant myself, I am routinely reminded of this – I have a US passport, a "high-skill" European Union work permit, and all the supporting institutional capacity that comes with that. If I want to get a new SIM card for my mobile phone, I go to the T-Mobil store with my passport and German ID card and walk out a few minutes later with a connection to the internet. When I need health care, I just go to the doctor with my biometric insurance card; when we registered the birth of our child, my identity and the associated paperwork were all accepted without question. Because I am a "good" migrant, technological change often makes everything that already works for me work better.

Juxtapose this with the life of an urban refugee or forcibly displaced person who has moved to a new city. This person may not have formal identification, which most countries require for getting a SIM card, so just getting online is difficult. Because of their refugee status, access to jobs, public health care, and education may be impossible. In such an environment, what development and humanitarian professionals call "innovation" risks merely being the use of technology to paper over and work around politically motivated decisions to make everything hard for refugees. Until we understand how technology fits into the daily lives of refugees, and learn from their perspective, we cannot easily know whether a new app or website serves any purpose for them. If it serves no purpose, then is it a good use of resources for international organizations and NGOs to develop a new digital tool?

I contend that it can indeed be a good use of resources to develop a digital tool *if we understand its purpose in the lived experience of the refugee.* To achieve that understanding, we need not only refugees' perspectives but also a perspective on the politics of technology and technological change. When we look back on the history of urbanization and technological change, it becomes clear that enabling urban displaced people to get a share of the benefits of technological change has been a deeply political process. Textile mills, steelworks, and factories all involved technological change that drew people to cities, but for urban displaced people in the nineteenth and early twentieth centuries, contentious and often violent labour politics were required to gain a share of the benefits these technologies delivered. For twenty-first-century urban refugees in growing middle-income cities, digital identity, online records management, and the gig economy offer opportunities to try to build a life, but ensuring that these technologies are economically, socially, and legally meaningful requires strong engagement in contentious politics.

This confluence of urban displacement, digitalization, and politics will change the ways that cities in developing countries grow economically and socially. Many of the theories from the twentieth century that explain urbanization and urban displacement and migration are rooted in industrial practices and political economies where manufacturing was a precondition for growth and drew in displaced people. Labour movements and the politics of economic inclusion were indirect outcomes of changes in industrial technology that required urban workers to be together at work and live close together in working-class neighborhoods. These physical spaces were breeding grounds for contention, places where the politics of urban development were shaped in such a way that displaced people could eventually force their own inclusion. At the same time, the administration of urban displacement was far more limited in scope – the practice of counting and managing migrants only started in the late nineteenth century, before expanding in technical and legal scope in the mid- to late twentieth century. In the twenty-first century, cities in the Global South are experiencing growth in an era when industrial practices are less centralized and more digitized. Today, due to technological and political changes, the perennial ingredients for economic growth are less relevant or available to the rapidly expanding cities of middle-income countries.

Urban displacement and technological change in growing cities are complex topics to grapple with, and identifying new trends in how these phenomena interact requires mixed methods, including a storytelling approach that cuts across disciplinary boundaries. I use a mix of historical, quantitative, and qualitative methods to identify new ways that digitalization will influence the ways that urban refugees will help shape the growth and development of cities in developing countries. Technology has often played a role in demographic change, and the human stories embedded in that change give life to the statistics and structured interviews that are the backbone of this book's case studies. The cities where the data were collected are also alive in their own ways; how they have grown (and are still growing) is as important to document as the results of the formal field research. The cities themselves, as hubs of industrial, social, and political history, provide the medium through which digitalization manifests itself in the lives of urban migrants. Beyond building theory, I am seeking to tell a story that has practical value for policy-makers and that brings current trends in migration and technological change to life for a general readership.

Twenty-first-century urban displacement can seem "new" in the eyes of technocratically focused development practitioners – indeed, development practices tend to treat the current state of rich world metropolises as a template to be replicated through technological means (Fuseini and Kemp 2015; Parnell and Robinson 2006). The historical overview I present in this book will help identify what is truly new in the digital world by integrating past experiences of technological change, urban displacement, and city planning. Historical reflection can also help mitigate the sensationalism around current refugee and migration debates, reminding us that indeed, we have been here before – it may have looked different two hundred years ago, but the fundamentals that drive people to migrate, and the technologies that facilitate these often rapid and unsettling social changes, are part of the broader human experience. Digitalization is indeed changing many things around us, but these changes, and the political and social responses they elicit, are things we have weathered before. Knowing this makes it easier to delve into the changes we are bound to see in the twenty-first century and to use empirical social science to make sense of them.

My goal in writing this book is of course to learn more about the ways that urban displacement and digitalization will affect the development trajectories of cities in the Global South. In drawing on the history of European and American urbanization and displacement, I also hope that this book will make it possible for people in cities everywhere to see new ways to engage in the politics of technological change. Digitalization offers a chance to revitalize urban society, to maintain translocal networks, and to develop new models of urban society. I hope that readers, by looking through the eyes of today's urban refugees, and by heeding history's reminders of how we can have cities that are good for everyone, will come away from this book with a sense of optimism for a future in which digitalization will make it possible for urban refugees and their host-community neighbours to seek opportunity in inclusive, vibrant cities.

Acknowledgments

This book was a five-year adventure to complete. When I conducted the first round of fieldwork in Bogotá in 2018, I did not have much of a vision beyond doing an interesting case study and turning it into an article. By the time I was doing fieldwork in Nairobi in early 2019, the idea for this book had started to form; by the end of that year, I was fortunate to have the resources available to do the rest of the data collection in Kuala Lumpur. This book is the outcome of noticing a number of threads connecting different fieldwork locations, as well as participating in different collaborative articles that came out in 2021 and 2022.

This book would not exist without the help of so many people at every step in the process. A book needs an editor, and Richard Baggaley at McGill-Queen's University Press has been great to work with. In academic writing, it is easy to get bogged down in minutiae, and Richard looked at early drafts and encouraged me to just tell the story. This was at a time when I was deeply involved in some thorny revise and resubmit processes, and it made a huge difference that he encouraged me to just *write*. Good writing is the outcome of a lot of feedback, and I had some great people supporting me in this. Lisa Marie Clifford, Thomas Flores, Jörn Grävingholt, Angieszka Paczynska, David Perry, and Mirja Schoderer all provided great insights and ideas for improving my book proposal and draft chapters, and provided encouragement while I was searching for a press. Evan Easton-Calabria and Judith Kohlenberger provided helpful advice and encouragement as I completed the manuscript and prepared it for review. Special thanks as well to Tabea Bork-Hüffer and Simon Peth at the University of Innsbruck, who invited me to give a seminar on the project in 2020; that seminar provided insightful feedback that helped me keep the writing momentum up during the pandemic. Many thanks as well to Julia Leininger, the head of my department, who was always there to help me find the resources as well as the time to make this book happen.

There are three case studies in this book. Many colleagues were involved in the collaborative effort of gathering data, writing papers, and managing the bureaucracy of getting resources in place. In Colombia, I worked with Sonia Camacho, Constantin Ruhe, and Rodrigo Taborda on the data collection, and later on an article about e-government in the lives of displaced people. Christian von Haldenwang, Robert Karl, and Xenia Grecia provided expertise and guidance while I was working on the Colombia case (Chapter 6). The data collection in Kenya was done with Jana Kuhnt, Abel Oyuke, Samuel Balongo, and the best post-graduate team I could have hoped for: Mirko Eppler, Stella Gaetani, Francy Köllner, Nyat Mebrahtu, Antonia Peters, and Carlotta Preiss. In Kuala Lumpur I worked with Katrina Munir-Asen to collect the interview data; she also provided amazing insights about the city itself and her experiences working for the UNHCR office there.

The infrastructure for doing this kind of research is significant, and local partners were key to doing the work safely and collaboratively. The team at IPSOS Colombia were always ready to find a sampling solution in a challenging environment, and they made it possible to collect a unique dataset in parts of Bogotá that otherwise would have been inaccessible. In Nairobi, Henry Nyanaro and Lucy Kiama at HIAS Kenya helped set up interviews and make sure that ethical and safety standards were in place during interviews and survey work. Abel Oyuke and Samuel Balongo's team of enumerators in Nairobi were also fantastic, collecting data arranging interviews in challenging conditions that required sensitivity and care. In Malaysia, the national UNHCR office was incredibly supportive of our work, helping us connect with refugee-led organizations and opening as many doors for us as possible. James Bawi Thang Bik, who represents the Alliance of Chin Refugees in Malaysia, provided a unique perspective on the challenges that come with being a refugee in Kuala Lumpur and the type of work that goes into leading a refugee-led organization in Malaysia. There were many other people in Bogotá, Kuala Lumpur, and Nairobi who made this all possible; drivers, good-humoured public servants, GIZ staff, and endlessly patient officials at the various agencies that grant research permits.

Of course books take time, including lots of travel for fieldwork, so I want to thank my wife Anne for supporting me throughout this process. My parents Walter and Victoria also played their part, reading sections and copy editing what I churned out. Finally, I remain deeply grateful to the refugees who shared their stories and their time: I hope this book does justice to their experiences and knowledge and, in its own small way, helps chart a path to a more inclusive world.

Support for the open-access edition of this book was provided by the German Institute of Development and Sustainability (IDOS).

PART ONE

Conceptualizing Technology and Urban Displacement in Theory and History

1

Urban Refugees in a Digital World

Arduous journeys to new cities in search of safety or economic opportunity are an enduring part of the human experience. These journeys are often undertaken with limited resources, and the decision to move is often made in desperate circumstances. Sometimes these circumstances are political, other times they are economic, and often they follow a disaster or violent conflict. In the background of all this human movement is technological change, which affects how urban refugees interact with administrative, social, and economic systems. Digitalization, which encompasses expanded access to computers, smartphones, and the internet, is changing the social, political, and economic fabric of cities in ways that demand a re-evaluation of how we understand urban refugees' roles in the economic growth and social cohesion of cities of arrival.

Throughout history, the people making these journeys have done so under different migration and citizenship regimes; even so, we can find similarities across the centuries. Displacement from rural to urban settings was part of the experience of landless Britons during the First Industrial Revolution, and in the nineteenth century, Europeans left for the United States seeking economic opportunity as well as refuge from political and environmental tumult. In the twentieth century, Black Americans moved from the South to the North to escape political terrorism and economic exclusion as well as to embrace the political and economic possibilities offered by northern cities. Cities have always been the places where people arrived and where opportunities for work and community were available; they are also where displaced people organized themselves, shaped politics, and fomented social change. Technology has been and still is a social and economic infrastructure that shapes the scale and scope, as well at the praxis, of how urban displaced people engage with the politics, economies, and social networks in cities of arrival. Given how I will be using historical and contemporary examples in this book, set in different legal and political environments, later in this chapter I discuss how I will be using the terms "urban displacement," "urban refugee," and "urban displaced people."

Technologized processes of social, political, and economic change led by urban displaced people can happen on a large scale, as evidenced by the 1909 Shirtwaist Strike, so-called because it was organized by garment industry workers – at the time, a "shirtwaist" was what we now call a "blouse." Many of these workers were urban displaced people who had arrived from Europe, often to escape violence and political persecution. As recounted by one of the strikers, Theresa Serber Malkiel (1910), 20,000 female garment workers employed in New York's blouse manufacturing industry went on strike against working conditions. The majority were Ashkenazi Jews who had fled pogroms in Eastern Europe. In New York City they faced down violence and threats from strikebreakers and police to force factory owners to renegotiate their contracts. Their success had a lasting impact on organized labour in the American garment industry.

Urban refugees in today's growing cities, many of whom have fled violence or unrest to seek opportunity in cities of arrival, are steadily shaping the communities that host them. However, technological change and digitalization have significantly altered in both scale and scope how urban refugees are shaping the cities they arrive in. During interviews with Somali urban refugees in Kuala Lumpur, I spoke with a young man who had been a baker before moving to Malaysia. He told me how sad he was to leave behind his bakery in Mogadishu and then took me on a tour of the bakery he had set up in the Somali community centre in the Gombak neighbourhood of Kuala Lumpur. He had acquired a set of industrial ovens, employed young Somalis in the neighbourhood, provided bread for stores in the city's Gombak district, and planned to launch a YouTube channel. The YouTube channel piqued my interest, and he explained that many Somalis watch YouTube, and that he wanted to use the channel to guide other urban refugees through the process of setting up a bakery. He loved baking, and digitalization provided him an outlet for sharing that with others, even as circumstances had pushed him far from home.

The Shirtwaist strikers and this baker from Somalia seem at first glance to be radically different people doing radically different things. I would argue, though, that they are doing similar things mediated by very different urban technology infrastructures. Both are trying to shape their work and social environments while navigating urban social life as displaced people. The technologies of production in the garment industry in New York City meant that tens of thousands of women worked close together in factories and sweatshops, and the physical proximity of those labour spaces made large-scale organizing possible. In contrast, the baker in Kuala Lumpur works in a space where digital technology magnifies his individual work. He may not be organizing large-scale labour strikes on YouTube, but his channel can be viewed globally and may help other bakers elsewhere in the city, or in other countries, set up their own businesses.

Writing a book about digitalization and urban migration is as much about engaging with the public and political debate on migration as it is about engaging with the academic discourse on the topic. Technological change played a role in migration patterns long before the digital era. While we may not have named or given causal association to technological change and displacement in historical contexts, changes in industrial production and the development of analogue surveillance technology are indeed examples of how technological change has influenced urban displacement. At the macro level, the First Industrial Revolution with its technological changes in production created a demand for urban labour in Europe and the United States – an example that demonstrates how discussions of technological change that treat the digital era as "new" risk failing to learn from processes that have been with us since the late eighteenth century. Industrial technological change and the technologization of consumer and manufactured goods had a significant impact on migration patterns throughout the nineteenth and twentieth centuries. This was not limited to industrial change: at a micro level, the ways we communicate, share knowledge, and transfer money influence patterns of displacement and settlement. Wire services have facilitated the sharing of money and ideas across geographic space, and advances in communication technology make it possible for migrants to maintain translocal social and economic ties. The digital era is marked by micro-level technologies that facilitate financial and social networks, but this does not mean that macro-level technological change has stopped being part of the process whereby urban refugees settle into cities of arrival. Supplanting the macro influence of industrial technology is the technology of surveillance and administration, as digital processes make it easier to manage people and space at scale.

Furthermore, digital technological change in the lives of urban refugees is not just a theoretical or conceptual sociological issue. The UN High Commissioner for Refugees (UNHCR), the International Organization for Migration (IOM), and the donor countries of the Organisation for Economic Co-operation and Development (OECD) are directing resources toward refugee management, and these political and administrative actors have shown a significant interest in the role of digitalization and new technologies in supporting refugee livelihoods. However, the historical perspective on technological change and displacement and the role of technology in public administration is often missing from the policy discourse. There is a tendency to think of the digital era in ontological terms, excluding by omission or commission the epistemological aspects of how technology influenced previous eras of urban displacement.[1] In the popular and policy discourse, modern urban displacement in developing countries has become something that "happens" in Africa, Latin America, or Southeast Asia. It is framed as a "new" phenomenon, albeit happening in volumes never seen before, and as a problem to be solved by "development," with expertise and resources coming largely from North America and Europe.[2] Public fear of refugees, a desire to "fix" the drivers of modern displacement, and historical amnesia regarding the West's relatively recent experience of multiple periods of large-scale forced displacement have combined to create a toxic dynamic between donor countries in the Global North and partner countries in the Global South. We cannot understand how digital technological change will affect future urban displacement unless we make the history of technological change and urbanization in the Global North part of the discussion.

To help bridge the historical arc of urban displacement and the geographic North/South divide, this book will draw on Langdon Winner's (1980) concept of technological artifacts "having politics." Society chooses technologies to meet collective needs based on political decision-making, and when these technologies operate in a society, they feed back into political processes. This is especially true in the context of international urban refugee policy. Host country governments and humanitarian agencies, for example, want to provide support to people, many of whom require some form of identity and registration. Sharing information, managing documents, organizing appointments – all of this can be done, or is being done, by agencies that work with refugees. Donor countries, largely in the Global North, want this identity data as well – after all, it plays a key role in controlling who comes and goes, thus reinforcing borders and surveillance; it also serves as evidence when adjudicating who receives refugee status. In both the Global North and the Global South, registration, identity, and administrative legibility go hand in hand with urban refugees' access to jobs, financial services, and social benefits. What makes digital administrative technology so pervasive is that the infrastructure is not simply built on enterprise-level computing apparatuses; it also uses private and individual sources of data to track and identify people. Administration is a "technology" unto itself, and the digitization of the means to administer a population influences urban refugees' economic and social behaviour in ways that are different from what urban displaced people experienced in the nineteenth and twentieth centuries.

DIGITAL URBAN SOCIETY: WHAT DOES TWENTY-FIRST-CENTURY TECHNOLOGICAL CHANGE MEAN FOR GROWING CITIES?

I propose two axes for evaluating digital technological change in contemporary urban refugees' lives: one axis is job-affecting, and the other is network/surveillance-affecting. These can take place simultaneously and even beneficially interact with each other. While urban displacement and digitalization are separate policy fields with their own cones of experts and international, national, and multilateral policy processes, these two fields touch on different levels. Indeed, there are hundreds of examples of how humanitarian and development aid actors integrate digitalization into displacement and refugee policy. So why do I focus on only job-affecting and networking/surveillance-affecting axes? Historically, rapid technological change during the eighteenth and nineteenth centuries reshaped urban labour structures, consolidating large volumes of workers in cities. These new urban populations generated demand for city administrators to collect demographic and health data in order to make rapidly expanding cities legible to the state. In the 230 or so years since then, work and surveillance have become intertwined, and the balance of digital technology's effect on jobs and surveillance serves as a starting point for understanding the complexities of how urban refugees are shaping contemporary cities of arrival.

Through the historical analysis and contemporary case studies featured in this book, I will use these root axes to show how the historical balance of technologized jobs and surveillance has evolved into the contemporary development and humanitarian programming directed toward urban refugees. For example, development economists and policy-makers examining the future of work focus on how digitalization creates new low- to medium-skill jobs in the gig economy for urban refugees. Humanitarian agencies are using mobile phone–based digital platforms for cash transfers to refugees and displaced people and digital identification technologies to provide people with IDs.

Over the past twenty years, telecommunications technology has spread rapidly, bringing internet connectivity to regions where access up to the mid-2000s was based on the availability of limited cable infrastructure. The same countries that are rapidly digitizing are also experiencing urbanization driven by internal and cross-border displacement. In the popular imagination, we see images of vast slums surrounding formal city cores in Africa, Southeast Asia, and Latin America, and we see displacement presented as a uniquely twenty-first-century challenge. From an urban displacement perspective, this raises an important question: how will cities in middle-income countries cope with the inflow of people, and what will be the political, economic, and social trajectories of these cities? The urban displacement phenomenon itself is not new; cities like Manchester and New York City were not populated through technocratic processes of skill sorting, and indeed had large informal settlements and slums where new arrivals often lived. What *is* new is a rapidly changing digital technology environment and a diminishing role for urban industry, which creates scenarios that are not well described by twentieth-century economic theories of urban migration that focus on job seeking.

Through the lens of modern narratives about cities and economic development, what does twenty-first-century urbanization look like? At one level, it can look quite scary. David Kilcullen (2013) paints a bleak picture of urbanization in which violent conflict and crime converge in spaces where people's needs cannot be met by dwindling resources and where social cohesion is frayed by increased digital connectivity. When we delete urban warfare from Kilcullen's narrative, Mike Davis's (2006) *Planet of Slums* is not significantly different in its outlook. Davis examines urbanization disconnected from growth or labour opportunity – masses of people living in dire conditions with no economic prospects, excluded from modern growth, and the social and political instability that comes with such conditions. However, cities are not all doom and gloom. In Jane Jacobs's (1961) book on the rise of fall of American cities we see how neighbourhoods that are effectively slums can rejuvenate themselves and thrive without external planning and finance. Indeed, the American theories of urban planning and investment in the 1950s and early 1960s, which often mixed technocratic planning, racism, and classism,[3] were antithetical to supporting healthy cities. Doug Saunders (2010) builds on this analysis, looking deeply at how urban migration in modern developing metropolises creates the space for people to take risks, seize opportunities, and build new lives. This reflects Saskia Sassen's (2001) analysis of how New York, London, and Tokyo became centres of global culture and capital. Over time, transnational and cross-border networks of people and institutions consolidated capital and financial networks. We can already see this type of translocal consolidation taking shape in Somali neighbourhoods like Eastleigh in Nairobi and Gombak in Kuala Lumpur – culture, capital, and social networks within the Somali diaspora support the growth of cities of arrival, expanding those cities' global economic and political footprints. When looking at the same cities and slums, Kilcullen, Davis, and Saunders see radically different social and political potentials. Technological change and increasing digitalization play a strong role in shaping these potentials, from the individual up to the systemic level.

To corral all of this I will be taking an Engaged Theory approach (Steger and James 2019), using historical, qualitative, and quantitative data to identify patterns regarding how urban refugees in middle-income metropolises use digital technologies and how digital technologies in turn affect their lives. Engaged Theory starts with the assumption that theory building is not an unbiased process – we seek out data based on presumptions about which stories and phenomena are valuable, then interpret those data based on our perceptions of the world around us. Development practitioners and policy-makers hope to leverage technological change and digitalization with the goal of creating healthy cities in which urban refugees can integrate and contribute, and to develop new theoretical assumptions about how cities in the Global South will grow in the digital era. To do this we have to bridge the gap between macro-development processes led by development agencies and the micro-sociological political and economic processes that take place in refugees' neighbourhoods of arrival. Without this bridge, and without empirical data from urban refugees themselves to help build the bridge, we risk repeating the technocratic paving-over of local knowledge, a phenomenon that spans Scott's (1999) analysis of late nineteenth-century France all the way to Jacobs's (1961) critique of planning in mid-twentieth-century American cities. While the grand method of the present book is Engaged Theory, its argument about what urban migration in developing countries in the digital age looks like is built on case studies and mixed methods fieldwork. This approach to data gathering allows for deeper analysis of individual-level lived experiences while also providing cross-sectional data to help inductively explore the theoretical scenarios that will be presented in Chapter 2.

Since the focus of this book is on how digitalization is impacting the lives of contemporary urban refugees, it is important to understand who we talked to and why. As often happens with contemporary laws and definitions, legal categorizations of "refugee" and "migrant" developed in the mid-twentieth century are not entirely fit for purpose. The definition of a refugee used in contemporary refugee status determination (RSD) processes is often too narrow to account for myriad legitimate reasons to seek protection; meanwhile, various categories of "migrant" are often narrowly defined in national laws. The term "mixed migration" perhaps best captures the kind of urban displacement we are witnessing in the Global South – people who are moving away from violence or political unrest, who fall within the scope of most refugee definitions, and also people who are moving away from economic deprivation and environmental change, who normally are categorized as economic migrants. Mixed migration, as we will see, also describes the Global North's history of urban displacement. That is why, for this study, we conducted surveys and interviews with poorer urban migrants, asylum seekers, and refugees. These people's lives are defined by impermanence: they often exist in legal grey areas, without formal access to social and economic systems. Throughout this book, we will be referring to our interviewees and survey respondents as urban refugees, so as to include both UNHCR-registered refugees and those who are not registered but would meet a common understanding of who a refugee is.

The decision about who to interview was not only categorical. We also factored in the historical context of technological change, which has always affected urban migration and development. Looking back, the urbanization that took place during the First Industrial Revolution occurred in tandem with enclosure policies that forced people off rural land; the Black diaspora in the twentieth century United States was escaping from white supremacist terror and political and economic exclusion. These examples amounted to forced displacement, even if that was not the term in use at the time. Mixed migration has an analogue too – economic motives, political turbulence, and famine drove the mass migrations of Jews, Germans, and Irish to North America. While the three contemporary case studies in this book are not perfectly analogous to developments in nineteenth- and early twentieth-century European and North American industrial cities, the attributes and income levels of urban displaced people across time provide us with some background for comparing how technological change and urbanization mixed in the past. This history can help us understand the digital era and urban displacement in the present and future.

INDUSTRIAL TECHNOLOGICAL CHANGE AND URBANIZATION: ENGAGING WITH HISTORIES OF DISPLACEMENT

This book grounds its contemporary analysis of technology in urban refugees' lives in historical events. Taking a historical perspective on technology and urban displacement accomplishes two things: it provides the intellectual framework for understanding why technological change and urban displacement should influence each other, and it helps show how technological and demographic changes have historically been central to the human political and sociological experience (see Levy 2008). In popular media and the political sphere, we often hear commentators say we are currently experiencing displacement and migration at volumes heretofore unseen and that these changes are something radically new. While limiting this discussion to transatlantic migration excludes the huge demographic changes that were simultaneously taking place in Asia during this time period, I will focus the historical component of this book on the British/European and American experiences of urban displacement. That is, I have chosen quite deliberately to keep the history of European and American urban displacement central to the narrative. This will serve to remind readers that what we are currently seeing in the

Global South is something that Europeans and North Americans experienced as well, pushing back against the sometimes selective amnesia that often pervades public debates about refugees and migration. While displacement dynamics in the twenty-first century present unique social and political challenges, urban displacement is hardly a new phenomenon.

The First Industrial Revolution, which began in the late eighteenth century, provides a jumping-off point for understanding how technological change in combination with changes in land management laws led to accelerating rural-to-urban migration in England. After 1785, when Edmund Cartwright introduced his water-powered loom, greater Manchester became a global centre of the cotton trade. The infrastructure changes that followed, such as gas lighting, meant that cities were more livable and that work hours could be extended. These industrial technological changes led to demographic shifts in England; however, industrial technology was only part of the story. Around the same time, landownership laws driven by changes in agricultural practices were being enacted with violent force; the Inclosure Acts created structured parcels of land, which smallholders rented from lords, and this drove up rents and reduced the amount of common land available to the rural poor. As more and more land became enclosed, rural Britons moved to towns and cities, where industrialization was creating new work opportunities. Through this mix of legal and technological change, British cities experienced a population boom during the nineteenth century.

When we scale up to international migration, the Great Migration that extended from the mid-nineteenth century to the early twentieth also saw technological change intersect with political, economic, and environmental upheaval; this brought about the massive displacement of people across borders. Technological developments in the late nineteenth and early twentieth centuries led to changes in transportation and communications, intensifying the industrial technological changes that began in the late eighteenth century. The time it took to travel between Europe and the United States shrank, and the flow of information between the continents increased considerably with the advent of transoceanic cables. In tandem with these technological changes, political and social factors in Europe combined to force many people to seek new lives in the United States. Political upheaval, often violent, as well as crop failures and famines in mid-nineteenth-century Central and Eastern Europe and Ireland pushed many people to emigrate to survive. Technological change combined with political and environmental factors led to forced displacement, and American cities grew in response.

Moving deeper into the twentieth century, there was another large movement of people, this time within the United States. The large-scale migration of Black Americans from the southeastern to the northern and western states, described by James Gregory (2005) as the Southern Diaspora, was driven by racism and political exclusion as well as by available jobs and political opportunities in American manufacturing cities in the northeast. This demographic shift fundamentally changed the voting alignment of northern cities and had a significant impact on the US Democratic Party (Grant 2020). In the later twentieth century, as industrial technology changed less rapidly so that less human labour was required, surveillance and administrative technology began to play a greater role in the processes and decisions of Black Americans to move north. Migration clubs – local groups in Black communities that organized journeys out of the south – drew on networks and information-sharing processes to ensure that when Black Americans arrived in northern cities, housing and work would be waiting for them. This type of organizing drew on methods of surveillance, data management, and communication; at the time, these were analogue processes, but still, they represented a technology of organizing. This is an example of how technology in the lives of urban displaced people need not be physical or industrial to have an impact on moving and settling into an urban society.

These examples help tell half the story, that of how technology has shaped the labour and industrial aspects of urban displacement. We can also see in these historical examples many of the drivers of contemporary urban displacement in the Global South. Political and social upheaval, economic shocks, and environmental change remain central factors in peoples' decisions to move to cities. The story of technological change and urban displacement is generally one of the poor and the vulnerable being forced to move. In many ways, the urbanization that happened from the late eighteenth century to the late twentieth is analogous to what we refer to in the twenty-first century as forced displacement. On balance, urban refugees in the 2020s do not look experientially all that different from many of the people displaced to cities during European and American periods of urbanization, industrialization, and political upheaval. The other half of the technological story concerns how cities and authorities responded to displacement and what role technological change played in administering and counting urban displaced people.

TECHNOLOGY AND MIGRATION ADMINISTRATION: KEEPING TRACK OF PEOPLE IN CITIES

When Ashkenazi Jews, Irish, and Germans moved to the United States in the mid- to late nineteenth century, there was no Refugee Convention, and the term "internally displaced person" (IDP) would not be coined for another 120 years.[4] What we would consider modern migration policy, built around restrictions to entry, is largely a twentieth-century phenomenon. Thus, the other half of the story is about the technology of administration, which, unlike industrial technology, is changing rapidly in the digital era and is radically shaping how urban displaced people move across borders and within cities of arrival.

The introduction of an increasingly wide array of visas and negotiated job and work migration programs has changed the ways that people move between countries and cities. Technology has played a key part in this, but to understand how we have gotten to the point we are with immigration and refugee administration we have to understand technology as more than hardware and software. Administration is itself a type of technology, a process augmented by changes and advances in measurement and counting tools. James Scott (1999), in his critical assessment of large-scale centralized efforts to render territory logical and measurable by the state, essentially describes early administrative technology – indeed, demographic statistics were one of the ways that eighteenth-century France attempted to measure and organize the population for tax purposes. It is rudimentary, and quite different from what we imagine "technology" in the twenty-first century to be, but demographic counting and statistical techniques are indeed a type of administrative technology. Unlike the power looms, blast furnaces, and later robotic manufacturing processes, administrative technology has often existed in the background, something that has come along incrementally in response to population-level needs.

From the late eighteenth century on, as industrial technology changed the nature of urbanization and production, there was a concurrent demand to make sense of national demographics. Long before they tried to control modern migration, states and municipalities were implementing other types of administrative systems to maintain control over populations. To understand how urbanization and the technology of administration evolved into modern migration and refugee policy, the book will start with an example from Foucault (1980, 166–82) that focuses on public health and the development of hospitals during the late eighteenth and nineteenth centuries. Foucault describes how public health management became necessary due to a mix of urbanization and industrial labour requirements; people moving to cities to work in factories had to be healthy enough to work, which meant that outbreaks of disease in dense urban neighbourhoods could have serious economic effects. So it made sense to use the technology of census taking to know who lived where, as a basis for tracking disease outbreaks. Demographic data were also key to adapting medicine to the increasing role of women and children in labour. The hospital evolved during the nineteenth century as the hub for containing, treating, and researching disease; especially for the Paris medical community, patients became subjects, whom physicians and surgeons "mined" in order to learn and refine their techniques. Scott and Foucault provide us with a way to imagine technology not as a machine in the physical sense, but as a mechanism of social control and management. This concept of technology is critical for understanding the evolution of displacement and urbanization, as well as the role that digitalization will play in future processes of urban displacement.

Understanding the idea of administration and statistics as technology is important when we move into the mid-nineteenth and twentieth centuries. The United States during the mid-nineteenth century was the first country to try to restrict the number of Catholics entering the country (it failed). This nativist strain of immigration politics was behind later efforts to prevent Chinese from immigrating, by setting rules such as literacy tests for potential migrants and then in the 1920s by setting quotas on the total number of admitted migrants from the Eastern Hemisphere. During the post–Second World War period programs for resettling displaced people were implemented; this was followed in the 1950s by adoption of the refugee convention. As waves of refugees from Hungary and Cuba were allowed to seek amnesty, the United States deported millions of Mexican labour migrants back to Mexico. During the 1980s and 1990s, immigration policy took a hard turn toward controlling the number of people crossing the US–Mexico border, a trend that has continued into the digital era. Why highlight the politics of US immigration policy? As noted at the start of the paragraph, administration and counting are technologies – we use them as tools to manage people. When a country decides to limit or manage border crossing, counting and control become key activities.

Statistics are a form of administrative technology that can be used to set policies and control populations; however, there also needs to be some kind of physical way a border patrol officer or immigration official can identify and count people. In modern migration policy, the principal travel document is the passport. The modern passport is a useful piece of technology for understanding the recent history of how migration and technological change are linked. As Winner (1980) argues, technologies have politics – we count different immigrant groups at the border because there has been a political decision to limit the entry of some groups. Counting is an administrative technology, and that technology then reflexively shapes political decisions. If politics demands counting, then counting demands documentation – thus, the modern passport. If the political environment demands greater levels of identifiability, passports become electronic and biometric. Biometric and electronic passports require devices to read them, so politicians have to invest in reader technologies. This is the cycle by which technology reflects politics. Urbanization during the Industrial Revolution created new public health problems, and the political economy of the time required healthy populations. Health statistics were the technology that made urban populations legible to the state, and the technology of health statistics led to public investment in hospitals. As people left urbanized Europe and Asia for the United States, politics demanded the counting of immigrants, and this over time led to increasingly technological passports. The political environment shapes what kinds of technologies are deployed to manage displacement, and the deployment of these technologies reflexively shapes how politicians invest in public resources. In the digital era, where technological change is taking place faster than politicians and regulators can keep up, what does the present and future of urban migration look like?

CONTEMPORARY DEBATES: FORCED DISPLACEMENT, URBAN REFUGEES, AND TECHNOLOGY

In the contemporary discourse on forced displacement, urban refugees, and the role of digital technology in refugees' lives, there is already historical, techno-social, and anthropological literature that grounds my arguments. As this book progresses I will be linking the themes covered by these authors to the history, contemporary cases, and conceptual analyses that bring everything together.

From a historical standpoint, Peter Gatrell's (2013) work on the evolution of the global refugee regime through the twentieth century focuses on how global conflicts and disasters intersected with an increasingly professionalized and governmentalized humanitarian agenda. Gatrell shows how refugees carry with them experiences of home in ways that have shaped contemporary political narratives about the global refugee regime. Evan Easton-Calabria's (2022) work on refugee self-reliance also uses a historical frame, examining how twentieth-century notions of order and modernization have fed into UNHCR's approach to refugee self-reliance as well as that of the global development community. In taking a historical approach, these books peel back the layers of political, economic, and social factors that undergird contemporary debates about refugees and displacement, showing us how otherwise unseen historical pathways have shaped modern refugee policy, intentionally or not.

This history comes alive in modern debates about the role played by digital technology in the lives of refugees. A key starting point is the role of digital technology in creating new pathways for refugees to find work. Andreas Hackl's (2021) analysis of digital livelihoods for refugees highlighted the opportunities for refugees to find work in the digital economy, as well as the barriers they faced. Those barriers are well illustrated in Rushworth and Hackl's (2022) analysis of how, when learning to code and work in the digital industry in Berlin, refugees faced legal and social hurdles to inclusion that went beyond a lack of technical skills. In part this could be attributed to an institutional culture that imagined digital work as a means of earning an income, to the exclusion of the other roles that work played in refugees' lives. Alencar and Camargo (2023) provide an example of this, based on work with Venezuelan displaced women in Brazil. Many women in that study found ways to integrate digital technology into their work lives, but many others faced social and economic hurdles, ranging from limited access to devices and the internet to being unable to work due to care duties.

Digital technologies have become an important part of social network–building as well as a means to maintain files and evidence of life stories and identities. Georgiou and Leurs (2022) present an affecting analysis of how mobile phones provide refugees with a repository of data and documentation about their journeys and lives

– their phones served as archives of displacement, journeys, and settlement in a new place. Earvin Cabalquinto's (2018) work on translocal familial and social ties highlights how digital technology is changing the way that geographically dispersed families maintain connections. Translocal families use mobile phones to maintain traditions, rituals, and intimate connections, although maintaining these digitally can be a challenge.

As the histories of urban displacement and technology merge with the current debates about the role of technology in urban refugees' and migrants' lives, we see a space for extending Gatrell's (2013) and Easton-Calabrias's (2022) work farther back in time and embedding it in technologized urban settings that have hosted displaced people since the late eighteenth century. This enables us to use contemporary empirical case studies of digital technologies in urban refugees' lives to understand how the future for cities in the Global South may look.

BOGOTÁ, KUALA LUMPUR, AND NAIROBI AS CASE STUDIES

To bring this history to life, three growing cities in middle-income countries were selected for data collection. Bogotá, Kuala Lumpur, and Nairobi are hubs of migration in their respective countries, and the work in those cities has allowed me to conduct cross-regional comparisons of the data collected from the urban refugees who reside in them. Note that this book is not a strict comparative analysis – the cities have been selected as much for their idiosyncrasies as for their similarities. The individual case studies are theory-guided and aim to explain the individual cities' unique circumstances (see again Levy 2008). The integrated analysis that follows the case study chapters will be using something akin to the diverse causal approach described by Gerring and Cojocaru (2016).

So, why did I pick these three cities? The first thing to highlight is what makes them similar: they are all capital cities in countries on the middle-income spectrum (measured in GDP per capita), they all have long histories of urban displacement, and they all have neighbourhoods and enclaves where refugees tend to settle. All three cities have full mobile data coverage, although there is variation in mobile phone signal quality in different areas. All three cities also host displaced people and refugees, and often those people are poor and have more than one reason to move (such as to seek work *and* flee violence). Many of these people could claim refugee status or already have. So what makes each city unique?

Bogotá was where this book started. In late 2017 there was a great deal of excitement about the peace process, which brought about a negotiated end to the country's fifty-year civil war. The initial question the team I was working with focused on was the potential that information communication technologies (ICTs) had for helping identify and support urban internally displaced people (IDPs). This was a policy-relevant question, since Colombia already had a formal process for registering and providing aid to conflict-affected IDPs. While urban displacement has a long history in Colombia, internal displacement over the past fifty years has been deeply influenced by patterns of violence and land grabbing. Even for those who were migrating to Bogotá for ostensibly economic reasons, violence likely featured somewhere in their migration process. Meanwhile, while we were doing our work in Bogotá, the exodus of Venezuelans across the border was growing, and we included these people in our survey. The drivers of flight to Bogotá can include losses of rural property through violence and the possibility of finding work and resources in the city. In the technology-for-development discourse, Bogotá has not been a hub of innovation the way the other two cities have been, but it still has reliable mobile and wired internet access and most people have access to a mobile phone.

Kuala Lumpur is the wealthiest of the three cities and the most advanced in terms of public infrastructure. In modern times, the city has also been a beacon for people fleeing conflict and political oppression in the ASEAN region. Some neighbourhoods and enclaves in the city have hosted people from as far west as Palestine and as far east as Vietnam. The groups interviewed for this book include Rohingya, Myanmar Muslims, Somalis, Chins (a Myanmar Christian ethnic group), and Ahmadiya Pakistanis. Kuala Lumpur has been a hub for people seeking safety and opportunity, yet the Malaysian government's official policy is not to recognize refugees. Malaysia is not a signatory to the refugee convention, and there is no legislative framework there for determining refugee status. It allows the UN High Commission for Refugees (UNHCR) to run a national office and administer all refugee status determination and resettlement processes, but this does not mean that refugees have formal protection. They are routinely arrested, and since they have no legal migration status they cannot participate in the formal economy or educational system. UNHCR does have the power to get them out of jail and to issue identification, but this happens in a legal grey area. As a result, many refugee groups have formed community organizations to meet social, legal, and health care needs. Internet connectivity, especially mobile phone internet, is generally good in Malaysia's urban areas.

The third case study is Nairobi, which has the lowest income per capita of the three cities, although the surrounding counties that comprise the metropolitan area, such as Kiambu County, are relatively well off. Nairobi hosts the largest number of urban refugees of the three cities, and just as in Kuala Lumpur, these refugees inhabit a murky legal space. Unlike Malaysia, Kenya is a signatory to the refugee convention and has a legislative framework for providing asylum, but it also has a convoluted legal framework regarding who must live in camps and who can reside in Nairobi. Simply put, Kenya has an encampment policy for all refugees; less simply, there are multiple avenues whereby refugees can gain permission to remain in Nairobi. As in Kuala Lumpur, urban refugees move to Nairobi and settle in ethnic and national enclaves, where community organizations extend them protection. They are not formally allowed to work, but the rules for refugees being self-employed are loose enough that many displaced people run small businesses. From a physical and economic perspective, Nairobi is also growing rapidly and is a hub of tech and innovation in East Africa.

Land grabbing, political strife, violence, famine – these drivers are part of the experience of modern urban refugees. They are also the things that drove people from the commons to the cities in industrializing Britain, across the Atlantic from Europe to North America, and from the American South to cities the North. Technological change meant new jobs, shorter journeys, and greater surveillance. As we move deeper into the digital era, Bogotá, Kuala Lumpur, and Nairobi will follow the same arcs of development, and people will continue moving to those cities and others like them. However, the technology will not be in the administrative background or contained within the arena of industry – it will be front and centre as new social networks are built online, new tools of administration track people, and the classic draw to the city, jobs, is digitally disrupted.

METHODS AND CASES ACROSS TIME: HOW HISTORICAL AND CONTEMPORARY ANALYSIS COME TOGETHER

Technological change has been a prominent background factor in urban displacement and in how cities are managed during periods of rapid population growth. How did these changes affect urban societies, including power relations between capital, labour, and the state? A qualitative analysis of the history of urban displacement that highlights technological changes can help point out which questions to ask of today's urban refugees, as well as the role technology plays in their urban lives. The cities in today's Global North did not emerge from an ontological bubble as bustling centres of business, culture, and politics. The British and American manufacturing hubs underwent evolutionary processes that can help us understand how metropolises may grow in this new digital era and the role migrants will play in shaping that growth. In Chapter 3 I will discuss in more detail the methods used to develop the historical cases.

While I will be focusing on the European and American historical contexts, it is important to reiterate that there is a rich literature on urbanization in Southeast Asia, Latin America, and Sub-Saharan Africa. Regarding Southeast Asia, there have been economic analyses of the links between commodity export and the globalization of supply chains and urban growth from the early colonial period to the present (Huff and Angeles 2011). Also, Rimmer and Dick (2009) have explored the development of Southeast Asian urban society through the lens of consumption and the privatization of public space. Latin America has at times encountered urban/rural mobility policies that have run contrary to rural-to-urban mobility patterns; for example, the Mexican government focused on supporting agrarian reforms that ran against global urban-industrial trends (Kemper and Royce 1979), and Brazil attempted to moderate urbanization trends that were driven by rural automation (Wagner and Ward 1980). In Africa, just as in Southeast Asia and Latin America, the urban context has been shaped by colonialism. This is apparent in the case of Cape Town, where population growth in the 1800s was organized around suburbanization and town blocks (Todeschini 2011). Comparative analyses of urban development in Ghana and Nairobi have shown the important role that expansion and suburbanization have played in the growth of modern capital and secondary cities – growth driven in part by the architectural and aesthetic politics of Pan-Africanism (Asabere et al. 2020; Otiso and Owusu 2008).

European and American influence on urban planning, economic development, and migration and refugee law since the Second World War has been significant. The International Organization for Migration (IOM) is headquartered in Geneva, and the UN Refugee Agency (UNHCR) has headquarters in both New York and Geneva; both those bodies have traditionally been led by Americans and Europeans. The World Bank in Washington, DC, and the Organisation for Economic Co-operation and Development (OECD) in Paris have both played a significant role in establishing the mindset that migration and displacement are to be understood as supporting economic development. The European/American history of industrialization, urbanization, and modernist development in the 150 years leading up to the Second World War and Bretton Woods shaped the economic and political cultures of these organizations. These institutions' activities continue to shape global refugee and development policies and norms, hence my focus on the European and American histories of urban displacement, which have implicitly and explicitly shaped the institutions that to this day set global policies and norms for managing urban displacement.

MIGRANTS, REFUGEES, AND DISPLACED PEOPLE: A NOTE ON TERMINOLOGY

When talking about people in the contemporary context, including those who were surveyed and interviewed for this book's case studies, I will be using the term "urban refugee." "Refugee" here includes people who have received official asylum status and also those who are not officially registered but would be considered refugees in the common sense.

In the historical context, I will be using the term "urban displaced people," since the administrative concept of "refugee" as a legal category did not exist, or did not apply in specific contexts such as Black Americans leaving the Jim Crow South for American cities in the North. The term urban displaced people allows me to talk about forced displacement in historical contexts such as industrial Manchester or turn-of-century New York City, without having to graft legally defined terms onto past times when modern refugee law did not exist. In focusing on the historical experience of displacement instead of the legal category of refugee, my goal is to show how the past experiences of displaced people map onto the experiences of contemporary urban refugees.

When discussing the general phenomenon – historical and contemporary – of people being displaced to cities, I will use the term "urban displacement." This refers to the broad political and sociological phenomenon of displacement to cities, as opposed to the identity of displaced people themselves.

THE FINDINGS IN PRACTICE

The histories of urban migration and of technological change speak to issues beyond academic inquiry. Thus a deeper understanding of how technological change has influenced urbanization over time, and an analysis of what makes digital technological change different, has a direct bearing on how we in turn understand today's key development and humanitarian policy issues. The historical arc also serves a broader purpose, which is to humanize the people who are moving to the growing cities in the Global South. It helps show that while the twenty-first century is introducing new variables to urban displacement processes, urban displaced people who worked in England's industrial Victorian cities, or who took one-way tickets across the Atlantic to North America, or who left behind political terror and economic exclusion in the American South, were not all that circumstantially different from the urban migrants seeking safety and opportunity today.

This is an inherently critical position to take; it is also why Engaged Theory is the grand method of this book. Digital technological change is the independent variable, and we want to understand how modern urban migration has changed in response to it. Developing an identification strategy for isolating how digitalization causes changes in urban migration is fine scientific practice, but for this knowledge to have a "real world" impact we have to identify the power dynamics and values that undergird this causal assumption. Historical analysis gives us the space to do this, as does taking time to theorize technology as both physical machinery and a means of administration. The later chapters of the book will critically examine examples of recent and ongoing digitalization efforts by organizations like UNHCR and the IOM to better understand how institutions' and individuals' valuation of digitization converge and diverge in practice. These chapters will provide a context for us to evaluate the ways that modern urban migrants relate to digital technology and identify whether the digital strategies of development agencies empower organic urban development or force failed models of urban planning onto refugee communities.

2

The Urban Context: Where Displacement and Digitalization Meet

Cities, historically and in the present day, have many attributes that make them the best social and economic option for displaced people seeking safety as well as the space to establish new lives. For urban refugees today in cities experiencing both rapid economic growth and accompanying socio-political instability, digitalization creates new economic and social dynamics. What does the future of refugees' role in urban development look like when digitalization reduces the need for physical labour and manufacturing? How will the exchange of ideas and cross-cultural knowledge be expanded, or constrained, in situations where people can maintain translocal social networks but the state can at the same time more efficiently monitor and control their physical movement? These two questions, which focus on the social components of urban displacement and the economic development of cities, are central to understanding how digitalization could change the relationship between urban refugees and the cities to which they move. Theorists like Lefebvre (2003), Jacobs (1961), and Massey (2005) have defined cities as more than agglomerations of buildings, parks, and infrastructure. Cities are also social networks, ever-evolving economic engines, and centres of political change. As metropolises in the Global South continue to grow at exceptional rates, the influence of digital technologies on daily life are changing not only economic patterns but also how citizens and governments interact in urban spaces.

Urban centres have always been hubs of cultural, economic, and political innovation. They are spaces where people from myriad cultures can gather, settle, and exchange ideas; they are centres of gravity for capital and by extension for research and development, and over the centuries they have provided public spaces for political activism and innovation. A key component of all this innovation has been the movement of people. Cities thrive when people migrate to them; this does not mean, though, that cities need not contend with poverty and social and political exclusion. Indeed, cities in the Global North went through their own periods of displaced people living in large slums and tenements. I do not want to romanticize urban fringes and slums since they often represent conditions driven by a politics of exclusion; I *am* saying, however, that historically they have also been places of urban activity and self-renewal. When we look at Jacobs's (1961) discussion of Boston's North End, which in the 1960s was by all accounts a slum, we see a space that featured tight social and economic networks and required little outside financing to renew itself and prosper. We want to understand not only how these urban social, economic, and political networks arose in Western cities during the late nineteenth and twentieth Centuries but also how cities in Latin America, Sub-Saharan Africa, and Southeast Asia have started taking shape and developing in the late twentieth and now early twenty-first centuries on their own terms.

Cities in the Global South today, like their northern peers, are also spaces for digital innovation. Given how cities attract financial and human capital, the opportunities for developing digital solutions for commercial and administrative uses are abundant. Cities themselves are hubs for software and technology industries, where the mix of educated workers, knowledge infrastructure, and financial capital makes it possible to set up firms. In the Global North, we see hubs of tech innovation in cities like San Francisco, London, Berlin, and Stockholm. The technology industry is expanding into urban centres in developing countries too: Nairobi is referred to as the "Silicon Savannah," and Southeast Asia has long nurtured robust technology industries (Simmons 2016). However, digitalization is not just about jobs – it manifests itself in cities in physical ways. One of the clearest changes we have seen globally over the past ten years is the expansion of the "gig" economy, where jobs and tasks are requested via smartphone-based software programs. When talking about a city, transportation is an example of a key sector where the gig economy has had an effect – firms like Uber have changed how people hail cars, shaken up the taxi industry, and affected traffic volumes on city streets. From an administrative standpoint, digitalization also plays a key role in the governance and control of urban spaces. E-government systems allow citizens to register addresses and pay taxes, while CCTV and big data computing allow authorities to monitor and track people in rapidly evolving ways. These digital changes present a number of opportunities and risks for urban refugees, who often live in precarious legal and political conditions in countries of arrival.

Digitalization is changing the political-economic nature of urban settings in ways that present new challenges and opportunities for urban refugees to influence and shape the social and economic fabric of the cities where they settle. These intersecting challenges, such as new modes of work and social/political organizing, will mean that cities in emerging economies are going to experience economic and social development in very different ways than their counterparts in the Global North did during the nineteenth and twentieth centuries. How will the shift to increasingly digital economies affect the role of migrants in shaping cities' economies, and how do we need to rethink our models of urbanization and economic development? From an administrative perspective, will digitalization create opportunities for integrating new arrivals, or will it merely harden exclusionary practices in new ways?

ECONOMIC DEVELOPMENT, CITIES, AND MIGRANTS

While this is not a book specifically about urban economics, that topic is central to how we have understood, and continue to understand, urban migration and displacement from the twentieth and into the twenty-first century. What do the lives of contemporary urban refugees look like? How do researchers understand the ways those people have woven themselves into the fabric of modern cities? This analysis will identify the ways that urban economies, and the refugees who help drive them, can help us understand the changes that digitalization could bring and what these changes mean for rethinking established economic theories of urban migration.

Differentiating "urban" from "city" is a key starting point. Lefebvre (2003),[1] in *La Révolution urbaine*, argues that the two terms mean different things. In his framework, a city is described thus:

> The city is vastly different. Indeed, it is not only a devouring activity, consumption; it becomes productive (means of production) but initially does so by bringing together the elements of produc-

tion. It combines markets (the inventory includes the market for agricultural and industrial products – local, regional, national, global: capital markets, labour markets, markets for the land itself, for signs and symbols). The city brings together whatever is engendered somewhere else, by nature or labour: fruits and objects, products and producers, works and creations, activities and situations. What does the city create? Nothing. It centralizes creation. And yet it creates everything. Nothing exists without exchange, without union, without proximity, that is, without relationships. The city creates a situation, the urban situation, where different things occur one after another and do not exist separately but according to their differences. (117–18)

The city is the space where otherwise atomized things come together to create new interactions. "Urban" is something different, though. Urban in this sense is the sociological process of a population self-managing within spatial units; this self-management then propagates the capital and physical aspects of the city. Working against this self-management is the state, which aims to control the city's space and economy from the top down. Lefebvre gives us two concepts to work with as we think about urban displacement and digitalization: urban society as the abstract space in which political and social contestation takes place, and the city as the physical administrative space in which urban society exists.

Jane Jacobs's (1961) work on what makes a healthy city and how cities' economies work provides a good jumping-off point. Jacobs contends that far from leading to healthy cities, the scientific urban planning that emerged in the early to mid-twentieth century essentially sucked the life out of them. A healthy city would often look chaotic to a planner or financier. The networks of characters, as she describes them in her chapters on sidewalks ("On Safety," 29–54; "On Contact," 55–73), are what make a city a self-managing social network. In a wonderful passage, she describes how Boston's North End in the 1950s and early 1960s in the eyes of city planners was a blight, a slum lacking in investment potential for private capital. However, when she visited she found a neighbourhood capable of revitalizing itself without outside support; people provided services such as painting and handiwork, there were cafes and restaurants, and there was life on the streets. It was a city space that, to draw on Lefebvre's urban society concept, was self-managing. The social connectivity of the neighbourhood itself created capital and economic activity; this is not to say the North End could not have benefited from administrative support or outside capital; the point is that it could adapt and support itself without these things.

Jacobs built on this social-spatial argument with her follow-up books on the economies of cities. In *The Death and Life of Great American Cities*, *The Economy of Cities* (1970), and *Cities and the Wealth of Nations* (1985), she pushed back against the status quo of urban planning. Essentially, she argued that cities are hubs of regional export production and that the more they export the more they can import from other regions. Importing new goods spurs people to develop new goods and skills, and local networks of entrepreneurs and producers in a city drive an adaptive export economy. When a city can no longer innovate new types of exports, it stagnates and dies away. Applying this theory to a national level, Jacobs then argues that cities are key to a nation's wealth. Cities export capital and technology to the regions around them and are able to adaptively create new businesses to drive regional economies. Having a national network of cities prevents large incumbent firms from taking over regions and homogenizing their economies, which would lead to economic stagnation.

In the twenty-first century, Edward Glaeser (2011) offers an updated look at how wealthy cities of the Global North have reinvigorated themselves and what the emerging futures of middle-income metropolises could be. He builds on Jacobs's work in a number of ways and expands his analysis to examine cities in developing countries. Most prescient for our purposes, he notes that cities create opportunities for poor migrants and refugees and are enriched by their activities as members of urban society. Cities present opportunities, and refugees are often willing to take risks that established residents would turn away from. Refugees are not just a source of labour, though; they represent human capital that can create new business and drive innovation, and they shape the politics of the cities in which they live. In the mid-twentieth century, we can look to New York City's boroughs and see the influence that displacement had on American political and economic systems over generations. Richard Feynman, for example, one of the great physicists of the twentieth century, was a child of immigrants and grew up in Rockaway, Brooklyn. It can be easy to point to luminaries, particularly men of European descent like Feynman, as an argument for openness to immigration and providing safe haven to refugees. However, poor displaced people, especially women, often drove systematic change. The New York Shirtwaist Strike of 1909 was led by female Jewish immigrants, many of whom had fled pogroms in Central and Eastern Europe (Malkiel 1910). The strike succeeded, which led to the renegotiation of contracts between industry and workers that shortened hours, and offered better pay and working conditions in New York's garment industry.[2]

This brings us back to the present: how does the flow of refugees and displaced people moving to today's emerging cities look to scholars and journalists working on issues of urbanization and development? Is digitalization creating the space for middle-income cities in the Global South to take developmental pathways that are less dependent on capital and industrialization and based more on existing social networks? Three contemporary books paint three different pictures: a dark outlook – cities in developing countries will be hubs of violent crime and conflict; an economic argument – cities will grow but without jobs, leading to permanent economic exclusion for refugees; and an ostensibly more positive outlook – the slums and refugee enclaves are challenging environments but also present great opportunities for migrants and host cities. These books do not necessarily have a digitalization focus; instead, they contextualize what future urbanization might look like. The digitalization aspects of urban displacement and development will be discussed vis-à-vis these contexts later in the chapter.

For cities in developing countries, the bleakest outlook is that urbanization is going to lead to increases in irregular warfare and violence driven by criminal activities and a lack of governance in urban centres. David Kilcullen (2013) lays out this scenario in *Out of the Mountains: The Coming Age of the Urban Guerrilla*. While the idea of urban warfare and political uprisings is not new, his insights about the role of new technologies in networking fighters and revolutionaries together are prescient. Economists often think of technological change in terms of increasing productivity and efficiency. In the history of technological change and urbanization this has generally been the case; for example, the power loom radically increased the volume of woven fabric an urban factory could produce. But digital change is different – instead of directly affecting the production of materials, new digital technologies network people together. Because these new apps and software packages are "free," huge numbers of people can suddenly communicate and organize at a scale that would have been impossible at the turn of the twenty-first century. Not every city is the hotbed of urban conflict and chaos that Kilcullen describes; that said, the tensions that are inevitable as cities develop, such as labour strife and political protest, are easier to feed and organize on digital platforms. This means that things can turn violent quickly if spoilers find a way into the information stream. So when we look at the future of digitalization and urban migration in the development of cities, we have to ask which will happen: will it be greater social cohesion, or a hardening of existing political or ethnic bubbles?

We cannot yet know what impact digital technological change will have on work in the growing cities of developing countries. Mike Davis in *Planet of Slums* (2006) argues that far from being the beacons of opportunity Glaeser describes, modern megacities in the Global South are increasingly marked by slums where the poor are cut off from limited municipal resources and exploited by the private sector and one another. *Planet of Slums* was published before the boom in digitalization in developing countries; still, Davis makes a valid point: technological change – including digitalization – that does not create jobs could have deleterious effects on urban migration and cities' economic development. In a world where new jobs require technical skills and advanced training and require fewer people to do them, will we merely end up with jobless urban displacement? Will those refugees who move to the poorer areas and slums surrounding cities be stuck in a state of permanent economic exclusion, as cities privatize and digitize services under the banner of "e-government" and a limited number global technology firms make money off the data that urban refugees generate as they use social media?

Doug Saunders (2010) provides an alternative argument: that modern slums, areas of arrival for refugees and displaced people, will not be left behind by the grind of the global economy and are indeed the most dynamic parts of cities. Saunders describes these slums and poorer neighbourhoods as they are – rough, often dirty and dangerous, but also places where opportunity exists. He picks up where Jane Jacobs left off, seeing the potential of emerging cities in labyrinthine districts that have fallen outside the scope of the city planners or that have been purposefully sealed off by their policies. In such places, people find solidarity as well as opportunity. The picture of neighbourhoods and slums in arrival cities painted by Saunders highlights opportunities for human development without ignoring the precarity that poor migrants encounter in their journeys and on their arrival.

The presence of this liminal space between precarity and opportunity has always been key to the development of cities, but does a digital future support the import/export processes described by Jacobs in *The Economy of Cities*? If the economy of emerging cities moves away from "making" things and becomes driven by the passive production of data, how will people be able move from precarity to stability?

The above three accounts of modern urban theory and developing cities lay out some of the possible directions that urban displacement and digitalization will push cities in as we move deeper into the twenty-first century. Cities are more than agglomerations of economic activity, though. As Lefebvre argues, and Jacobs elaborates, there are sociological factors that drive the survival of cities as social constructs. Cities are more than hubs of economic innovation; they are also hubs of social and cultural (re)generation. Technology plays a role in how urban societies manifest themselves, and digital technologies create new avenues for people to network and for the state to administer space.

DIGITALIZATION IN URBAN SOCIETY AND THE ADMINISTRATION OF CITIES

Economic development and commercial activity are central to the purpose of cities and vital to their functioning, providing a draw for people to move to them, but a healthy city is based on more than just economic production. Healthy cities balance social networks of people in different neighbourhoods with effective administration and public service delivery. Over the past two hundred years, technological change has shaped how urban migrants create social networks and how authorities attempt to administer and control city space.

Lefebvre's work was relatively abstract and conceptual. He discussed how "urban society" stands in opposition to state power and control. In this regard, there are many tangible examples of urban societies organizing and engaging in political contestation. Over the past fifteen years this contestation and organizing has taken an increasingly digital turn. While not exclusively confined to urban spaces, the violence that broke out in Kenya during that country's 2007 election provided an early glimpse into digital political organizing. Text messaging served as a mass medium for propagating rumours and organizing violence; but then, both during the violence and in its aftermath, that same technology became central to many digital peace-building efforts. A defining example of urban digital protest as political revolution arose in 2011, when it toppled governments in Tunisia and Egypt. In Egypt, the urban space of Tahrir Square was the physical hub of the protests, but the protesters made masterful use of social media and blogs to combat the state's efforts to break their movement. After Tahrir Square, governments adopted those same tools, which, as it turned out, were equally useful for surveillance and control. I will examine that side of the debate later, but first I want to unpack some examples of digital urban social action that are not political revolutions and how urban refugees fit into these networks.

Building urban social networks, social signalling, and maintaining translocal networks are all processes that migrate well into the digital space.[3] Especially for those who have recently arrived in a new city, access to a mobile phone can have social implications beyond mere communication. In Bangladesh, Andrew Wong (2009) developed what he called an "urban footprint" model to show how poor urban migrants moved from accessing mobile phones to engaging in more advanced digital behaviours and social activities as their individual lives became increasingly woven into the life of the city. The phone became a way to connect to different groups and activities; it also signalled to others that this person was part of a wider urban community. Not all digital urban activity that is contentious is revolutionary, however. Giota Alevizou (2020) examined grassroots organizing among migrants in Ward's Corner, a working-class part of Tottenham, London. Facing redevelopment of the block where their shops were located, they established a digital platform to engage with others, share their experiences of the neighbourhood, and discuss their goals, as well as their fears of what redevelopment would bring. They then used the content generated in this digital space to seek new avenues for asserting their rights in the face of political and economic pressure. These are examples of urban societies taking advantage of the digitized city space to build social networks and pursue shared social and political goals.

Digitalization in urban contexts is not simply about forming political action networks, though. Urban refugees play an important role in generating local and translocal media cultures. Georgiou (2013) talks about how cities become places where the media create spaces for contestation and cooperation around political and social narratives, what Leurs (2014) calls "digital throwntogetherness." The digital urban space is one in which refugees maintain connections to home while building local networks. Ethnic news and entertainment media, created and consumed by a specific ethnic group, often emerge in urban refugee enclaves (Matsanani, Katz, and Ball-Rokeach 2010). In my own fieldwork this could mean anything from ethnic language news services on YouTube, to a media producer in a refugee community finding a way to patch a local football match from an obscure league into the satellite feed so that people could watch a game on TV from far away. Urban refugees seek media from home, and in the cities where they now live, they have found ways to find it.

On the other side of the coin is municipal administration. The city is itself becoming increasingly digital – the "smart city" – and administration is going online in the form of e-government. While these changes may not be taking place with an express focus on urban migrants, they affect their lives in unique ways that long-term local residents do not encounter. While there is still some debate around what we mean by the term "smart city," for the sake of this section I will use a technologically focused definition. Smart cities integrate information communication technologies (ICTs) and internet devices into their physical infrastructure with the aim of gathering large amounts of real-time data on things such as energy use and sidewalk and road wear and tear; they also use sensor systems to autonomously control mass transit vehicles. At its maximally technological, the smart city is built from the ground up and thoroughly integrated across hardware and internet connections. This includes cities like PlanIT in Portugal, Masdar City in the UAE, and Songdo in Korea (Albino, Berardi, and Dangelico 2015). However, the planned smart city that has garnered the most attention and overt controversy was Google's Quayside development, which ended up being cancelled. Envisioned as a partnership between the City of Toronto and the Google subsidiary Sidewalk Labs, this project ran into strong objections largely centred on the way the integrated technology will gather data on residents and how a private firm will use those data (Cecco 2019; Kofman 2018). Industry-built and technology-centric smart cities offer positive surface-level possibilities for e-government and efficient citizen services; but they also herald a dominance of planning over life as it is actually lived, a dominance that for Jane Jacobs represents everything that would lead to the death of a city. Such planned cities would be "bloodless," and besides that, their surveillance technologies – video and facial recognition, different types or sensors collecting health data, and so on – present particular problems, in that citizens' data would be accessible by public authorities as well as by private sector actors (Graham and Wood 2003).

The private sector aspect is especially troubling when viewed critically – what do private sector firms really *owe* citizens? The narrative of smart cities as highly efficient, complex networks places firms like IBM at the centre of everything (Söderström, Passche, and Klauser 2014). The smart city is a massive captured market in which public services produce data that are of value to large firms, citizens have no choice about whether to provide those data, and administrative entities have access to it for the purpose of surveillance. Given how bleak this sounds, are there any positives to the smart city concept? Smart cities can be hubs for the rapid sharing of human knowledge (Albino et al. 2015), and the integration of e-government services can help reduce things like graft and corruption (Vu and Hartley 2018). But there are also inherent security and privacy risks: smart cities are still populated by citizens, and there will be inherent tensions related to privacy and data security, how data will be shared, and the appropriate use of artificial intelligence in complex digital systems (Braun et al. 2018).

WHAT DOES THE FUTURE OF CITIES LOOK LIKE IN AN ERA OF DIGITALIZATION AND URBAN DISPLACEMENT?

If global demographic data are correct, the world will continue to become increasingly urban. During the nineteenth and twentieth centuries, urbanization models and theories of economics and sociology generally focused on the city as an economic and production hub. Moving to the city for things like family reunification or as a personal lifestyle choice were tertiary to the economic aspects of urban life. When technological change drove advances in labour-intensive manufacturing, it made sense for models and theories of urban displacement to focus on the search for higher incomes and greater work opportunities. Even when there were sociological drivers at the meso and micro levels that affected urban refugees' decision-making, the general concept held: people move to cities to find work, the economic activity gets turned into new products and businesses, and associated technological changes feed into new jobs for new urban migrants. Analogue industrial technology facilitated this process, whether it entailed increasing the speed of fabric production or the transition from sail to steam. In the digital era, by contrast, technological change does not aim to facilitate industries and services; it aims to disrupt them.

Can a city experience the same economic development trajectory if digital technologies are designed to concentrate capital while decreasing the number of jobs required to generate economic activity? This problem exposes the fact that twentieth-century models and theories of urban migration and healthy cities rest heavily on a number of assumptions about the role of technology in economic development. The Harris-Todaro model (1970), which assumes that people move to cities seeking higher incomes, runs into headwinds when technological change does not generate new jobs or works to depress wages. Jane Jacobs's theory of cities as exporters of new products and businesses does not work if city dwellers – and refugees in particular – are atomized from one another by gig economy apps that pay so little per task that people cannot build up sufficient capital to invest in new businesses. These problems create the space to ask whether the nature of digital technological change is such that refugees come to cities for reasons that are not, at their core, economic. Instead, digital technologies connect refugees to family, local networks, and social support organizations in ways that would have been impossible in the pre-digital era. Urban refugees can organize politically and socially in highly efficient ways, using things like WhatsApp groups – indeed, being connected in real time to community leaders can mean the difference between a long stay in immigration detention or an advocate responding quickly to make sure a refugee's rights are protected. A refugee, seeking safety, may well be drawn to a city by the opportunity to create and take part in what Lefebvre might have viewed as a digital urban society.

There is a flip side to the networking opportunities that digital technologies afford refugees when they arrive in slums or ethnic enclaves. Social media, mobile phone–based messaging services, and e-government services are easily used by governments and illicit actors to surveil communities. While the surveillance powers of governments are often discussed in terms of refugee control and bordering, the surveillance risks associated with human trafficking are also significant. Many urban refugees undertake their journeys with the help of smugglers and traffickers. Like governments, these criminal entities have a vested interest in the surveillance and control of refugees. For the state, surveillance is about controlling who comes in and who can access public and private goods legally; for smugglers and traffickers, it is about keeping track of which refugees are using their networks and ensuring that those refugees pay, be it in cash or in labour. Poor refugees, especially those who are fleeing violence or persecution and who have had to cross borders illegally, can end up suffering the worst of both types of surveillance. In the digital era, the city could cease to be a place where urban refugees find social networks and safety in slums and ethnic enclaves and instead evolve into a space where the state pushes them to the edges, where illicit actors can prey upon them.

These changes in the technological background of city spaces invite a re-evaluation of why refugees come to cities and what these changes mean for the economic development trajectory of middle-income cities. How are the overlapping roles of economic and labour opportunities, and social networks and surveillance, affecting the decision-making and experiences of urban refugees in the digital era? How do these experiences feed back into the development of cities? To understand how the constellation of technological change and urban migration will affect developing cities, I propose four potential future urban displacement and development scenarios. The scenarios are based on the varying levels of job growth and social networking/surveillance; these are two key background features of urban life that technology has influenced in analogue history and the digital present. Do digital technologies present new opportunities for work and wage earning that can raise refugees up to the middle class, thereby fostering an export- and innovation-oriented city? Or are the manufacturing jobs that drew past urban displaced people disappearing, replaced by digital translocal social networks that attract migrants to urban areas instead of jobs? The four scenarios in Figure 2.1 will be used to ground the analysis of the case studies later in the book and to drive the discussion of future theoretical and practical directions in the role of urban displacement and the economic growth of cities.

The scenarios in figure 2.1 are potential urban outcomes based on how digitalization will affect jobs and social networks for urban refugees. They reflect the premises long embedded in development and urban planning – that economic growth is central to good devel-

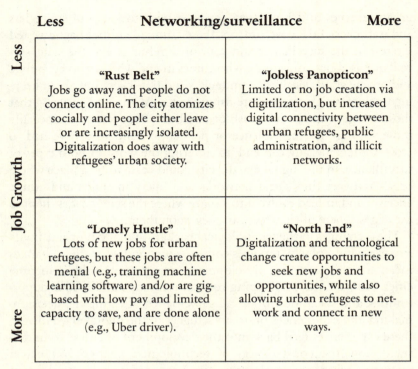

Figure 2.1 Scenarios for digital technological change and urban migration in developing countries

opment, that individual and community-level empowerment through greater access to information and resources is better than centralized solutions, and that digital technological change should bring about these positive outcomes. Thus, we have four scenarios:

1 "North End," named after Boston's North End, which Jane Jacobs (1961, 8–13) describes as the kind of bustling and lively urban space that represents cities at their most organically vibrant. Regardless of its status as a slum in the 1950s and 1960s, the North End had the social networks and skills to revitalize and update itself. This is the direction Saunders sees slums taking in the twenty-first century. While far from perfect, the areas of cities that urban refugees move into are an entry point from which they can find a place in urban society. Digitalization offers new ways for urban refugees to establish social networks,

which can help them locate housing, social support mechanisms, and initial jobs. These networks provide not only economic and social opportunity but protection as well. Urban refugees who are moving into large urban centres occupy a particularly vulnerable position in society; often they are unprotected by the law, so they are easily exploited in workplaces or at risk for trafficking. By having a community around them, they gain protection from the people Jacobs describes as the "characters" in a city who occupy sidewalks, storefronts, and stoops. From the administrative perspective, digitalization offers new ways for refugees to apply for protection status if they are fleeing violence or persecution, as well as to engage with municipal authorities. From an economic perspective, digitalization opens up new avenues for entering the job market for workers who in the past would have worked in urban manufacturing. This can take the form of "gig economy" jobs such as driving or delivery services intermediated by smartphone apps. Another avenue for new digital jobs for urban refugees is through firms like SamaSource, which hire people to help with basic coding and machine learning tasks. The narrative is that through these activities, urban refugees pick up new skills and use those skills to open new businesses and create city exports. In this scenario, which reflects Saunders's perspective on arrival cities, there is a healthy balance between urban society and economic activity, facilitated by digital technological change.

2 "Jobless Panopticon" describes jobless city growth combined with the expansion of digital networks. The Panopticon is an approach to prison building that Foucault (1977) cited as a mechanism for maintaining surveillance and control. In such a prison, the prisoners can always be observed, but they cannot see the observers – they never know for sure if they are being observed, and thus they behave as if they are always under observation. In this scenario, digitalization does not bring formal jobs, but it does bring the opportunity for people to network and to stay in contact with one another, as well as for communities and the state to monitor urban refugees' activities. The idea of a Panopticon is not inherently "bad," although passive surveillance can stifle freedom if deployed to do so. Instead of a "bad/good" dichotomy, what digital technology does on an unmatched scale is support and enforce accepted modes of

behaviour within communities. As an alternative to the Panopticon, social digital networks in slums and arrival neighbourhoods can keep track of who comes and goes as a means to foster safety. When an urban refugee who is otherwise invisible to state apparatuses of protection such as the police or social services disappears, their sudden absence from a community's digital social networks could well trigger a search for them. In this scenario, there is a tension between the social benefits of digital connectivity as a means for communities to surveil themselves, and digital connectivity as a way for governments and illicit actors to control urban refugees. On the economic side, digitalization does not bring people into economic networks or provide labour opportunities; at the same time, the lack of jobs or economic opportunities could be a catalyst for digitally networked social or political unrest.

3 "Lonely Hustle" is a city where urban refugees may find formalized work through digital means such as driving for Uber, or doing menial computing tasks such as training machine learning software, but they are highly socially atomized through this work.[4] The sense of community through work, and the requisite opportunities to innovate or combine skills, do not manifest themselves in this scenario. Jacobs would critique such a scenario as a planner's city, an entirely pre-planned city with no regard for the natural ways that urban spaces develop to encourage social networks and internal economic regeneration. The digital perspective on this kind of planning could be the modern smart city, where computing and digital connectivity aim to maximize the efficiency of how the city operates, possibly at the cost of impeding it from supporting healthy urban societies. While there is still the capacity for surveillance, it is unlikely that the state is doing the surveilling since the economy of this scenario would be oriented around jobs that are not done in collective spaces and thus do not support labour or social organizing. Davis's description of economically excluded slums where urban refugees are sequestered and excluded resonates in this scenario. In this type of digital city, it would be hard for poor refugees to meet through work, to share knowledge, or to build the wealth to start their own businesses. The economic development of cities in this scenario is not driven by urban displacement; instead it is driven by large technology firms that make the bulk

of their money off of data trading and by acting as intermediaries between governments and citizens, and labourers and customers. This scenario is the opposite of what Lefebvre would consider an urban society; here the state and capital dominate the city space and citizenry.

4 "Rust Belt," named after the central and northern urban industrial regions of the United States that used to produce steel, is a city where digitalization is not creating jobs (and may be erasing them) and the population is not using digital technology to build any kind of urban society. Those who can escape are doing so, leaving behind cities with depleted fiscal capacity, brain drain, and limited resources to meet the needs of those who cannot leave. From a development perspective, this is a "bad" scenario. There is outward migration as people are forced to seek livelihoods elsewhere, as well as forced immobility for those who want to leave but cannot. There is probably not much that technological change can do to improve things in this situation. The drivers behind this scenario are likely to be major systemic shocks; for example, as COVID-19 made it impossible for small businesses to operate in poor neighbourhoods and slums in Sub-Saharan Africa, many people left cities and returned to smaller towns and rural villages. For middle-income countries in the Global South where municipalities do not have strong revenue streams and surpluses to support businesses and residents, this kind of shock can be profoundly damaging. As people make the initial decision to move away, digital social networking tools can have a compounding effect. Evidence from Bangladesh indicates that after disasters in urban areas, poor labourers use their mobile phones to navigate back to semi-rural and rural areas where there is the chance for work. Here, digital technological change plays a direct role in dismantling urban society, leaving a shell of a city behind.

These are of course highly stylized scenarios developed using the imagery and empirics from different authors' concepts of urbanization and the life of cities. They provide a set of theoretically grounded heuristics to guide the analysis of the case studies that appear in later chapters. The case studies are based on survey and interview data about urban refugees' experience of digital technology in their lives –

these urban refugees theoretically are a core component for the regeneration of healthy cities, contributing labour and social connections to established urban systems. They are not disconnected from the urban spaces they live in, and their experience of technology as it relates to their social, economic, and political lives is a key part of understanding the development trajectories of their host cities in the digital era. Their responses in the aggregate can tell us about how they perceive the cities around them – whether the role of technology in their urban lives creates the perception of a North End, a Jobless Panopticon, a Lonely Hustle, or a Rust Belt. Indeed, we may see elements of different scenarios emerge in the case studies. To help understand why I selected the three cities for this study, and how the respondents were selected, we next examine how past technological change led to urbanization in cities in what is now referred to as the Global North.

HOW THE HISTORY OF URBAN MIGRATION AND TECHNOLOGY HELP BRING THE SCENARIOS TO LIFE

The cities of the past provide key data for understanding the present and future effects of digitalization and urban displacement on city development. At the start of First Industrial Revolution, technological change created new industrial processes that in turn demanded higher volumes of labour. This had a significant impact on the decisions displaced people made to move to cities; it also did much to shape the physical spaces of those cities. Tenements and slums were prominent features of late eighteenth- to mid-twentieth-century metropolises, serving as the entry points for newly arrived labourers. Early city planners were addressing the circumstance that cities were turning into crowded, dirty, unhealthy agglomerations of mostly poor displaced people; such spaces required physical and administrative rationalization. But industrial technological change did not just create the conditions for absorbing labour and producing goods. Indirectly, technological change created the conditions for organized urban society, especially labour movements. Factories and their associated machinery had become spaces where labourers gathered in large numbers; with social mass came the power to organize and demand rights.

Organized collective action in factories was not facilitated directly by technology the way it is today (i.e., through social media). That said, one consequence of industrial technological change was that it brought large numbers of poor labourers into contact with one another, and into contact with unionists. In later periods of large-scale migration, the conversion from sail to steam meant that an Atlantic crossing took days instead of months – again, a technological change that facilitated the migration of huge numbers of poor and working-class Europeans to American cities. Industrial technological change took another turn in the twentieth century as robotics and automation changed the demand for urban labour. In this book, the experience of earlier migrants will be nested within an analysis of wider systemic technological changes, helping show that while it was not the main purpose of technological change to create new urban societies and networks, this was indeed an outcome.

History also provides a few levels of perspective on digital change, urban displacement, and the development of cities that can help us evaluate the data collected in the present. The first level, and the one this book focuses on, is that of the individual urban refugee. History provides many examples of people moving to cities, often in response to a mix of economic incentives and push factors such as environmental shocks and political unrest. In modern parlance, we would say these people are part of mixed migration flows – people are on the move for reasons that reflect traditional migration choices as well as reasons that reflect forced displacement. One way that the historical analysis of urban displacement can help in this regard is by abstracting away today's legal and definitional characteristics assigned to different types of urban displaced people such as labour migrants, refugees, and the internally displaced. In the nineteenth and early twentieth centuries these legal or typological categories generally did not exist; migrants came to cities for a mix of reasons and integrated in whatever ways were available. As a result of this flow of urban displaced people, cities like Manchester, New York, and Paris developed into urban centres that have at various times struggled and flourished but have remained hubs of urban society. These urban displaced people shared many demographic and experiential attributes with today's urban refugees in the Global South, so understanding technological change in these past circumstances can help frame contemporary analyses of digitalization and urban displacement.

3

Technological Change, New Displacement Patterns, and Urbanization

The history of technological change as part of urban life offers a lens through which we can understand how theories of urbanization developed during the twentieth century and thus better understand how digitalization and digital technological change can create new drivers of urbanization, as well as avenues for urban refugees to integrate into cities of arrival. Much of the literature on urbanization and economic development has focused on the labour- and income-based motivations for moving to cities; the role of technology in creating these economic drivers has received less analysis. This chapter will fill that gap, showing how technological factors influenced urban refugees' movement to, arrival in, and integration into growing cities well before the digital era, starting in the late 1700s.

This chapter will use three examples of technological change, in combination with other social and political factors that helped create the conditions for large-scale urban displacement and migration. The first era we examine is the First Industrial Revolution in late eighteenth-century England. As the textile industry integrated new technologies like power looms into the manufacture of thread, urban factories in what is now Greater Manchester had to hire more and more workers. However, it was not just the opportunity to work that brought people to the city; also during this period, property laws were changed so as to eliminate rural commons where non-landowning people had long been able to extract resources or hunt for food. Many rural poor now faced the threat of being charged with trespassing or poaching and in effect were forced to move to cities. We then move forward into the mid-nineteenth to early twentieth centuries, a period of significant migration from Europe to the United States. Changes in transportation technology meant that transatlantic journeys could now be measured in days instead of months. Also, the ships could move many more people, and railway systems meant that cities in what would become the American Steel Belt became increasingly accessible from coastal urban centres like New York City. Again, though, it was not just pull factors of economic opportunity and easier travel that led to migration; many Irish and Germans were fleeing famines caused by crop failures and environmental shocks; around the same time, Jews in Central and Eastern Europe were fleeing antisemitic pogroms. This chapter's historical journey concludes in the mid- to late twentieth-century United States. The Great Migration, a massive movement of Black Americans from the southern to the northern United States, came at a time when manufacturing became increasingly less manual and the technology involved in moving to a city became administrative and surveillance-based. Like those displaced in England and Europe, African Americans were moving north for reasons besides economic opportunity; they were also responding to the racism and political terror they faced in the Jim Crow American South.

Rural-to-urban migration theories – for example, the Harris–Todaro (1970) model – have tended to focus on jobs and income as pull factors. What makes the urban displaced people in these historical periods relevant to modern discussions of urban displacement is the political and environmental push factors that contributed to their decisions to move. Many of these displaced people were poor and disenfranchised, and they often faced threats to their safety and physical health in their places of origin. These "push" factors are not directly related to technological change but are central to developing a historical understanding of how technology fits into larger patterns of displacement. That is why I will not be arguing that technology is *the* singular pull factor today – while technological change has played a key role in setting the economic conditions for urbanization, people's decisions to move are complex. Indeed, reducing such decisions to economic ones risks erasing the role played by trauma and disenfranchisement, both of which shape how urban refugees adapt and create homes and livelihoods in cities of arrival. Industrial and transportation technologies are woven into these people's stories, and understanding how this fabric of technological change and urban society has been woven is key to understanding and empathizing with today's urban refugees and the digital world in which they are making their journeys.

The relationship between industrial technological change and the sociopolitical drivers of urban migration also provides a basis for understanding the evolution of administrative technology and migration management (see the next chapter). Thus, these three historical cases do more than shed light on industrial and social changes that led to urbanization; they also provide a frame of reference for how statistics as a component of public administration evolved as a technology of control. As cities grew, authorities needed to make their swelling populations "legible" to the state. We do not often think of statistics and identity documentation as technologies, but indeed they are means for controlling and managing populations, and they reflect the economic and sociopolitical conditions that created a demand for them. Industrialization did much to create the early conditions that demanded quantitative tracking of populations, and over time administrative and surveillance technology extended itself until today it has as much influence on urban refugees' lives as the opportunity to find work and economic opportunity.

THE HISTORICAL METHODS EMPLOYED

While this is not a book of history in a formal or methodological sense, history plays a key role in building the overall narrative of how technological change affected urban displacement over time. Thus, I draw on a set of historical methods to guide my narratives of the interplay between industrial and administrative technological change in cities where displaced people settled. Historical causality, the use of secondary sources, and the use of objects from the digital collections of museums come together to show how urban technological change in England, Europe, and the United States shaped contemporary understandings of technology in society, as well as the reasons displaced people move to cities.

Frans van Lunteren (2019) argues that historical analysis is not just descriptive, but uses empirical knowledge of historical events inferentially and hermeneutically. The goal is to understand through historical data how processes unfolded. This book concerns itself with how technological change, both industrial and administrative, became embedded in urban contexts, thus creating the conditions in which urban displaced people shaped the social, political, and economic trajectories of cities of arrival. Drawing on Ermakoff's (2019) concept of a genetic approach to historical causation, I will take a "genetic-lite" approach to the historical analysis in this chapter and the next. The genetic approach to historical causality describes an inquiry that focuses on patterned processes leading to an outcome. What I look at in this chapter and the next is the pattern of industrial techno-social processes that brought urban displaced people into cities, thus spurring the authorities' demand for technologies to administer these rapidly growing urban populations. I refer to my approach as "lite" because I am not demonstrating rigorous statistical causality, but instead using literature, digital records and archival data, and artifacts from museum collections to describe a long-term industrial to administrative shift in the role of technology in urban displaced people's lives.

To that end, my approach will be largely archival and based on secondary sources. Ventresca and Mohr (2017) note that an archival approach can draw on a broad variety of sources, ranging from physical documents to digital and electronic databases, news and media, and statistical records. I draw on these as well as descriptions of museum-held technological artifacts to build an understanding of the technological tools that urban displaced people were using, in particular in Manchester and New York City. The use of artifacts has been contentious among academic historians, but as Chavis (1964) and Schlebecker (1977) argue, physical artifacts can tell us things about the society and the individuals who used them. This is particularly true when we are trying to understand how technologies created pathways for urban displaced people to shape their cities of arrival, as well as why industrial technologies may have brought people to cities but administrative technologies could be what defines the future of urban displacement in the digital era.

FROM THE COMMONS TO THE CITIES: ENGLAND AND THE FIRST INDUSTRIAL REVOLUTION

England from the early 1700s to the mid-1800s was a fount of industrial innovation and technological advancement. London may have been the centre of government and banking, but it was in secondary cities such as Manchester, Newcastle, and Birmingham that urbanization and manufacturing took off. These were centres of specialization, with Manchester becoming a hub of textile manufacturing, Newcastle specializing in steel and metallurgy, and Birmingham having a mix of manufacturing industries. As Hahn (2020) shows in her recent book on technology in the wider context of the Industrial Revolution, it was not just that technology was created and economies were reshaped; the main story was that technology did a great deal to reshape the structure of local communities, the politics of domestic labour relations, and international trade relations. The Industrial Revolution brought about a huge systemic shift in the global political economy, so to help keep this case contained, and to keep my focus on technology and urban displacement, I will look largely at Manchester during this period, because factories, machinery, and technology all played key roles in its urbanization (Lloyd-Jones and Lewis 1986).

Referred to as "Cottonopolis," Manchester grew from 10,000 inhabitants at the start of the eighteenth century to 89,000 by the start of the nineteenth, rising to 700,000 by 1901 (British Library 2014). As its nickname indicates, many of these new inhabitants moved from rural areas to work in Manchester's booming cotton industry. The city already had a large number of textile warehouses and was located on a network of shipping canals that positioned it to integrate cotton storing, weaving, and shipping as the technology for producing textiles at mass scale came into use. Indeed, it was the integration of production, warehousing, and shipping, and the close proximity of villages where cotton was spun, that created the conditions for Manchester to become "Cottonopolis" (Lloyd-Jones and Lewis 1986, 1988; Hahn 2020). The Bridgewater Canal moved finished cotton thread out for warehousing and shipping; it also brought raw cotton in from the American slave states and the West Indies to satellite towns such as Oldham, Rochdale, and Bolton, where people specialized in spinning thread and making textiles. Along with growing industry came a parallel trading and banking industry, as large commodity exchanges were established in Manchester during the 1800s. Without the physical and financial assets of the city, and without transportation capacity and networks of surrounding villages that produced finished materials, the technological changes of the time would not on their own have turbocharged Manchester's textile industry.

The invention and integration of new industrial-grade weaving technologies created a strong demand for labour in Manchester. Why was cotton so important in this context, and how did that importance create the space for rapid technological innovation? As a material, cotton is light and strong – good for clothing, but also useful in industrial applications – for example, it could be bonded with rubber to create belts for conveyor mechanisms and spinning machinery (Levitt 1986). From a technological standpoint, though, turning raw cotton into useful thread was a time-consuming process that required highly skilled workers. Prior to mechanization, spinners used spinning wheels to create thread; the problem was not the quality of the thread, but that it took someone working with a hand spinning wheel too long to create enough thread to meet demand. James Hargreaves invented the spinning jenny in 1764 that allowed a single worker to spin multiple spools at once, creating more yarn with higher consistency. Around the same time, his fellow Lancastrian Richard Arkwright created his own mechanical spinning machine, which used a water wheel to drive the spinning machinery. That machine became known as the water frame and was the technological basis for setting up factory production of cotton thread (Science and Industry Museum 2022). Samuel Crompton, also from Lancashire, invented the spinning mule in 1789, which merged aspects of the spinning jenny and the water frame, which meant that the machine could produce consistent thread at a finer gauge than could be achieved by hand spinning (Science Museum Group 2022).

The mechanical spinning of thread brought about the urbanization of the entire cotton industry. The spinning machines, along with much of the factory spinning that took place in the late 1700s and into the 1800s, were in southern Lancashire and northwest Derbyshire. Today's Greater Manchester metropolitan area is made up of towns from historic Derbyshire, Lancashire, and Yorkshire. Thread- and textile-producing towns in Lancashire like Rochdale and Oldham (which are now administrative units of today's Greater Manchester) were not part of the urban core of Manchester in the lead-up the Industrial Revolution. What the urban core of late-1700s Manchester provided was the logistics, infrastructure, capital, and labour to make, store, ship, and finance the rapidly growing global cotton trade. The city of Manchester started to grow around networks of canals, factories, warehouses, and storage depots. Indeed, canals were the key piece of transport infrastructure linking Manchester to the port of Liverpool, from which goods were shipped abroad. While Manchester was not traditionally a canal city, investments in canal basins such as the Rochdale Canal helped link it to the east of England and represented wider means for transporting materials and goods to support expanding industry (Maw, Wyke, and Kidd 2009, 2012). The sheer amount of cotton thread and textiles, transport and storage infrastructure, capital, and manufacturing capacity became a draw for other technological advances, such as the production of rubberized waterproof fabrics pioneered by Scottish chemist Charles Macintosh (Levitt 1986). Technologizing and industrializing the process of producing cotton thread in the counties around what became Manchester's city core led to demand for transportation and warehousing. Having the raw materials and capital in one city meant that people like Macintosh came to Manchester to realize the potential of their own textile-based technologies. We see at this point a bustling city, and the foundation for an urban society – but to understand what that urban society looked like, we have to explore who (beyond inventors) was moving to Manchester at the time it was industrializing.

To create the city that Manchester became during the nineteenth century, a mix of skilled and unskilled labour was needed. Running the machinery in spinning factories, such as the water frame, required technical labour. Of course, technical labour needed to be supplemented with physical labour – goods and materials needed to be moved, and infrastructure needed to be built. Able bodies were needed in large numbers. It is self-evident, though, that a city needs a mix of labour to grow and develop. Perhaps more interesting, then, is who moved to Manchester and other cities in England during the First Industrial Revolution. One factor we can examine is skills. Up to now, I have focused on the cotton industry, but there is far more to making that industry work than just spinning and weaving. As Lloyd-Jones and Lewis (1986) show in their analysis of the economic structure of early nineteenth-century Manchester, the complexity of industrial production was such that master weavers and factory owners required a wider variety of labour; banking, food and beverage production, chemical production, and all variety of builders made up the city's labour base. This mix of skills meant that the population of industrial Manchester reflected a wide range of life experiences and demographic backgrounds. If the work these people did was what constituted the city as a geographic administrative space, the mixing of their backgrounds and lived experiences is what created the urban society that Lefebvre would describe in his twentieth-century work.

Emma Griffin's (2014) biographical history of how the Industrial Revolution shaped the lives of labourers highlights not only the privation and tragedy that marked the lives of the working class but also the opportunities that industrialization opened up. Many of the changes and opportunities that arose were part and parcel of how technology changed the nature of political and labour organizing, at a time when laws affecting landownership and poverty were forcing people to move and reshaping social and economic networks. What did all this mean for Manchester and other English industrial cities? One major demographic change was that young people, particularly men, began moving to the cities. Williamson (1988a, 1988b, 1990) showed how over multiple generations in the early 1800s, English cities were stocked and restocked by young people. The emerging technologized urban society of cities like early nineteenth-century Manchester skewed young, as a boom in labour demand drew domestic migrants from rural areas. These young people had a mix of displacement and migration experiences. Also, in an era when minorities in England were generally distrusted, Manchester became a hub of Jewish society (Williams 1985). Williams (1985) describes the efforts the Jewish community undertook to build trust and push back against the antisemitism and xenophobic politics that were part of English politics and society. This community was a mix of people from outside Manchester, many of whom had been displaced by antisemitic politics and violence, and who now carved out a space for themselves in the expanding urban society and economy. Jewish communities, many of whose members had fled antisemitic pogroms and violence in continental Europe in the late nineteenth century, would play a role in major industrial labour movements one hundred years later in the United States.

Coming back to Manchester, and English urbanization overall in the late eighteenth and nineteenth centuries, it is important to understand how technological change shaped and was shaped by land, economic, and wartime politics. It is not just that technological change created economic opportunity in cities, although work as a pull factor was certainly part of the story. One factor that has been and continues to be debated is the role of the Enclosures Act, which led to the legal privatization of agricultural commons during the 1700s and 1800s. The idea of enclosure was to consolidate agricultural land so that it could be industrially farmed; this was achieved by landlords buying out leases on existing fields and merging those with the common lands on which peasants farmed. The acceleration of enclosure, and the formalization of it through parliamentary acts, had the effect of forcibly displacing poor tenant farmers and peasants who relied on the commons for food. As industrial technology shaped urbanization in cities like Manchester, agricultural technology and techniques drove changes in how land was amalgamated and who controlled its use. For the poor, the changes in industrial technology created urban jobs while changes in rural industrial technology forced many into unstable living conditions. Technology, property laws, and capital aligned to create large volumes of what amounted to internal displacement; many of these people ended up in cities, either permanently or as urban displaced people passing through.

It is important to avoid thinking uni-causally about technological change, urbanization, and internal displacement in England during the Industrial Revolution. Indeed, the evidence that rural enclosure pushed people off the land and into the urban labour supply is mixed. Chambers's (1953) foundational article on the relationship between enclosure and labour supply in England from the late 1700s to the mid-1800s showed that urbanization was far more demographically and economically complex than a linear rural-to-urban labour migration. When we look back at Griffin's (2014) biographical work on labourers in the English industrial period, something that comes up often is the regularity of moving. Often from very young ages, people moved for work, were kicked out of housing or off land, or were sent to poorhouses. Internal displacement, then, would be an apt way to describe the working-class experience of the early to mid-industrial period in England. What cities like Manchester evolved to represent for many people who were displaced was stability, albeit stability at a very tenuous step on the socio-economic ladder. For the Jewish community, the city provided space for a synagogue, which it could then build around in relative safety (Williams 1985). Labourers who moved to urban centres were also having children, and those children were surviving at high enough rates to grow up in cities, which further added to urban population growth (Chambers 1953; Williams 1988). Technological change in urban industries did more than change the economic structure of cities; it also generated a background social infrastructure that in turn drove major demographic, social, and political changes.

Thanks to industrial technologies, capital coalesced around production centres like Manchester; meanwhile, workers who had once been independent artisans or poor farmers found themselves working in large numbers at close quarters. Spinning and weaving technologies created demand for workers across a wide range of sectors at a time when oligarchic property policies were displacing rural populations and when English politics were growing increasingly reactionary and xenophobic. However, as Griffin points out in her biographies from this period, for the poor industrialization was not just a period of violence and displacement. It was also a period of expanding opportunities for political, economic, and social engagement. The Jewish community of Manchester found opportunity and safety in urban society, and workers formed unions and pushed for rights in the face of state-organized violence, although women remained excluded from these processes (Gershon 2016; Valverde 1988). Technological change had set in motion the expansion of urbanization, and it was the displaced poor whose labour and activism in a technologized context built England's cities. Moving forward to the 1900s, the role of displaced people would be central to shaping American urban politics as well. Along with industry, transportation technology would make New York City a beacon for those displaced from Europe – and displaced women would play a key role in labour strikes that were central to American labour reform.

FROM EUROPE TO NEW YORK CITY: THE GARMENT INDUSTRY AND URBAN DISPLACEMENT

New York City, Philadelphia, Pittsburgh, and other large American cities in the nineteenth century drew migrants from across Europe, particularly Germans, Irish, and Eastern European Jews. All of them were seeking better economic prospects as well as fleeing political violence, economic shocks, and famine. As in the previous section, I will focus on an exemplar case, New York City, to ground a wider discussion of how displacement and technology shaped turn-of-the-twentieth-century American urban society. One reason for selecting New York City is that it was the centre of the American garment industry from the late 1800s to the mid-1900s; thus as we move forward in time from Manchester, the "Cottonopolis," we will see how technological change revolutionized the production of thread and cloth and then the production of ready-made clothes. Another reason for selecting New York City and the garment industry is that it provides an example of how urban society becomes a place of refuge and opportunity for minorities displaced by violence and xenophobia. New York City's garment industry was largely staffed and run by

Ashkenazi Jews who had fled Eastern Europe and Russia to escape persecution and pogroms (Klier 1989).

During the Industrial Revolution in England, most of the urban displacement had been internal; by contrast, New York City hosted large communities of international urban displaced people. The city today has five boroughs: Manhattan, Brooklyn, the Bronx, Queens, and Staten Island. Between 1900 and 1910 the two largest boroughs were Manhattan and Brooklyn, with populations in 1910 of 2.3 million and 1.6 million respectively. In that decade they also had large migrant populations: 48 percent of Manhattanites and 35 percent of Brooklyners were foreign-born. The Bronx had around the same percentage of foreign-born residents as Brooklyn (35 percent) but one-quarter as many residents overall (around 426,000) (Gibson and Lennon 1999). With these numbers in mind, I will focus on migration and displacement in Manhattan and Brooklyn. Where did these displaced people come from? Most of those who were Jewish had come from the Russian Empire, Romania, and, later, Austria-Hungary. While Jews came to New York City in huge numbers between 1880 to 1910, they were not the only people who left Europe under varying degrees of duress and settled in American cities. Famine and environmental shocks in Ireland and political upheaval in Germany drove millions of people in those two countries to immigrate to the United States, with many of the Germans moving to large cities in the American Midwest (Library of Congress 2014) and many of the Irish immigrants staying in New York City and other cities on the American east coast (Library of Congress n.d.). Two types of technology shaped urban displaced people's arrival in and influence on urban society in New York: transportation – steamships had a profound impact on transatlantic ocean crossings – and sewing machines, which revolutionized the ready-made garment industry.

Shipping technology changed the volume and nature of transatlantic immigration and had a significant impact on the American industrial revolution (Hirschman and Mogford 2009). The displacement described in the preceding analysis of Manchester and England as a whole was primarily domestic, whereas the urban displaced people arriving and staying in New York City in the 1880s to 1900s were crossing not just international borders but entire oceans. Voyages that in the late 1700s would have taken six weeks and included a fair amount of variability in arrival times had been shortened to one or two weeks with significantly more reliable arrival times. How steam technology fit into the history and politics of immigration from Europe is just as important as the mechanical function of steamships as people movers. The surge in immigration from Ireland to the United States in response to the famine of 1845 brought about a scaling up of steam shipping. Cohn (2015) focuses on how the transition from sail to steam affected the routes between Europe to New York City; using passenger manifests, he shows how quickly the technological changeover happened. The demand for transit was surging prior to the American Civil War; after that war, however, uncertain political conditions in the United States slowed investment in steamship building. Once the production of ships picked up, though, more people could make the crossing, since steamships could carry far more passengers. Cohn (2015) shows that by the 1880s, all immigrants arriving in New York City were doing so by steamship (see also Keeling 2013; National Museum of American History n.d.a).

As of the mid-1800s, most immigrants from Europe to the United States intended to move west and start homesteads. After the Civil War, though, more and more displaced people and immigrants stayed in cities to work in industry, and in New York City in the late 1800s the garment industry was where many urban displaced people ended up working. Steamships had changed the way people reached New York; now the sewing machine changed the structure of the garment industry. Around the same time that urban displaced people began arriving and seeking work, garment manufacturing was evolving into an outsourced industry: contractors could set up shops in tenements, where the workers could produce ready-made clothes, with the larger garment companies then handling the finishing and distribution (Gotham Center for New York City History n.d.). Between the 1870s and 1900, the Lower East Side of New York City was a densely populated hub of "sweatshops" – apartments where garment contractors made ready-made clothes. It was the sewing machine that made these sweatshops possible, and many urban displaced people arriving with some basic sewing knowledge found work in these shops (National Museum of American History n.d.b). The sewing machine, a seemingly mundane piece of technology, had made this contracting system possible, and that system in turn responded to demand for more clothing (Stamp 2013; Monet 2022). To meet that demand, clothing production moved from the Lower East Side north into the Garment District, to factories where hand shears were replaced by Eastman cutting machines (Eastman Company n.d.). Clothing manufacture was becoming increasingly technologized.

In New York City's garment industry, and in other growing American industrial cities, displaced people from Europe were the labour force. Their voyages across the Atlantic were often one-way until the further advances in steam technology in the late 1800s made it both possible and practical to make return voyages to Europe. In the mid-1800s, massive numbers of Irish fled their island due to the 1845 potato blight and the resulting famine. More than one million Irish died during that famine; overall, Ireland's population shrank from 8.2 million in 1841 to 4.7 million by 1891 (Library of Congress n.d.). Meanwhile, many of the German immigrants to the United States during this era were leaving behind political turmoil and the lack of economic opportunity. This displacement reached its peak in the mid-1800s, but after the Civil War both Irish and German immigrants continued coming to the United States, with many settling in New York City. The violence and environmental catastrophe these urban displaced people left behind in Europe are analogous to many of the factors that are displacing today's urban refugees and displaced people. But with regard to New York City from 1880 to the 1910s, there is one demographic group that stands out both for its experience of displacement and for its unique role in the technologized garment industry: Eastern European Jews (History of New York City Project 2020).

Ashkenazi Jews in that era faced a rise in violent antisemitism in Europe and the Russian Empire (Klier 1989). They were not the first Jews to arrive in New York City; in the mid-1600s, Jews fleeing the Spanish and Portuguese Inquisitions had ended up settling in the Dutch colony of New Amsterdam, which later became New York City (Warner and Wittner 1998). In the early to mid-1800s, Jews from what is now Germany started arriving in New York City, leaving behind the discrimination they faced in Europe; there they established an upper-middle-class community as well as B'nai Brith, a fraternal organization that provided aid and social services to the community. Unlike their German counterparts who arrived in the first half of the nineteenth century, Ashkenazi Jews arriving from Eastern Europe spoke Yiddish; they were also more ideologically diverse (Fordham News 2017). Within the Lower East Side community, there were dedicated socialists, Zionists, and Orthodox. Many were poor, and living conditions on Manhattan's Lower East Side could be abysmal. The relationship between the German Jewish community that lived in Upper and Midtown Manhattan and the Central and Eastern European Jews who settled in the Lower East Side was at times strained and paternalistic (Caro 1974). Regardless, the latter community grew, and its members would play an important role in reshaping labour conditions for garment workers both in New York and in the United States as a whole.

The Jewish communities in late nineteenth- to early twentieth-century New York City, like their historical peers in industrial Manchester, had been displaced to a new urban setting, where they now established communities at a time of industrial, technological, and political change. Having left behind discrimination and violence, they now lived in a city where there were constant tensions between opportunity and exploitation, welcome and discrimination. The evolution of the New York City garment industry from being contractor and sweatshop driven to working out of factories and lofts, and the technology that supported that transition, is part of the story of how people displaced to New York City created a new urban society. It was an urban society in which labour rights and the fight for safe and fair working conditions was central.

The transition from sweatshops to garment factories had an impact on the working conditions faced by urban displaced people. Garment production was done in dangerous conditions, with long hours, and there were significant disparities between the jobs men and women held within the industry, manifesting in wage suppression and labour exploitation. The women most exposed to those disparities were Jewish and Italian immigrants, and it was Jewish women who organized the Shirtwaist Strike of 1909–10. Many of these women had been involved in labour unions and labour action in the countries from which they had been displaced, so they had experience with labour organizing. The very technology of the garment industry created the urban space for organizing: people worked in close quarters in sweatshops and factories, and contractors ran their businesses out of tenements. The labour organizing that was conducted in this context involved high-risk, confrontational action led by immigrant women, including Theresa Serber Malkiel, a strike participant who left us a detailed written account (1910). Prior to the strike, one of the labour leaders, twenty-three-year-old Clara Lemlich, had been hospitalized after being beaten by management-hired strike-breakers while on the picket line (Sanchez 2021). Like Lemlich, most of these women were young and poor, and they faced down strike-breakers hired by the factory bosses as well as the police, who were sympathetic to the factory owners and often colluded with them. The strike grew to 30,000 participants and led to significant reforms in New York's garment industry. The social networks and connections that developed within the Jewish Lower East Side community, built around a particular industry and its accompanying technologies, over time turned into concerted collective labour action that achieved tangible gains for industrial workers.

We continue the journey into the twentieth century with another example of displacement, this time returning to internal rural to urban movement. The Great Migration from 1910 to 1970 saw millions of Black Americans move from the Jim Crow South to cities across the northeast and midwest, drawn by economic and social opportunities that were unavailable in the formerly Confederate southern states. This opportunity is only half the story, though; many were pushed to leave by intense racist political terror and violence, an ongoing legacy of the white supremacist, chattel slavery roots of the American South. While industrial technologies were fairly well established in the cities Black Americans arrived in, the technological change I will focus on is the networks of administrative technology, grouped under the umbrella of surveillance. Community administration and the data collection that accompanied it were part of the Great Migration and together serve as a stepping-off point for understanding how demographics, statistics, and public administration played, and continue to play, a central technological role in urban refugees' lives.

THE SOUTH TO THE NORTH: LATE TWENTIETH-CENTURY INTERNAL DISPLACEMENT IN THE UNITED STATES

By the mid-twentieth century another large demographic shift was under way: Black Americans were leaving the American South for the large industrial cities of the north. Driving this migration was economic opportunity in the cities where European immigrants had been arriving since the mid-nineteenth century, combined with a desire to escape the racist political terrorism they would continue to face if they stayed in the states of the former Confederacy. The Great Migration was not the first period during which Black Americans moved to northern cities and established urban communities. Throughout the Antebellum era in the United States, Black slaves escaped to the North on the Underground Railroad, where they set up networks to help other escaped slaves move north and in doing so established Black cultural and political institutions in northern cities.

New York City, Philadelphia, and Rochester, among other cities, became centres of Black organizing and urban society well before the Emancipation Proclamation ended legal slavery. These Black urban societies were created with technology, but not technology in the sense of artifacts like spinning jennies or sewing machines. The technology that made it possible for slaves to escape to the North was information and networks. The Underground Railroad itself was a technology of information management and logistics, a system that enabled around 100,000 Black people to flee slavery in the South. Lacking a formal map of the routes for moving north to Canada, the Underground Railroad relied on word of mouth, coded messages, interdependent networks of free Blacks, cells of Abolitionists, Native Americans, and members of the clergy to establish meeting points and safe houses for the journey north (Gara 1961). While this chapter focuses on the Great Migration of Black Americans to northern cities long after the American Civil War, remember that it was the Underground Railroad that created the information networks and surveillance systems that were crucial to the safe movement of Black Americans out of the South during the Jim Crow era.

The post–Civil War decades saw an initial uptick in the movement of Black people with the end of slavery and the implementation of federal reconstruction policies. By the 1870s, though, federally managed Reconstruction had largely ended and a racist backlash had started that put in place laws restricting the political, economic, and social participation of Black people in the former Confederate states. This intermediary period from the 1870s to 1910 that came after the abolition of slavery but before the Great Migration saw large movements of Black Americans to Kansas. In 1874–75, Black people started moving to Kansas, although initially not in a large-scale, organized manner (Grant 2020). However, this movement prepared the ground and infrastructure for an organized large-scale movement of Black people to that state in 1879, referred to as the Exoduster Movement (Painter 1977). During this period, Black people were moving not only to Kansas, led by a Black entrepreneur from Tennessee name Pap Singleton, but also in smaller numbers to northern and midwestern industrial cities (Grant 2020). Grant provides us with a comprehensive analysis of how, in the mid-twentieth century, the Great Migration, especially after the Second World War, fundamentally reshaped the role of Black Americans in urban politics as they moved to northern cities. Her work helps show how information sharing and the distribution of social networks created the infrastructure to support the movement of 6.5 million Black people from the South and integrate them into urban societies in the North and Midwest.

After the Second World War, industrialization and production technology had more or less stabilized as features of the urban environment. In turn-of-the-century New York City, rapid technological changes were taking place in garment production; in contrast, by the mid-twentieth century, industrialization was complete. Factories and manufacturers still needed labour after the war, but industrial technology was no longer shaping urban migration the way it had up until the late nineteenth century. Instead, the technologies that played a key role in facilitating the Great Migration came under the umbrella of surveillance and provide a number of analogues to how we think about digital technology in the lives of today's urban refugees. This is not to say that translocal networks played no role in facilitating movement between Europe and the United States in the 1800s, or from rural to urban settings in England between the late 1700s and the mid-1800s. By the later Great Migration period, though, we see a change in the salience of networks and technologies of information sharing. For Black Americans in the United States until the end of the Civil War, the only option if they hoped to move was essentially to smuggle themselves to the North along a network of secret trails and safe houses. This required incredibly robust and secure information sharing, planning, and surveillance. After the Civil War, as Grant (2020, 39–68) explains, even though such movement was now legal, networks, translocal information sharing, and surveillance continued to play important roles in Black people's northward movement. Early on, migration clubs organized group transportation and temporary housing (Grossman 1989). Later, Black-owned media published in the North and distributed in the South provided information about life in the North to Black people who wished to leave the South. Churches and civil society organizations were also a core part of the networks that supported Black migrants. Upon arrival, Black migrants were registered to vote, and the Democratic Party courted them aggressively in northern and midwestern cities. Surveillance technology was central to making the Great Migration work: communities in northern cities needed to know where people were in the South in order to send them printed materials, churches needed to know whom to expect and when, and after they arrived in northern cities, political parties needed to find them in order to register them as voters so that they could join those parties. These networks were not technological artifacts like a spinning jenny or a steam engine, but they were technologies in the sense of information management and community oversight.

Compared to the other examples in this chapter, the demography of these Great Migration newcomers was more diverse. Drawing on work by Painter (1977) and Wilkerson (2010), Grant notes that the Great Migration was a leaderless movement; there was not a central figure like Harriet Tubman guiding escaped slaves north, or Pap Singleton organizing a large migration to Kansas. However, there were social networks and institutions that supported migration, and these were potentially key to the diverse demographics of people who moved. When professionals like doctors and lawyers went north, they often worked with migration clubs to bring people along, since they were going to need networks of clients if they hoped to establish practices. Labourers of course went north too. All of this meant that the urban societies that Black Americans established in northern cities were created around communities that had diverse educational, professional, and economic backgrounds. We could attribute this to the shift in the role of technology from being industrial to serving as a means to link networks of displaced people across space. In a context in which "technology" is networks and information, people organize around the skills and professions they need in a new city for the community to function.

Having established who moved, and the role that non-artifact technologies like social networks and surveillance played in facilitating movement, I now shift focus to why Black people who moved to northern cities during the Great Migration are analogous to modern urban refugees and displaced people. In her work on how the Great Migration shaped urban Democratic Party politics, Grant discusses the role of push and pull factors in decisions to migrate; these hinge on economic opportunity, and the pull factors of full citizenship and voting rights, balanced against the argument that existing Black communities in the South should be built and maintained. Many Black people would have left the South because of organized white supremacist terrorism, backed as it was by Jim Crow laws, which mandated that Black people be segregated from Whites. In practice this meant that Black people were forced to go to separate schools, were excluded from voting, and had their movements and lives controlled by racist authoritarian state governments. This level of oppression on its own would likely have served as grounds for seeking and receiving asylum in another country under today's refugee laws.

However, racist political terror in the Jim Crow South was not confined to statutory law. The Ku Klux Klan (KKK) was the largest of many white supremacist terrorist groups that emerged after the Civil War, and its stated purpose was to enforce white supremacy through violence. A national organization, the KKK was perhaps the most organized perpetrator of violence against Black people, but to understand how ingrained white supremacist violence was in southern society we have to understand the role that mob violence and lynching played in daily life. A lynching describes an event in which a mob extrajudicially murders someone for violating laws or social codes, and white supremacy in the South was the social code that trumped all others. Lynching could be directed at individuals, like fourteen-year-old Emmet Till, who was tortured and murdered for whistling at a white woman; see Tyson (2017) for a wider analysis of Till's murder. It could vary in regional intensity; see Meyers (2006) on lynching in southern Georgia. It could take the form of massacres such as those in Wilmington, North Carolina, in 1898 (see Cecelski and Tyson 1998) and Tulsa, Oklahoma, in 1921 (see Messer 2021). Roberta Senechal de la Roche (1996) argues that while lynching may have taken place in a context of poor Whites' resentment of growing Black prosperity, it served fundamentally as a mechanism of social control for elite Whites. Mutilated bodies were left hanging in trees for the express purpose of signalling what could happen to those who were perceived as having deviated from the white supremacist norms of the Jim Crow South. If you were Black, northern cities offered economic and political opportunity unavailable in the South, while staying in the South meant always living with the acute risk of violence and death.

As with the previous examples, central to the experience of Black Americans during the Great Migration was political exclusion and violence. They shared this experience with the factory workers in England, whose labour organizing was met with violence by the volunteer Yeomanry cavalry forces, and with Ashkenazi Jews, who were fleeing pogroms in their Eastern European home countries. In this way, the historical examples of urban displacement in this chapter provide a number of analogues to the experiences of exclusion and violence that are part of contemporary urban refugees' and displaced people's lives in Bogotá, Nairobi, and Kuala Lumpur.

FROM INDUSTRIAL TO ADMINISTRATIVE TECHNOLOGY IN URBAN REFUGEES' LIVES

These three historical examples help illustrate the role of technology in setting the conditions in which urban displaced people come to cities and form pockets and enclaves of urban society. Two factors tie these otherwise rather different cases together: the nature of displacement and the experiences of the displaced, and the evolution of technology, from its use in industry to its use in organizing.

The first factor is important for understanding the link to the modern case studies that come later in this book. In much of the literature on the early industrial period in England, the first Great Migration from Europe to the United States, and the second Great Migration and Southern Diaspora in the mid-twentieth-century United States, the people on the move were often referred to as migrants or immigrants. Yet when we look more deeply into the conditions that led to their moving to new places, we start to see parallels with modern concepts such as forced displacement. In late eighteenth- and early nineteenth-century England, the restructuring of common land use, along with changes in industrial and agricultural technology, forced many poor and landless Britons to move. Today we might refer to this as development-induced displacement, a concept that arose in the 1990s and that has evolved over the past twenty-five years (see McDowell 1996; De Wet 1996; and more recently Adeola 2020). The Jewish communities that played such a key role in New York City's garment industry in the late 1800s and early 1900s were often fleeing antisemitism and pogroms in Eastern Europe and the Russian Empire. In a modern framework, many of the Ashkenazi Jews arriving in New York City back then would likely have qualified for refugee status. The Black Americans who were part of the Great Migration from the American South are not generally viewed as having been internally displaced. If we unpack the conditions in the Jim Crow South, though, they faced high-intensity political terror and violence – lynchings were common, and white supremacist legal structures had stripped southern Blacks of political and economic autonomy. If they wanted to experience full citizenship and freedom from racist violence, Black Americans could *not* stay in the South. In each historical case we see factors that drove people to cities that are analogous to those that forced drove people to the case study cities later in this book.

From the perspective of technological change in urban settings and in the lives of urban displaced people, there is also a narrative arc that the next chapter will explore. In Manchester, technology was industrial: it mechanized and sped up the process of producing things, in this case cotton thread. It also magnified the importance of urban space, since factories benefited from proximity to tertiary services, transport infrastructure, and high-density housing for workers. By the time we reached New York City, the shift from producing thread and raw cloth to producing ready-made clothes and finished products came with the rapid expansion of sewing machine and cutting technology. This meant that the nature of urban enclaves and urban society also changed, as work was done within ethnic migrant communities, often in apartments and dwellings. The changes in technology meant that the garment industry relied on a different structure of urban society, built around ethnic enclaves. It also meant that the people displaced to New York City could organize politically in ways that were different from English labour organizing – men in skilled and managerial factory jobs dominated English industrial organizing, whereas the decentralized nature of New York City's sweatshops created space for women to play a leading role in labour organizing. By time we reach the Great Migration in the United States, a different type of technology was coming into play – organizing, networking, and surveillance technology. While labour and work played a role in how Black Americans settled in northern cities, the organization of travel and the administration of movement played a key role in shaping Black urban society.

Essentially, surveillance technologies allow governments, communities, and households to keep track of individual movements at a micro level while tabulating demographic and geographic mobility of populations at a macro level. The role of surveillance technologies in public administration, statistics, demographics, public health, and border control has significant effects on how and why displaced people settle in urban settings and how many of these people are able to make the journey to a city of arrival. As we move through time, statistical and demographic technologies evolve alongside the technologies used by individuals in a world where people are on the move.

4

Digitalization and Urban Administration: Evolutions of Surveillance

As we move away from the nineteenth and twentieth centuries and into the twenty-first, we find that technology has become a feature of urban displacement; society is shifting away from being based on industrial artifacts and toward practices of surveillance and networking. The Underground Railroad and, later, the migration clubs of the Great Migration were developed around hubs and networks of people collaborating to help move migrants from one place to another. The former network was illegal; that latter was a means by which groups of Black migrants were able to arrive in a new city as a somewhat intact community. Both these networks relied on surveillance technology to function: they kept lists of people on the move, maintained information about safe places to stop during a journey, and had networks in place to help newly arrived people settle. In their different ways, both represented types of surveillance. A process or method of surveilling or counting for the purpose of administration is, in essence, a "technology."

Clearly, surveillance can be menacing or sinister, as when state security services tap phones or monitor people's movements. But it can also refer to things like communities whose members use WhatsApp to check in after travelling from a meeting so that everyone knows everyone else is safe. In the late eighteenth century, the development of public statistics to track population growth and health was a form of surveillance technology. It seems that analogue and digital technologies have been behind almost all aspects of public and collective administration since the early days of industrialization (Thompson and Bates 1957). Some of this, as James Scott (1999) points out, involves the state trying to make the goings on within its geographic and economic borders manageable. State statistics help identify how many people are working and what they are producing and thus make it possible to plan fiscal policy and public investment. Scott extends his analysis back to the 1700s, which helps us get a sense of how far we have come in terms of the technology of counting and surveilling. He provides a basis for understanding the role of counting and surveillance in the operations of the state. To narrow this large topic down to the level of counting and surveilling urban displaced people, I will focus on the development of urban statistics and public health.

Public health in industrializing urban centres became a critical topic for policy-makers and researchers of the time. Rapid population growth had led to the development of slums and tenements, which in England during this period led in turn to outbreaks of waterborne and pulmonary diseases. Tracking these outbreaks, and by extension keeping track of how many people were arriving in working-class neighbourhoods and slums, and from where, was vital to keeping a factory-driven urban economy functioning. To put this into tangible perspective I will revisit industrial Manchester, drawing on Pickstone's (1985) historical analysis of public health and hospital development over the course of that city's industrialization. Public health serves as an example of how the state – or in this case the city – can use surveillance to make sense of displaced populations. I start with this history as a means to set the stage for developments in the late nineteenth and twentieth centuries, when surveillance technologies and public statistics were tailored to support policies directly related to immigration and refugee protection.

While border controls and restrictions on freedom of movement are not unique to the United States, I will focus on that country for the sake of presenting a single historical example. In the mid- to late 1800s in the United States, waves of xenophobia led to laws that banned immigration from particular countries and parts of the world. These exclusionary immigration laws, which came and went, targeting different groups at different times, required both the technology of counting and the technology of passports if they were to be enforced. Again, we do not commonly think of these things as technologies, but indeed they represent surveillance technology in both statistical and documentary form. Passports in particular have been become highly technologized, and I will be looking at how computer chips and biometric data have become key technologies in modern passports.

Statistical tracking and passports are part of life for all people who cross borders, so to bring this part of the book to a close and set up the next one I will spend time focusing specifically on how surveillance technologies are used and deployed in contemporary urban displaced communities. Unlike business travellers, tourists, or people moving to new countries with work visas, displaced people and refugees must contend with an often highly invasive level of technological administration and surveillance. My analysis will cover the role of international organizations in these technological processes, as well as that of the private sector, and will also analyze how displaced communities themselves use surveillance technologies to manage and govern their own members. I will close the chapter with a synthesis of the historical analyses in this chapter and the last and provide some leading points to take into the next section of the book, where we will look at the lives of urban refugees and displaced people in specific cities as they are affected digital technology.

STATISTICS AS TECHNOLOGY: MAKING INDUSTRIALIZING CITIES ADMINISTRATIVELY LEGIBLE

Early in the industrial era, rapid urbanization forced political and administrative leaders to re-examine the role of demographic statistics as a policy tool. In discussions today we do not tend to think of public statistics and demographic data collection as technologies; it is more common to think of "technology" in terms of physical artifacts or internet technologies. Yet the collection of public statistics is in fact a type of surveillance technology. To better understand this, I will examine how government authorities gathered data on people as well as what statistics signified as a tool for managing rapidly growing cities. Questions of political economy will come up in this analysis: On whom do we collect data? From whom do we collect it? Why is that data of importance? During the Industrial Revolution, data were collected on workers and their health and family status, since healthy workers were important to an economy that demanded more and more labour. This helps us understand why health and hospitals were so important to growing industrial cities and provides a tangible example of how surveillance technologies in urban refugee and displacement contexts evolved over time.

Public administrators have been integrating computer systems for data collection and processing since the 1950s (Thompson and Bates 1957). Large-scale enterprises, both public and private, have found ways to make complex systems legible as a whole. Governments use statistics and measures to manage the complexities of state administration and thus have become increasingly "datafied." One example is Norway's national digital data management system (Tøndel and Anthun 2013); another is governance agencies' outsourcing of data management to data science firms like Palantir.[1] It is debatable whether this "datafication" and focus on measurement and manageability translates into better outcomes for citizens. There is a risk that the turn to statistics and computers as means to render populations legible to the state will have a reductive or dehumanizing effect – that people will become numbers instead of unique actors within a polity.

Unless there is citizen involvement in the development of digital and statistical systems for delivering and managing public resources, data technologies risk reinforcing the role of the state as a surveillance entity instead of provider of public goods. Webster (2012) discusses this using the metaphor of the X-ray machine. The collection of citizens' data for the purposes of planning state operations and services is inherently a type of surveillance, in that it attempts to see through and into the inner workings of complex social systems. Webster argues that to derive the greatest collective value from these systems we must constantly evaluate the trade-off between privacy and visibility. This trade-off and the contestation between citizens and the state regarding statistical surveillance long predates digital computing. Statistics as a surveillance technology for making space and populations legible to the state were central to the modernizing endeavour of urban industrialization and city planning.

Since this book focuses on the role of digital technological change in urban refugees' lives and their connections to contemporary cities of arrival, I will not attempt a full historical account of the role of statistics and surveillance in administrative development. Instead, I will draw on James Scott's (1999) overview of the development of the administrative state to highlight the history of measurement and statistics as technologies of governance as a starting point. Scott's work is particularly useful, for he shows how counting and measurement led to the creation of national citizenship in France and examines how modernist notions about administrative legibility influenced urban planning and city redevelopment in ways that favoured state control and dominance of the population. Since he was analyzing the industrialization era, we can use his findings to understand how counting and measuring became central to the management of growing cities, then later to the control of borders, and to data collection for humanitarian purposes in today's context. Scott opens with an analysis of how France during the 1700s undertook the onerous process of standardizing measures across various estates and subnational legal spheres. I say *onerous* because measurement is a reflection of both empirical reality and sociopolitical interests. Scott explains that if someone is measuring volume, for example, questions arise as to how dry or wet something is, and whether it can be "crowned" as opposed to made level with the top of a container, and so on (1999, 27–9). The state finds it worthwhile to struggle with these distinctions, since drawing them allows it to set a uniform tax code and track the volumes of commercial products moving within and across its borders. Uniform systems of counting and taxing also create uniform definitions of citizen. When the power to tax and count rests with the national government, people become identifiable by the fact of their residence within the geographic space of the country, rather than their subregion.

In the late eighteenth century in France and Germany, the focus was initially on counting and taxing agricultural goods, such as grains, as well as timber and the like. Then as industrialization and urbanization started taking root, counting *people* became equally important, and this strengthened the political will to reimagine the physical attributes of cities. Organized labour movements were going toe to toe with the apparatus of the state, fighting for a broad reorientation of workers' rights and political agency. In response, governments both national and city-level tried to make urban populations statistically legible and urban landscapes more linear and rational. Georges-Eugène Haussmann's "reinvention" of Paris between 1853 and 1870, commissioned by Napoleon III, expanded the city physically and modernized its infrastructure. This was necessary, as the population of Paris had doubled in the first half of the nineteenth century (as had that of many other European cities) even though the city remained the same physical size. This had led to crowding, as well as public health issues, besides making it hard for the state to enforce order. The enforcement of order was an important aspect of Haussmann's project, but so was the ability to monitor things like public health, and that is still the case in today's digital world (Graham and Wood 2003).

How, then, did cities during the industrialization era develop statistical and demographic systems of surveillance? How did this uniquely affect people who had been displaced to cities? And how did the technologies of surveillance of people crossing borders and moving to cities evolve over time? In the late nineteenth century, we start to see national immigration policies develop on the back of national citizenship. Statistics and counting remained important technologies, but now they shifted their focus away from who was already *in* cities and toward who was being displaced *to* cities. The idea of setting quotas was part of the American experience, so I will be using the historical track record of American immigration policy to map how the modern passport came into being as a technology of surveillance and border control.

URBAN EPIDEMIOLOGY AS TECHNOLOGY: PUBLIC HEALTH DURING THE INDUSTRIAL REVOLUTION

During the period of industrialization, both in continental Europe and in England, much of the movement to cities was initially domestic. While some people who moved to Manchester – Jews, for example – came from abroad, the majority of people moving to newly industrializing cities were arriving from the surrounding countryside. In many places the notion of national citizenship either was in its infancy or did not exist at all, since many European states were still confederations or agglomerations of various kingdoms and principalities.[2] As urbanization took root and industrial technology changed the nature of labour, people displaced to cities began living in tenements, where proper sewage and wastewater systems were lacking, disease was often rampant and hard to control, and urban birthrates were rising. English cities like Manchester, London, and Newcastle, as well as continental cities like Paris, suddenly needed to be able to keep track of populations in ways that had not been necessary prior to industrialization.

Medicine as a profession, and medical systems generally, evolved significantly throughout the nineteenth century, although as Starr (1977) has pointed out, health care would not become a major component of national economies until the twentieth century. Prior to industrialization, medical treatment typically was provided in the home. Modern hospitals for the urban working class and the impoverished evolved from religious charities and poorhouses, which provided social and medical services as late as the late eighteenth century. At that point, as industrialization and urbanization began to take hold, treatment of disease began to be part of medical practice; hospitals grew in size, ceased being religious centres, and became "medicalized" (Mann 2020). Some of this medicalization of hospitals was a consequence of teaching and training, which led to the professionalization of medicine. This, however, was not an apolitical change; in this time of urbanization and industrialization, medical doctors had begun playing a key role in medical/social reform. Rose (1971) writes that many doctors in nineteenth-century England viewed the sheer volume of disease and death among the urban working class as an insult to their profession and a blight on social progress.

Technology does not evolve in a vacuum. Here, it is important to understand why public health and hospitals were relevant technologies for tracking and monitoring urban displaced populations in England and France. Technological change on the industrial side of things demanded a large, urbanized labour force. Given the logic of capital, a labour force that was repeatedly rendered incapable of working due to the transmission of air- and water-borne pathogens could result in serious losses for factory owners, exporters, and investors. Foucault (1980) writes that the politics of health in the eighteenth and nineteenth centuries revolved around new methods of counting, organizing, and administrating the body, of both the individual and the population. How did this manifest itself as a technology?

> What is the basis for this transformation? Broadly one can say that it has to do with the preservation, upkeep and conservation of the "labour force." But no doubt the problem is a wider one. It arguably concerns the economico-political effects of the accumulation of men. The great eighteenth-century demographic upswing in Western Europe, the necessity for co-ordinating and integrating it into the apparatus of production and the urgency of controlling it with finer and more adequate power mechanisms cause "population," with its numerical variables of space and chronology, longevity and health, to emerge not only as a problem but as an object of surveillance, analysis, intervention, modification etc. The project of a technology of population begins to be

sketched: demographic estimates, the calculation of the pyramid of ages, different life expectations and levels of mortality, studies of the reciprocal relations of growth of wealth and growth of population, various measures of incitement to marriage and procreation, the development of forms of education and professional training. Within this set of problems, the "body" – the body of individuals and the body of populations – appears as the bearer of new variables, not merely as between the scarce and the numerous, the submissive and the restive, rich and poor, healthy and sick, strong and weak, but also as between the more or less utilisable, more or less amenable to profitable investment, those with greater or lesser prospects of survival, death and illness, and with more or less capacity for being usefully trained. The biological traits of a population become relevant factors for economic management, and it becomes necessary to organise around them an apparatus which will ensure not only their subjection but the constant increase of their utility. (1980, 171–2)

In an era of contestation around work, labour, and rights against a backdrop of technological change, the surveillance of urban displaced people manifested itself in the form of demography and well as measures to address public health and the urban environment. Indeed, given that industrial technology was beginning to change how labour was organized, and given that urban societies were beginning to embrace a new politics of class, the state needed to surveil urban populations not just to track disease outbreaks and maintain public health but also to control and coerce those populations. Haussmann's broad Parisian boulevards gave the police and the army the advantage in street battles, and this aligned well with the French state's interest in countering popular revolutionary movements. Across the English Channel the political motivation to surveil aligned with the government's increasing xenophobia and wartime footing, besides making it easier to respond with force to labour unrest. Surveillance through public health and medicine, and investment in public infrastructure, served multiple purposes. It increased the state's capacity to provide health services and respond to disease outbreaks, while serving the desire of the state to maintain security and order.

Over time, the internationalization of urban displacement and migration shaped how public health data were made transferable across borders. The 1891 Immigration Act in the United States barred entry to people carrying contagious diseases. Yew (1980) and Birn (1997) describe how immigrants were medically evaluated on their arrival at Ellis Island in the early twentieth century, showing how these "line evaluations" were just as efficient as exclusionist and racist policies at keeping out immigrants, in that diseases came to be associated with poor urban immigrants from southern and eastern Europe. As noted earlier, to count border crossers and bar the unwanted, there needs to be a technology in place for gathering data. At Ellis Island, the surgeons working for the US Public Health Service would visually inspect immigrants and, if they saw no signs of disease or disfigurement, send them on to immigration registration officers. Those who were sick could be deported or quarantined. The management of vaccine records and immunizations for the purposes of crossing borders was formalized between the 1930s and the 1950s; this led to the World Health Organization creating the International Certificate of Vaccination and Prophylaxis (ICVP), more commonly known as the Yellow Card. While the ICVP has evolved since its initial approved version in 1956, it retains formatting that allows physicians to enter standard data on a traveller's vaccination status. Nigeria, Zimbabwe, and a handful of other countries have created digital versions of the ICVP (WHO 2020), and the COVID pandemic has spurred the development of globally recognized digital COVID vaccination passports (Dye and Mills 2021). From the end of the nineteenth century and throughout the twentieth, public health surveillance became a cross-border technology, overlapping with the functions and politics of the main of border management: passports.

PASSPORTS AND THE TECHNOLOGY OF BORDER CONTROL

Later into the industrial period, displacement to cities started to become cross-border. While migration to the United States followed many pathways, and included rural migration, by the late nineteenth century many of the new arrivals in coastal cities like New York City were coming from Europe. Immigration control, and its often attendant xenophobia, is not historically unique to the United States; still, I will focus on the US case since the evolution of its immigration policies in the late nineteenth century provides a bridge to my later analysis of refugee counting and registration during and after the Second World War. At a time when city-level demographics and health statistics were solidifying as tools for administrative surveillance in England and France, the US government was dealing with migration to both the east and west coasts of the country. This led to laws setting race- and nationality-based quotas, strengthened border control, and thus the technology necessary to count and track who was entering the United States. I will focus on laws that restricted cross-border movement, set quotas, and established standards for passports and documentation. Those who are interested in a comprehensive analysis of all the principal American immigration laws should visit the website of the Migration Policy Institute (MPI 2013).

After declaring independence in 1776, and then winning the Revolutionary War against the British in 1783, the US government in 1790 set out its first immigration and naturalization law, the Naturalization Act. Essentially, one needed to be a "free white person," have good moral character, reside in the United States for two years, and swear allegiance to the US Constitution (MPI 2013). Shortly after this law was put in place, the first deportation law came into effect, the Alien Enemies Act 1798. This law, which granted the president the authority to detain and deport any male citizen of a hostile country during times of war, would be used during the Second World War by President Franklin Roosevelt to forcibly intern Americans of Japanese descent. It is still in place. Few changes were made to US immigration policy until after the Civil War, at which point changes came rapidly. The Immigration Act of 1864 set in place the rule that labour contracts formed abroad were enforceable in US courts; this was part of an effort to encourage immigration in response to a post-war labour shortage (Cohn 2015).

The ensuing rapid rise in immigration from Europe and Asia fostered a xenophobic backlash in the coming decades. The Immigration Act of 1875, also known as the Asian Exclusion Act, made it illegal to bring contract labourers from Asia to the United States. This was followed in 1882 by the Chinese Exclusion Act, which banned Chinese labourers from entering the country for ten years, prevented those already in the country from naturalizing, and from 1892 required Chinese nationals to obtain immigration registration papers. Between

1903 to 1917, new exclusion laws barred anarchists, all Asians except Filipinos, and people over sixteen who could not read from entering the country. The 1921 Emergency Quota Act capped immigration visas at 3 percent of the sending country's population, continued to ban Asians, and capped annual immigration at 350,000 arrivals. In 1924 the National Origins Quota Act further limited visas, set the new quota at 2 percent of the sending country's population, capped new visas at 165,000, and banned entry for Asians and anyone who did not qualify for naturalization.[3] As we will see in the next section on refugees, these quotas were among the main reasons many Jews fleeing Nazi persecution were denied entry to the United States and had to return to Europe. It was not until 1943 that the Magnuson Act repealed the Chinese Exclusion Act and not until 1952 that the Immigration and Nationality Act removed race and nationality as bases for excluding immigrants. In 1965, the nationality-based quota system was replaced with a seven-point preference system; finally, after multiple rounds of ad hoc refugee laws, the United States adopted the UNHCR definition of refugees and removed them from the immigration preference system.

All of these laws required the means to count people, categorize them by race and/or nationality, and document this information. In the pre-digital era, this was of course done with paper. Chinese residents of the United States needed to obtain registration papers, and people entering the country from the 1920s onwards needed visas, which would be counted against their home country's quota. But for the immigrants and displaced people themselves, the key document was and remains the passport. Passports are the original technology of border surveillance. Passports in some form have existed for centuries, often as written documents from one sovereign to another requesting that their subject be granted safe passage across a border (Lloyd 2003). In the 1500s the idea of a passport likely had less to do with immigration quotas and more to do with diplomatic relations, but this started to change in the 1800s and fully changed in the mid-twentieth century. That is when we start talking about passports and visas as a means for counting and tracking the movements of people across borders. After the First World War, the League of Nations proposed a global standard for passports; in the United States, it was the Emergency Quota Act and 1924 Immigration Act that cemented the importance of a standardized document that showed an individual's nationality (Pines 2017). From this standard, the passport as a piece of administrative and surveillance technology has evolved to include computer chips, biometric data, and increasingly artful ways to prevent forging.

Computers and biometric technologies have since been introduced alongside statutory and legal standards. Sticking with the United States as an example, the 2002 Enhanced Border Security and Visa Entry Reform Act required the development of an electronic system for sharing information about entry and deportation to and from the United States. As the system of surveillance demanded it, the technology of the passport advanced – machine readability and computer data chips make a passport, and by extension its holder, legible to computing systems that track the numbers moving across borders. However, technology has politics, and contemporary passports are not simply tools for digitizing information about the movement of an analogue human. As noted by Pines (2017) and O'Byrne (2001), the passport serves a symbolic and political purpose. In an increasingly mobile world, a passport represents someone's "stateness"; instead of being a document easing mobility, it often serves to indicate that the holder is unwelcome to cross a border. The concept of "bordering" and the technologies associated with it are central to critical research and theory of migration and immigration policy. Those who suffer the least from bordering are those with the "right" passport, one that has been issued by a wealthy nation and is fully kitted out with the latest digital and biometric technologies. Urban refugees often fall on the other end of the spectrum; they often lack any kind of national documentation, and digital systems of border control have made them increasingly illegible to the state, which forces them into conditions of danger and legal precarity as they try to build lives in cities of arrival.

DIGITAL TECHNOLOGY IN THE LIVES OF TODAY'S URBAN REFUGEES IN THE GLOBAL SOUTH

Much of my discussion in the previous sections has focused on the general surveillance of public processes through data collection, demographics, and public health services, as well as the role of passports as a documentary and surveillance technology in border management. All these things have historically been central to the lives of urban refugees and displaced people. For contemporary refugees and displaced people, though, crossing borders can be arduous and very often dangerous; many are doing so without passports or identity documentation, and the politics of asylum and refugees over the past five to seven years have become decidedly more reactionary and xenophobic (Nwabuzo and Schaeder 2017). While the most dangerous journeys, or at least those that receive the most media coverage, follow Mediterranean routes from the Middle East and North Africa to Europe, there is no shortage of hardship for refugees and displaced people moving *within* Latin America, Sub-Saharan Africa, and Southeast Asia. Urban refugees who lack documentation or passports risk detention if they are found by police; to avoid this, many of them cross borders in remote areas, often paying smugglers to help them do so. Those who have made it across the border then have to claim asylum if they wish to have refugee status, or move to an enclave where they can settle into ethnic or national networks without registering.[4]

Humanitarian agencies, principally the UN High Commission for Refugees (UNHCR), provide registration and protection services to people who have crossed a border and are seeking asylum. Since many asylum seekers and displaced people lack formal identification documents, the UNHCR acts as the interface between them and the host government, establishing background information about asylum seekers, providing identification documents, and in effect making them legible to the state. Other organizations do this too, including the World Food Programme (WFP) and the International Committee of the Red Cross (ICRC). Humanitarian organizations are not only the agencies that handle refugee registration; at times, national governments and even municipal authorities provide registration and social services to urban refugees. What is important to understand is that surveillance, which includes registration, identity documentation, and biographical data collection, is a critical technology in the management and administration of refugees and communities of displaced people, particularly in the Global South.

Based on this we can now explore in greater detail how digital surveillance, accessed via devices ranging from mobile phones and tablets to laptops and sensors, increasingly slots into the daily lives of refugees. While this book focuses on urban refugees, I will also touch on examples and theories that are based on the experiences of refugees living in camps. To counterbalance the analysis of institutional technology and innovation, I will also explore how refugee and displaced communities use digital technology in their own ways. This institutional versus community comparison is helpful in understanding the ways that communities and institutions interact and cooperate in digital spaces. The institution-versus-community dichotomy also helps highlight how institutions understand processes of innovation in very different ways than urban refugee communities.

The English-language concept of "refugee" dates back to seventeenth-century France, when the Protestant Huguenots fled religious persecution, seeking asylum in England (Hornak 2017). However, until after the Second World War there was no global legal framework for recognizing refugees. A stark illustration of this lack of global framework was the world's failure to provide refuge for Jews and other groups who were being persecuted and murdered in Nazi Germany during the 1930s and 1940s. Immigration policy had evolved significantly since the late nineteenth century, and visa quotas based on nationality and ethnic and religious identity were common (USHMM 2022). Initially, the Nazi regime pushed Jews to emigrate, but because of the quotas put in place by the United Kingdom, United States, Japan, Australia, and other destination countries, mass emigration was impossible. In response to the increasing violence and persecution, and the large numbers of German, Austrian, and Czech Jews trying to flee, the Allied countries organized the Evian Conference to set out quotas and policies for receiving refugees fleeing the Nazi regime. Statutorily, many Jews could not gain admittance to safe countries since they could not obtain immigration visas, despite clearly being refugees by any common definition.[5] In the aftermath of the Second World War, the UNHCR was founded to organize aid and resettlement services for 11.3 million "Displaced Persons" in Europe who could not return to their home countries (Kirchoff 2006). The 1951 Refugee Convention represented the first international legal effort to establish who a refugee was; it also established that signatory states could not deny entry to someone claiming asylum based on that definition. Later, the 1967 Protocol relating to the Status of Refugees extended the geographic scope of the 1951 Convention beyond Europe, making it a global norm (OCHCR 2022).

Immigration quotas required new technologies for counting and tracking who was crossing borders. Ways had to be found to count and surveil these people. There needed to be procedures for applying for asylum, documenting applicants' residence status, and adjudicating cases. "Refugee" was a new category of person, and these people had to be made legible to the state. In the 1950s in West Germany, millions of displaced people were trapped in cities like Hamburg, having been forced to come to Germany as slave labour; they all needed to be made legible. They were not citizens of post-Reich West Germany, but neither were they immigrants in any way that immigration law at the time understood, and the 1951 Convention was meant to serve as the mechanism for making them legible as a persons within the West German state. The UNHCR office in Bonn, Germany, was in charge of registering Displaced People, adjudicating their claims, and organizing their housing and support; eventually, these tasks would be taken over by the German state. The 1951 Convention and 1967 Protocol formed the legal and normative basis for how signatory governments would formally register and count people crossing their borders to seek asylum and refugee status. These historical roots, and the administrative and institutional technologies that were used to identify, register, and manage refugees, undergird many of the ways that the UNHCR and international humanitarian organizations today use digital technology and media in their work (Seuferling and Leurs 2021).

As noted earlier, surveillance technology does not need to be digital. The legal and administrative process for making refugees legible to the state in 1950s West Germany used paper. Within a given office, there were systems in place for organizing paperwork so that individual claimants' files could be found, annotated, and updated; later, as computers evolved, the documentation and adjudication of asylum requests became increasingly digital. The UNHCR and other humanitarian agencies that work with displaced people and refugees digitize their operations in large part to increase their capacity to manage registration and identification documentation. This activity maps onto the way that states try to control the number of people entering through traditional migration channels, which are documented and controlled by passports, physical and digital borders, and contested political discourses (see, for example, Chouliaraki and Georgiou's [2019] work on digital borders). Digital registration currently includes names, images, and biometric data such as fingerprints and retina scans. Once these data are gathered and refugees are made legible to the state – or to the UNHCR when it acts on behalf of the host state – refugees can access things like health services, food aid, and cash assistance. The move to digitalize services for refugees is happening worldwide. For example, health services for refugees in Malaysia are listed on a website managed by the UNHCR (Martin-Shields and Munir-Asen 2022), and access to food in the Kakuma refugee camp in Kenya is managed through a mobile phone–based cash distribution system called Bamba Chakula (Martin-Shields 2021). In Jordan, biometric identity systems have been used to manage the distribution of cash assistance for Syrian refugees (Kramer 2021).

For humanitarian institutions the technological goals are legibility, efficient resource allocation, and continual auditing (see Scott 1999). For urban refugees themselves, though, digital technologies are how they are able to join social and economic networks in the cities where they have settled. Koen Leurs has done significant work on the creative ways that displaced people use mobile phones and social media to create life worlds outside the constraints of refugee existence. For them, smartphones are personal archives, places to store personal effects such as photos as well as PDFs of administrative documents (Leurs 2017). Leurs has also described how LGBTQ refugees express themselves creatively in digital spaces (Patterson and Leurs 2019) and use translocal digital social networks to maintain a sense of hope when they are stuck in transit and waiting to continue a journey (Leurs 2014). The ways that institutions imagine refugees use digital technologies, and the ways that refugees actually do use them, provide insight into how refugees appropriate the tools of surveillance and administration for their own purposes. Refugees in Kuala Lumpur had developed social media groups where they shared information about potential police raids on workplaces, in this way turning surveillance back on the state (Martin-Shields and Munir-Asen 2022). Refugees in Brazil who were participating in digital job programs reported using those programs to help them find safety and stability in a new place; for them, the digital work itself was not the most important part of the program (Alancar and Camargo 2023). Refugees who cannot afford a mobile phone can use SIM cards to store food aid credits – that is how Bamba Chakula works – although this can be more trouble than it's worth (Martin-Shields 2021). In the Kakuma refugee camp in Kenya, shops and kiosks would let refugees use a shop mobile phone to cash out the credit stored on the card, often for a small fee. The techno-individualization of food aid creates opportunities for entrepreneurialism among some refugees; but other refugees inevitably end up with less net aid after cashing out their SIM cards (Martin-Shields 2021).

In many of the same ways that urban displaced people working in England and the United States organized political movements in technologized workspaces, today's urban refugees use social media and digital technologies to access affinity groups, build translocal solidarity networks, and advocate for their rights. This often takes place in parallel with or completely outside the ways that humanitarian agencies and host states use digital technologies for registration, surveillance, and record keeping. During industrial era, factories provided the physical space for labour movements to do their organizing; today, social media provide virtual spaces for urban refugees to reimagine and create ideas of what life is or could be in the places where they have settled. At the same time, the digitization of humanitarian services and service provision has led to an individualistic restructuring of social safety nets. As Bhagat and Roderick (2020) note, placing private technology providers between economic and social resources and the urban refugees who need those resources generates a neocolonial power structure where private interests in the Global North get to decide who is worthy of credit or who can access social services. In the digital world, urban refugees face a new technological tension: they are building new social networks and developing new notions of urban identity and society, but even while they are doing that, the digitization of humanitarian services and institutions often privatizes and limits access to the humanitarian social safety net.

APPLYING THE HISTORY OF TECHNOLOGY AND DISPLACEMENT TO THE PRESENT

How does all this background history of industrial and surveillance technologies in the lives of urban displaced people help us as we move on to the modern case studies in Part 2? In Chapter 2, I presented four stylized scenarios for how digital technological change could increase or decrease labour opportunity and surveillance in cities, and how this would impact the role of urban refugees in host cities' development. Here, again, are the theoretical/empirical scenarios:

> *Rust Belt*: Less job growth, less networking/surveillance. Jobs go away and people do not connect online. The city atomizes society, and people either leave or are increasingly isolated. Digitalization does away with urban society.

Lonely Hustle: More job growth, less networking/surveillance. Lots of new jobs, but these jobs are often menial (e.g., training machine learning software) or are gig-based with low pay (e.g., Uber driver) and are done alone.

Jobless Panopticon: Less job growth, more networking/surveillance. Limited or no job creation via digitalization, but increased digital connectivity among urban refugees, public administration, and illicit networks.

North End: More job growth, more networking/surveillance. Digitalization and technological change create the means to seek new jobs and opportunities, while also allowing urban refugee communities to network and connect in new ways.

Through an analysis of Bogotá, Nairobi, and Kuala Lumpur's economic and political histories of hosting refugees and displaced people, we will explore how digital technology is shaping refugees' lives in these cities, and how in turn these refugees are shaping those cities.

PART TWO

Contemporary Case Studies and the Digital Future of Urban Displacement

5

Methods in the Contemporary Context: Case Studies and Data Collection

History provides a number of analogies to modern urban migration in developing countries and can help reduce some of the sensationalism in modern debates about migration. To bring the conceptual and historical analysis into the present, data were collected in three cities from middle-income developing countries – Bogotá, Kuala Lumpur, and Nairobi. This chapter explains the case study methodology and selection criteria and then discusses how data were collected for each city. As noted in the opening chapter, these cities were not selected to be comparative cases; rather, they are meant to stand on their own as inductive examples sharing comparable attributes. Thus, I will explain why each city was selected, what its unique attributes are, and how all three can be related to one another. The second part of the chapter will discuss how data were collected in each city. The case studies contain a mix of original quantitative and qualitative data to help us understand how digitalization is affecting the daily lives of urban refugees. Besides explaining why this empirical approach made sense, this chapter will discuss what the data collection teams learned about urban refugees' daily lives while they were conducting the data collection. This is essentially a meta-level analysis of what we learned through the process of data collection.

Case studies are an increasingly common approach to understanding the dynamics of both migration and technology; they also provide a canvas for telling the stories of the urban migrants who were interviewed during the data collection. While generalizability and theory building are important, the human stories within these case studies are what can motivate better development practice. Generalizability helps us understand why people use different types of apps, for example. But it is the stories embedded in the case studies that provide the human element that gives meaning to the general patterns. Those stories remind us of what is at stake for many modern urban refugees. It is important to understand in general terms which conditions lead to greater technology use, but the individual stories remind us that *how* we make information available digitally can have life-or-death consequences for the most vulnerable urban refugees.

Data gathering processes also shape how researchers view phenomena. Some of the most affecting parts of the fieldwork for this book involved evenings out with the research teams and enumerators, hearing about their experiences of doing interviews, and listening to their reflections on how participating in the research was reshaping their views on urban refugees. Since one goal of this book is to identify ways to change the politics around urban displacement, unpacking the experiences that local researchers shared is worthwhile. At the start of this project, this kind of reflective practice was not something I or my colleagues anticipated, but as we did the work it increasingly became clear that this sort of reflection could deepen our knowledge of how praxis can help us use research to create social change.

CASE STUDIES IN MIGRATION AND DIGITALIZATION RESEARCH

Digitalization and urban displacement are both complex topics, so when they are brought together it can be difficult to study them both generally and in detail. For engaging with the complexities of these two phenomena, case study methods make a great deal of sense. We can retain the complexities of the phenomena and use case selection criteria to bound them. Causal analysis on displacement patterns requires us to dive into a specific aspect of the displacement process, and likewise with digitalization – understanding the causal relationship between technological change and a social phenomenon generally requires something like a survey experiment or randomized control trial. These methods would be too narrow for the aims of this book. This section will provide examples of case studies in displacement and digitalization research, starting with displacement, then looking at digitalization in developing countries, and then highlighting examples of how these two phenomena have been studied together. From this review I will move on to discuss the cities examined in this book, explaining how I will mix inductive case study methods with a diverse analysis that brings together lessons from each city and proposes which scenario we are likely to see broadly emerge for urban migrants in digitizing middle-income cities.

The study of urban displacement has historically been rooted in economics and has correspondingly had a strong quantitative, rational-choice orientation. A classic model of rural-to-urban migration was developed by the economists John Harris and Michael Todaro (1970) and essentially assumes that the decision to migrate from a rural setting with full employment to an urban setting with limited employment is rational if there is an expectation of higher income in the urban setting. This model has spawned a wide-ranging debate in the development economics field, leading to quantitative analyses of its treatment of formal versus informal urban labour sectors (Stark 1982) and, more recently, consideration of factors besides expected income, such as social networks and connections (Bhattacharya 2002). Economic methods and logic have also been used to understand the effects of economic development in rural areas on the decision to move to cities. Yap (1976, 1977) showed that policy efforts to prevent or manage people moving to cities had little impact on actual urbanization outcomes; policies did not stop migrants from moving to cities and integrating themselves economically. If we fast-forward to the 2000s, this pattern remains the same even if the policy approach is not displacement management *per se*. Beauchemin and Schourmaker (2005) showed that in developing countries, active economic investments aimed at improving living conditions in rural areas had no effect on people's decisions to move to cities; indeed, they tended to *encourage* those decisions. Looking into the future with an urban labour migration focus, Seto (2011) argues that a mix of social and policy factors will continue leading people to migrate to cities in Africa and Asia; social networks and the attractions of capital and innovation to urban areas mean that coastal megacities will continue attracting large numbers of urban refugees.

Methodologically, how do other disciplines outside economics approach urban migration? One way that researchers have looked at the social and spatial effects of urban migration is by embedding qualitative social science methods in case studies. Weisner's (1976) analysis of urban/rural networks in Kenya uses sociometric data to show how clan networks and social status affected patterns of male urban/rural migration patterns. The nature of urban settlement is another area that has received case study treatment; an example is

Johnstone's (1983) analysis of how social and political factors led to reflexive patterns of urban development and squatting in Malaysia. Interpersonal linkages in Thailand played a key role in the flow of rural villagers to urban centres. These linkages come with their own hierarchies and power dynamics that influence rural/urban migration (Fuller, Kamnuansilpa, and Lightfoot 1990). Also, documentary and observation methods have been combined to help us understand the political aspects of regional urban migration policy; Filomeno (2017) used the case of Baltimore to examine how local immigrant communities and local governments fostered inclusive city-level immigration policies. The literature on urban migration shows that case studies with embedded mixed methods are a valid way of understanding urbanization and urban refugees' behaviour and decision-making.

The fields of information communication technology for development (ICT4D) and science, technology, and society (STS) have had a far more mixed methodological background, owing to the broader range of disciplines working in these fields. While case study approaches are commonly used across disciplines, the methods embedded in the individual cases vary significantly. The fields of engineering and informatics often take a technology-centric, technical approach to ICT and STS research – this of course makes sense, as these fields focus on the implementation of technological solutions. Electronic learning and health systems are useful examples of such research. Using the case of Pakistan, Kanwal and Rehman (2017) gathered data from a selection of university students to evaluate users' experience of online e-learning software; on the e-health side, Déglise, Suggs, and Odermatt (2012) evaluated SMS text message–based software programs for telemedicine in developing countries, showing their efficacy from a technological perspective. Social scientists also often rely on case studies with embedded empirical methods to understand the links between technology, society, and politics. Joel Simmons (2016), in his book on the relationship between technology, politics, and economic development, used comparative case studies of Singapore and Thailand to explain how differences in political and party institutions create long enough horizons of the future to validate investment in national-level research and development. An example of a micro-level case study of technology and society is Wallace and colleagues' (2017) analysis of how ICT access and use increases social cohesion in rural villages; they used northern Scotland for their study. Across engineering, informatics, and social science, the efficacy of case studies with embedded empirical techniques as a method is clear. So how can these methods be deployed when studying the relationship between technology and migration/displacement?

The study of technology and displacement has drawn on a mix of methods, again relying heavily on case studies. Kabbar and Crump (2007) used a sample of newly arrived refugees in Wellington, New Zealand, to identify factors leading to ICT use; they found that education *and* gender divides among ICT users. In Australia, Alam and Imran (2015) found that while there is potential for ICTs to support greater social inclusion of newly arrived refugees, greater government and community efforts are needed to increase access to ICTs and opportunities for training on how to use them. In the UK, refugee women who participated in community internet projects were reported to experience greater empowerment within their communities; also, they found the internet useful for locating networks and building a narrative about their life in the UK (Siddiquee and Kagan 2006). An example of social media's role in the migration and integration of refugees can be found in the Netherlands, where access to social media helps refugees build and maintain existing and new social networks in their new communities, which can have knock-on effects on wider social integration (Alencar 2018; Dekker et al. 2018). In the following section, I lay out why I selected the three cities I did and describe the mix of interviews and survey work I conducted with my colleagues in these cities.

WHY THESE CITIES?

At first glance, Bogotá, Nairobi, and Kuala Lumpur are an odd mix of cases to look at. They are on different continents and have different government systems and different cultural and historical trajectories. However, for the purposes of this book, there are underlying factors in each of them that are interesting both individually and in terms of comparison. Since the topic of technological change and urban migration is a global one, choosing these three different cases gives us some variation to help understand how digitalization and urban migration interact. While I am not taking a formal positivist comparative approach, there are a number of factors that led me to select these cities. Those factors are key for understanding how these modern middle-income cities align with the historical, demographic and technological analyses in previous chapters.

Table 5.1
Comparative factors between cities

City	Capital (Y/N)	4g LTE connectivity (Y/N)	Urban refugee enclaves (Y/N)	Internal and/ or external urban refugees in analysis?	Signatory to Refugee Convention) (Y/N)	Refugee encampment policy (Y/N)	Experiences of violence among urban refugees?
Bogotá	Y	Y	Y	Internal and external	Y	N	Civil war
Kuala Lumpur	Y	Y	Y	External	N	N/A	Violent persecution
Nairobi	Y	Y	Y	External	Y	Y	Civil war

Source: Author.

In the historical chapter about urbanization, cases of both internal and cross-border migration were used. Internal migration during the First Industrial Revolution primarily took place from countryside to industrial urban areas. There were structural policy decisions that resulted in people being economically displaced from rural land and effectively forced to move to cities. During the 1800s, European migrants left food-insecure and politically tumultuous countries in the hope of finding safety and opportunity in the United States. During the Great Migration period, political violence and economic exclusion drove millions of Black people from the southern United States to the industrial midwest and northeast. In Bogotá, Kuala Lumpur, and Nairobi, we similarly find that the urban refugees in these cities have been displaced internally and across borders. For many in Bogotá, political economic factors that included ongoing violence played some role in the decision to migrate to the city. In Kuala Lumpur and Nairobi, cross-border displacement spurred people to settle in national or ethnic urban enclaves.

When we shift perspectives and focus on the experiences of the individuals we interviewed and surveyed, we find that the relationship between violence and displacement spans the historical analysis of technological change and urbanization. In Bogotá, many respondents highlighted a mix of factors that went into their decisions to come to the city. These included seeking work, being near family, and seeking safety from violence. In Nairobi and Kuala Lumpur, we spoke mainly with people who either were registered refugees or would reasonably be considered cases of concern by agencies like the UNHCR and the ICRC. The experience of fleeing violence is often correlated with being poor and living in situations of legal and administrative limbo. This is particularly felt in Nairobi and Kuala Lumpur; in Kenya, refugees and asylum seekers are not forbidden by law to settle in cities but are meant to remain in camps, while in Malaysia, refugees and asylum seekers have no formal legal status. Fleeing violence or being displaced, and seeking economic and social opportunity, are factors that have driven people to urban centres historically and that continue to do so, as evidenced by all three cases in this book.

Across cases we see how individuals' lives and the nature of the cities they live in intermingle. In all three cities there are enclaves where urban refugees and urban displaced people settle. Bogotá is the unique example in this analysis because it is mainly internally displaced Colombians who settle in these enclaves, although some Venezuelans have settled in them as well. In Kuala Lumpur and Nairobi these enclaves are generally grouped by nationality. The data from these two cities were gathered largely from people who had fled violence or disasters and crossed national borders, so the natural approach to settling would involve finding others from the same home country. The strategy of settling with co-nationals is also important for urban refugees – since settlement for refugees and asylum seekers in both cities is either illegal or not legally defined, safety, work, and social opportunities are organized within the enclaves. In many ways, we see Massey's (2005) concept of "throwntogetherness" manifest in distinctly tense ways, with refugees becoming part of the local urban society even as hostile laws and politics drive what Gawlewicz and Tiftachel (2022) refer to as "thrownapartness." Digital technology in the urban context creates new tensions and opportunities that urban refugees must navigate in cities of arrival.

EMPIRICAL METHODS WITHIN THE CASES

The cases provide a framework for going deeper into the experiences that urban refugees have using digital technologies in their daily lives. To explore the role of digitalization in the lives of urban refugees, I and other research collaborators conducted 136 structured interviews with urban migrants in Nairobi and Kuala Lumpur; we also ran two original quantitative surveys in Bogotá and Nairobi and were provided with UNHCR survey data from Kuala Lumpur. This mixed-method approach is designed to be descriptive and to provide a basis for categorizing cities within the theoretical scenarios outlined earlier. This section will lay out what was done during the data collection and why; it will also delve into the challenges that arose and how those challenges have helped us learn about the lives of modern urban refugees in developing countries. Since data collection was not completely the same across cases, each case study is designed to stand alone, drawing on what data are available. Thus, the following descriptions of data collection will be city to city.

As noted in earlier chapters, this book focuses on cities that are in some phase of being middle-income and on the role of urban refugees in these transitions. Referring back to the historical cases, much of the urbanization that took place in the late eighteenth to mid-twentieth centuries involved poor displaced people. Often these people had been forced off land, were fleeing famine or violence, or were being persecuted in their home countries. While it is difficult to make perfect comparisons, many of these urban displaced people would likely have fit the profile for some kind of protection status, perhaps as refugees or IDPs. If we move forward to the growing cities of today that David Kilcullen, Mike Davis, and Doug Saunders talk about in their books on urbanization, many of the people moving to these cities also have these attributes. The people we surveyed and interviewed were generally poor and often either had formal refugee status or were "irregular" migrants who would satisfy the UNHCR's definition of "people of concern." The legal statuses of our respondents varied by location and context, but efforts were made to ensure that their attributes were similar across cases.

In Bogotá, we organized a survey of short-term Bogotá residents (coded as "internal migrants"), long-term residents whom we considered "locals," and Venezuelan migrants. These data were originally featured in Martin-Shields and colleagues (2022) to highlight how the time that migrants spent living in the same neighbourhood affected access to ICTs and the internet. The team, which included Sonia Camacho and Rodrigo Taborda from Universidad de los Andes and Constantin Ruhe from the University of Frankfurt, worked with the polling firm IPSOS to design a snowball sampling approach that covered the five principal districts of the city that are considered districts of arrival for migrants. Snowball sampling is not optimal, but it is acceptable (Shultz et al. 2014), and as we developed our sampling strategy we learned quite a bit about the gaps in urban population data and the challenges that arise when trying to develop a randomized sample of urban migrants. Our initial strategy was to work with the national registration office for internally displaced people (IDPs); in response to the large-scale internal displacement arising from the Colombian civil war, the government and municipalities have set up a network of centres where IDPs can register and receive protection and social support services. We had hoped to use the registration list to develop a random sample of urban IDPs; unfortunately, though, the negotiations around accessing the lists and contact information of IDPs fell apart owing to political and privacy concerns. At that point, we involved IPSOS and began considering alternative sampling strategies.

We wanted to have a dataset that would enable us to compare ICT and internet access between groups based on whether they were urban displaced persons or "locals." Given that we lacked access to the formal IDP registration, our first challenge was to identify displaced people: among the Colombians living in Bogotá, who is an urban displaced person and who is a "local"? We could find no formal temporal definition of "internal migrant"; our solution to this was to code as urban displaced people a cohort of respondents who had moved to Bogotá over the past seven years.[1] While not a perfect solution, this would at least represent a group who had arrived recently enough not to have been counted in the last census. This cohort included IDPs and economic migrants. Anyone who had lived in Bogotá longer would have been considered "local." Across both the migrant and local cohorts, the respondents were generally poor. During the data collection process we were also able to collect data from a cohort of Venezuelan urban displaced people. These respondents were relatively recent arrivals, having left Venezuela due to the economic and political upheaval in that country. In the end we were able to collect a dataset that included eight hundred responses from the three cohorts. These data will be used descriptively in the case study and supplemented with legislative documents and mobile internet speed data to develop a picture of how urban migrants access and use ICTs in Bogotá.

The terminology in the Bogotá case study differs from the other two case studies due the legal status of IDPs and Venezuelan displaced people in Colombia. Neither of these groups are recognized formally as refugees under Colombian law, so in this case study I will use the term "urban displaced people" instead of "urban refugees" when describing the population that was surveyed.

Data collection in Kuala Lumpur was conducted through semi-structured interviews with forty-six refugees and six semi-structured practitioner interviews; these were supplemented with survey data collected by the UNHCR's Malaysia office. The data were featured in an article on digitalization and refugee self-reliance (Martin-Shields and Munir-Asen 2022), and the interview research was done collaboratively with Katrina Munir-Asen. We worked with the UNHCR Malaysia community outreach team to connect with leaders within the main refugee communities in Kuala Lumpur. While a large number of nationalities are represented among refugees in Malaysia, we focused on the largest groups, which are currently the Rohingya, Myanmar Muslims, Chins (Myanmar Christians), Somalis, and Ahmadiyah Muslims from Pakistan. The interviewees ranged in age from eighteen to sixty-five; half of them were male. We specifically wanted a mix of educational levels, and we did not select specifically with regard to whether someone owned a particular kind of technology. This was not a probabilistic sample, and indeed in this round of data collection we were more focused on hearing in greater depth about people's experiences of technology and what it meant to them in their daily lives. To bridge language barriers we worked with translators who had experience helping community members deal with the UNHCR and NGOs and would thus have experience translating technical and administrative content.

Since a central question in this book is how digitalization makes cities legible and accessible to urban refugees, we also collected data on mobile internet speed in those parts of Kuala Lumpur where refugees tend to settle. This was motivated by my experience in Bogotá, where there was significant variation in the speed of mobile internet access in different parts of the city. Our method for collecting these data involved following a pre-planned driving route through the city, taking multiple observations in different parts of each refugee and migrant neighbourhood. We used an app called SpeedTest,[2] which checks upload and download speeds using the nearest cellular towers. Overall, internet speed was sufficient to use apps like WhatsApp and Facebook; in poorer outer neighbourhoods, though, there were pockets of extremely slow coverage. This did not present a fundamental barrier to access. However, it does point out that in both Kuala Lumpur and Bogotá, idiosyncrasies in infrastructure development can lead to digital exclusion. This will be discussed at greater length in the Bogotá and Kuala Lumpur case studies (in Nairobi, mobile internet speed was very consistent across the city).

The fieldwork in Nairobi consisted of structured interviews with refugees as well as a survey of urban refugees and their Kenyan neighbours. The structured interviews were done with refugees, facilitated by colleagues from HIAS Kenya, an NGO that provides psychosocial services to urban refugees in Nairobi. The research team I worked with in Nairobi did thirty structured interviews with refugees from Somalia, South Sudan, and the Democratic Republic of Congo. The interviews were structured in much the same way as those conducted in Kuala Lumpur; they covered basic questions about ICT and internet access, how and why people use digital technology, and how technology fits into their daily lives in Nairobi. The selection of respondents was similar to that of Kuala Lumpur as well, with a 50/50 split between men and women and an age range of eighteen to sixty-five. In both cases the choice to have a wide age range was a good one; the results were surprising, given the pervasive narrative about young people being "digital natives."

The survey data collection in Nairobi took place over two weeks in April 2019 and was done in cooperation with Abel Oyuke and Samuel Balongo, who are Afrobarometer regional managers based at the University of Nairobi. As in Bogotá, we wanted to capture a cross-section of urban refugees as well as a cohort of their Kenyan neighbours. This would allow for comparison between urban refugees and locals with regard to ICT access and digital inclusion. Along with questions about digital behaviour, we asked questions about social cohesion, perceptions of inclusion, social networks, and economic status. Developing the sample of urban refugees in Nairobi was easier than in Bogotá since the migrants we were surveying were not Kenyan – many of them were registered with the UNHCR or lived in enclaves with those who were registered. The sample was designed to be proportionally representative of all the nationalities for which there were UNHCR data in Nairobi. To find respondents, the enumerators worked with community representatives to identify housing blocks where migrants lived, mapped the blocks, and developed a random walk pattern through the buildings and neighbourhoods. The sample of Kenyan neighbours was developed using existing population maps and a random walk pattern in buildings and neighbourhoods.

In all three cities, we were collecting data from respondents who would be classified as vulnerable or high-risk. An ethical review of research protocols was conducted for all data collection processes. Survey instruments and interview questionnaires, as well as processes for privacy protection and anonymity, went through ethics reviews both in Germany and in each country where research took place. As part of the research protocol, protection officers or social workers who worked in the cities reviewed the quantitative and qualitative questionnaires to make sure that questions did not unnecessarily broach sensitive topics. All qualitative interviews were conducted at sites where a social worker or community worker would be available in case a respondent needed to debrief after the interview. For all interviews, translators were briefed on the questionnaire, gave feedback about sensitive questions, and helped the research teams pick up on cues that a respondent might be uncomfortable. Working with local counterparts and giving them the power to shape the data collection process helped build trust with the research teams; it also underscored that the comfort and safety of the respondents was paramount. For the survey in Nairobi, given the grey legal circumstances of many of the respondents, enumerators followed an informed consent procedure developed with legal experts at the Refugee Consortium of Kenya (RCK) to make sure that respondents would not put themselves in legal jeopardy by participating. All enumerators had a letter from RCK explaining this, as well as the contact information for RCK's legal aid team. Further details about how the policy and legal environment shaped the data collection procedures in each city will be covered in the case studies.

INSIGHTS FROM THE DATA COLLECTION

While doing the data collection, through the act of research itself, the team members in the different countries and I learned a number of things about the nature of urban displacement and technology. This included insights into the ways that laws and social status feed back into how we count people and measure demographics, and how the act of participating in research and data collection affects the ways that researchers and enumerators understand the lives of urban refugees. These insights are part of thinking about research in an engaged way – the process itself generates critical observations that are central to binding research with change making in the real world.

I will offer some general insights on this to set up the case studies and then go into greater detail about how these actionable lessons manifested themselves in specific places.

The survey work reminded us sharply that demographic data are not values-free and that population counts reflect national politics and values. Also, we had a chance within the teams to see how the definitions applied "in the real world," when counting urban refugees and urban displaced people led to gaps in population data. For example, when we did our survey work in Bogotá, the question of who counts as an urban displaced person proved a challenge to answer. How do you find people who fit a particular demographic profile when that profile is not counted in official statistics? Contrast this with the urban migrants we interviewed in Kenya and Malaysia; many of these people were officially refugees or fit the profile of refugees. These populations were well counted, and even when they did not show up in national statistical surveys it was possible to find and survey them. The politics of counting in these cases were striking, and they would have an impact on how I interpreted the data in the case study chapters later in this book. Defining and counting different classes of urban refugees, especially when they are unregistered, is not merely a methodological exercise. To understand how digital technological change in urban refugees' lives will change the trajectory of developing cities, we have to address the politics of who is counted in population statistics.

Another aspect of doing the field research in these three cities, especially as it applies to Engaged Theory, related to how the very act of doing research with urban refugee communities affected the enumerators and researchers. During debriefs and team dinners, people discussed how hearing people's stories during enumeration changed their views on urban refugees. It was striking to hear team members say they had never met a refugee and that their views up to then had been entirely shaped by the political debate, and that being with people in person during the research significantly changed their views of what urban refugees experienced and what they could bring to the cities where they now lived. This kind of attitudinal change, and the autoethnographic experiences of the research team members, were not core areas I was focusing on when developing the different data collection processes. Yet the act of doing research can have an important impact on how we view the social world; the experiences of the research team in Nairobi in particular will be expanded on in the case study chapter.

The history of urbanization and technological change from the Industrial Revolution and the Great Migrations helps us understand how technological change affected the lives of urban displaced people in earlier times. Now we want to understand what the future holds for cities like Bogotá, Kuala Lumpur, and Nairobi and how the increasing volume of urban displacement will feed into their vibrancy as the technological world changes in the background. The case studies in the following chapters fold together history, the built urban environment, the politics of human mobility, the experiences of urban migrants, and digital technological change. We get the chance to see how these changes look through the eyes of urban refugees themselves and to embed their experiences in the physical and historical urban environment. Doing so allows us to start to understand the scenarios these cities will face in a digital future and how the people who move to them may thrive, or struggle, as they build urban livelihoods.

6

Bogotá: ICT Access in the Neighbourhood

We begin the journey through the case studies in Bogotá, Colombia, a city of 7.4 million people, situated on the Bogotá Savannah, a plateau high in the Andes Mountains. It is the capital of Colombia, as well as the country's economic and manufacturing hub, and it contains a sprawling mix of architecture, interspersed with parks, all of it linked by freeways. Luxury high-rise buildings grip the foot of the Eastern Hills, a mountain range running north to south that is the *de facto* border of eastward city expansion. The central and eastern parts of the city are wealthier and more commercial. Low-slung working-class neighbourhoods spread west onto the plateau, while mixed developments of formal and informal settlements extend up and over the city's southern slopes. From the peak of Monserrate, you get a panorama of Bogotá's expanse; given the city's 2,640 metre elevation, this view often comes with fog rolling off the mountains in the morning; in the afternoons, massive shafts of sunlight cut through the high clouds and illuminate the city's skyline.

The low-slung localities on the west and south sides of the city, running up the mountain slopes and into the passes, are where we collected much of our data. These localities – Usme, Kennedy, Bosa, southwest Suba, and others – are where migrants and displaced people arrive and begin integrating into the city. It is in areas like this, ranging from poor to working class and with a mix of formal and informal development, that Doug Saunders (2010) sees potential despite the challenges the people face, and where Mike Davis (2006) sees economic exclusion at work on the edges of the urban core. The historical development of these localities, including their physical infrastructure and industry, is part of what has made them localities of arrival for urban displaced people.

In Colombia the driver of urban displacement, especially for the rural poor and working class, has been violence. Even for those seeking work in cities, violence in the provinces followed by a fifty-year civil war in the rural and jungle regions was at least an intervening factor. Internal displacement has been a key feature of Colombian demography; as many as nine million people today have been displaced (UNHCR 2023) as a result of ongoing and historical violence. Even those who came to a city seeking work in earlier times may have done so because of outbreaks of violence in their rural home areas. Displacement has deleterious effects on household income and savings, so many urban migrants arriving from regions affected by violence are likely to be poor and in need of protection services similar to what refugees would receive. Colombia has led the way with providing registration and support services for internally displaced people, with offices at the municipal level managing registration. The challenges raised by displacement mean that urban migrants access and relate to technology differently than their non-displaced neighbours – while urban displaced people do indeed have access to digital technologies, a key question is how they use technology to establish networks and whether that extends to using digital government services.

Bogotá, and Colombia generally, is fairly advanced among peer countries for internet connectivity and is ahead of many wealthier countries in terms of e-government and computer-mediated public administration. So, what does the technology space look like in Bogotá, and how do urban migrants access and use technology in ways that are different from their local neighbours? Before diving into the data collected from urban displaced people themselves, it would be helpful to outline the current state of technological access more generally. During the fieldwork for this book I had time to collect data on mobile internet speeds around the city, and this will help tell some of the story. From locality to locality, mobile internet speeds varied quite a bit. The temporary market departure of the Uber ride-hailing service will also be analyzed, since app-based ride hailing and delivery services are an increasing part of the infrastructure of cities. Finally, technology use and access is not just about internet speed and available apps. Rules and regulations regarding what is required to purchase a mobile phone and an internet connection can have a significant impact on who can get internet access. Over the years, Colombia has introduced rules for mobile phone and SIM card registration that have the potential to make it harder for urban displaced people to access mobile internet connections.

The background information about the history of Bogotá, both the physical city and the urban migration there, and its technology infrastructure provide the context for exploring how individual urban displaced people responded to survey questions about technology use and access in their daily lives. By combining our research with demographic and economic data, as well as information on why they were displaced, we can begin to develop a picture of how technology fits into their daily lives and how this extends to how they relate to the city. How do they seek work, develop social networks, and access administrative and e-government services? Unlike with the other two cases, the majority of the urban displaced people who responded to the survey were Colombian. This provides some insight into how much the basic condition of being an urban refugee or displaced person influences technology use and access.

These layers of information about the nature of the city, the state of technology, and the ways that migrants use that technology bring us to the scenario-generating exercise. Does technology use and access in Bogotá lead to greater networking, new job opportunities, or more surveillance? This first round of scenario generation will help set the stage for the case studies of Kuala Lumpur and Nairobi.

BRIEF HISTORY: BOGOTÁ AND URBAN DISPLACEMENT

The data that were collected from a mix of urban displaced people and their long-term resident neighbours gives us a snapshot of how digitalization affects urban migration and the development of cities. This is a deeply social question, and networks of family and friends play a key role in the answer. However, before we explore the data we need historical context for how Bogotá developed as a city and how urban displacement evolved in the second half of the twentieth century. When examining the history of urban development in Bogotá, we see the city evolve through multiple attempts at planning and *urbanismo* in the mid-twentieth century, followed by rapid growth in the late twentieth century.

Robert Karl's (2017) history of politics and violence in Colombia helps us understand how interwoven Bogotá as an urban centre is with the arc of Colombian political culture. His historical account of political violence in Colombia starts in Bogotá, which Colombians considered an "early-twentieth century Athens." It was the seat of the *país politico*, the society of politicians, and the *país letrada*, a subset of the *país politico* that included writers, journalists, and lawyers. But the city is not just a space occupied by an intellectual political class; for Clara Irazábal (2008), the Plaza de Bolívar de Bogotá, a central square in the tradition of Spanish settlements in Latin America, has played a public role as the gathering place for celebrations and political movements. As the population of the city and the surrounding farms grew, a period of urban planning began to take shape. There was a strong European influence on development, driven initially by Rocardo Olano's 1917 proposal to adapt his Medellin Futuro (Medellin Future) plan into a Bogotá Futuro (Bogotá Future) plan that would modernize the city between 1923 and 1925 (Castro 2013). In the 1930s, Austrian planner Karl Brunner (1939) applied his *Manual de Urbanismo* to the Bogotá Futuro plan; his focus was on creating an urban space that was rational and that would encourage social inclusion and access to services for all members of urban society. After Brunner, Le Corbusier was hired to bring a different modernization plan to Bogotá, again based on a rational model. Sandra Cortes (2009) points out, though, that all this planning was for naught – through the mid-twentieth century these plans led to patchwork development as city authorities changed and municipal budgets were unable to support the investment required to implement them.

In parallel with this planning, the semi-rural areas on the south and west sides of the city developed along their own trajectories. The current localities of Bosa, Kennedy (known as Ciudad Techo until 1963), Usme, and Ciudad Bolívar were slowly integrated into the expanding city, ceasing to be hardscrabble farming plots. Ciudad Bolívar, known in the 1930s as Paseo Bolívar, was settled by the poor, and this presented both planning and moral conundrums to Brunner. He contended that the unplanned state of the settlement led to crime and social ills, compounded by a lack of access to public services and physical risks with building on the slopes. Austin Zeiderman (2016) provides one of the most in-depth analyses of how planning gave way to city authorities viewing Bogotá's southern and western settlements, particularly Ciudad Bolívar, through a lens of risk management. The city used the southern hills as quarries, stripping the forests and extracting rock and sand to build the city itself. Once the extraction was done, poor migrants and locals moved out to these hillsides and built their own small homesteads. Over the years these settlements became denser, until they now reach down to the formally developed areas in Bosa and Kennedy. Over the decades, these settlements have been built, populated, cleared by the authorities, and rebuilt and repopulated. It is in these formerly peripheral localities, now formally integrated into the city, that networks of urban displaced people have arrived since the mid-twentieth century.

Displacement into Bogotá is highly mixed. There are internally displaced people (IDPs), who receive specific status as a result of the internal conflict; internal migrants, arriving in response to economic stress (with varying levels of choice versus force); and, more recently, an influx of forcibly displaced people from Venezuela. While there has been research on Colombian urban migration from a labour perspective (e.g., Aysa-Lastra, 2011; Calderón-Mejía and Ibáñez, 2016), Colombia is an interesting contemporary case because of the mix of migration drivers – people are displaced by violence and then forced into onward migration due to economic or social circumstances.

William Flinn's (1966, 1968) early research, organized with the National University of Colombia, provides qualitative empirical insights into the lives and motivations of migrants who were moving into areas of Bogotá that city planners like Karl Brunner wanted to rationalize using mid-twentieth-century city planning techniques. Flinn conducted his research in El Carmen, which at the time was a semi-formal settlement, not formally part of the city of Bogotá. One key observation we draw from the historical data is how politics, urban/rural divides, and violence are all interconnected. Waves of political violence in the 1940s and 1950s that targeted supporters of the Liberal Party forced hundreds of thousands to flee their homes, often to cities. The numbers were so high that city planning authorities in Bogotá called their city Ciudad Asilo (City of Asylum) or Ciudad Refugeo (City of Refuge); during the 1950s the population of Bogotá doubled, from 500,000 to over 1,000,000. Many of these migrants were coming from rural areas in neighbouring departments, particularly Cudinamarca and Boyacá, and worked in trades. Flinn's finding about the friendship and kinship connections among urban displaced people is important to bear in mind when we consider the role played by technology in shaping and influencing urban displacement today. During the 1960s, many of the displaced people arriving in districts like El Carmen had existing friendship and kinship networks in Bogotá, and these networks often provided material support during the initial settling-in period. These could be considered pre-digital local and translocal networks, and they represented a social foundation upon which neighbourhoods in Ciudad Bolívar, Usme, Bosa, and Kennedy have regenerated over time.

From 1950 to 1990 the boundaries of the city expanded, and these localities became part of the city proper (Rueda-Garcia 2003). El Carmen, which during Flinn's research was on the outskirts of the city and was a mix of irregular housing and limited infrastructure, is now firmly within the city limits between the large thoroughfares of Avenida Boyaca to the east and Calle 45 Sur to the north. While our survey work was done in localities like Bosa, Kennedy, Tunjuelito, and Suba, areas that have been absorbed into the city, there are poorer settlements on the southern mountain slopes where many urban displaced people arrive. Settlements akin to El Carmen in the 1960s are now on the mountainous southern and western boundaries of Ciudad Bolívar; examples include neighbourhoods like La Torre, Los Alpes, and Altos de la Estancia. Zeiderman's (2016) analysis of the modern politics of risk management and urban planning in Bogotá highlights how these settlements have evolved. They often involve organized *invasiones* (invasions): settlers move in, occupy land, and quickly build on it. Over time, one wave of settlers is relocated into public housing due to the risk of landslides, only for the next wave to move onto the same space.

This precariousness had an effect on our research. Merely finding people who have been displaced to urban areas is difficult for two reasons: first, the neighbourhood of arrival is not a long-term place to settle, and second, people displaced by violence are often highly marginalized. This pattern continues today; in May 2020, riot police evicted residents of Altos de la Estancia, demolishing their houses (Griffin 2020). While residents were offered public housing, fear of living in close quarters during the COVID pandemic led many to try to stay in their homes. As forced evictions have gone forward, many have been left homeless. As an outcome of this precarious existence, many urban displaced people who have fled violence or economic collapse make an effort to keep a low profile. Compounding all this, displacement due to violence has had a significant negative impact on household income and assets (Ibáñez and Vélez 2008), which means that IDPs arriving in Bogotá are likely to be poorer than their neighbours.

In these circumstances a mobile phone and a digital connection to friends, family, or community organizers can be key to an urban dis-

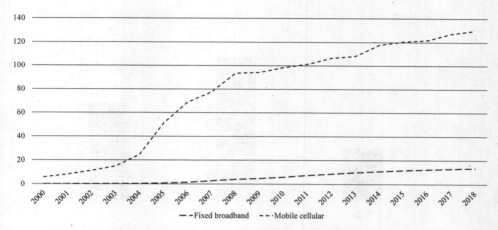

Figure 6.1 Fixed broadband versus mobile cellular subscriptions per 100 inhabitants in Colombia
Source: International Telecommunications Union (ITU) (2020).

placed person's safety and security. To understand how technology affects urban displaced peoples' relationship to the city and urban society around them, the following section provides an overview of technology access, investment, and policy in Colombia nationally and in Bogotá specifically.

TECHNOLOGY IN BOGOTÁ

National statistics can provide some wider context for internet and technology availability in Bogotá. Overall, Colombia is a well-connected country, and the past twenty years have seen significant growth in access to the internet. Figure 6.1 shows that most people access the internet via mobile phone. New cellular subscriptions began to soar in 2004. Fixed broadband (e.g., through fibre-optic cable) has grown far more slowly; only 15 out of every 100 Colombians had a fixed-line internet connection in 2018. Around 64 percent of Colombians use the internet; women do so marginally more than men (figure 6.2).

There is a significant difference in access is between rural and urban settings (Erb 2019). The costs of fixed telephone line internet are lower in cities, and the value for money is much greater – a US$30 per month, home internet subscription in an urban area gets the subscriber around 30Mbit, while the same subscription in

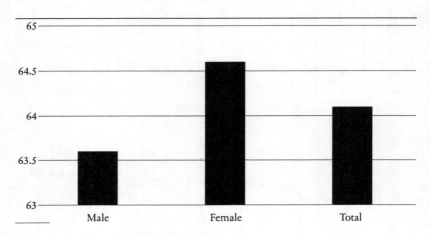

Figure 6.2 Percentage of population accessing the internet by gender, Colombia, 2018
Source: ITU (2020).

a rural area comes with only about 2Mbit.[1] I was able to gather some data on mobile internet speeds around Bogotá. I examined a mix of localities – those where migrants were interviewed, but also wealthier districts. I identified an estimated "middle" of these localities and conducted two upload- and download-speed checks. The results are shown in table 6.1 alongside the official socio-economic strata for the areas where the measurements were taken. The strata are not official measures of income *per se*. Rather, they are based on aspects of the neighbourhood that correlate with wealth: 1 is low, 6 is high. Plainly, mobile internet speed is higher in the wealthier strata.

These differences in mobile internet speed in different localities perhaps point to differences in how migrants use their mobile phones. Urban displaced people in Bogotá (and we will see the same thing in Kuala Lumpur and Nairobi) are not evenly distributed across localities – generally, they arrive in neighbourhoods like Usme, Kennedy, and Suba, and stay there. Even within these neighbourhoods, there is variation in the quality and durability of housing and infrastructure, and this has an impact on internet and technology access. However, statistics do not tell the whole story; to fully understand how technology fits into migrants' lives, we have to look at technology policy in Colombia.

Table 6.1
Mobile download and upload speeds using 3G roaming services across neighbourhoods in Bogotá

Neighbourhood	Download speed (Mbps)	Upload speed (Mbps)	Social strata
Usaquen	6.03	1.06	6
Chapinero	4.22	1.06	4
San Cristobal	3.23	0.73	3
Fontibon	3.05	0.29	3
Engativa	3.08	1.39	3
Suba	2.10	1.78	3
Tunjaulito	2.97	1.93	2
Kennedy	0.86	0.66	2
Usme	1.55	0.33	1

Collected using SpeedTest app software for iPhone, November 2018. *Source*: Author (internet speeds); data on strata from Gonzalez (2017).

The government has taken steps through internet and communication technology policy to address the differences in internet access across the country, with the result that Colombia has become a leader in internet access and e-government among its peers. However, other aspects of public policy have had unintended negative consequences for migrants who wish to access digital technologies. Plan Vive Digital (Live Digital Plan) is the Colombian government's strategy for bringing internet connectivity to the whole country (MinTIC 2020). This initiative fits within the government's broader strategy regarding digitalization and e-government. Since the late 1990s, that strategy has been viewed as a success in Latin America (Porrúa 2013). The national government took a number of policy-level steps to achieve that result. The long-term goal of expanding e-government in Colombia has enjoyed consistent political backing and financial support across administrations. It seems that the government now understands what citizens need and want from online portals, including e-government portals. It makes sure those needs and wants are met and that the average person is able to use them. Another component, perhaps self-evident but often forgotten, is investment in human resources: the Colombian government has made a concerted effort to ensure that ministries have staff with the programming and development skills to maintain e-government services so that they function well.

Plan Vive Digital is the connectivity component of the Colombian government's broader digitalization efforts. When the Santos administration came into office in 2010, there were barriers to internet use on the demand *and* supply sides (Vega 2013). These barriers included a lack of fibre-optic infrastructure, low capacity for public investment in such infrastructure, a sense among the public that the internet was not useful in daily life, and high costs for internet access. The strategy for addressing these issues included expanding internet infrastructure, subsidizing internet access through public–private partnerships in low-income areas, expanding the government's e-government portals to cover more services, and expanding Computadores para Educar (the Computers to Educate program, CPE). In the latter stages of the Santos administration, the Kioskos Vive Digital (KVD) program was launched as part of an initiative supported by UNESCO to provide kiosks where people in rural areas could access the internet. The idea behind this was to foster a broader digital culture. These kiosks were installed in schools, shops, and community centres (UNESCO n.d.). The KVD program largely succeeded at providing communities with internet connectivity, access to e-government services, and training. The response in communities with kiosks has been correspondingly positive, although the program has been hampered by inconsistent funding, with the result that many communities that would benefit from a kiosk have yet to receive one (1 World Connected n.d.).

One major hiccup in the wider digitalization strategy has been in the policy and regulatory space with regard to ride-sharing apps. Uber, one of the largest such apps in the world, was fined by Colombian regulators for unfair business practices; the case centred on whether Uber was providing commercial transportation services without proper licensing (Acosta 2020). After the December 2019 ruling, Uber decided to shut down its services countrywide as of the end of January 2020. The solution that allowed it to restart services demonstrated the complex nature of technology regulation; essentially, the Uber app in Colombia now connects customers with cars rather than drivers; in legal terms, the driver is now just the agent who provides the car. This case highlights the challenges inherent in digitizing an economy. Colombia has done quite well at developing infrastructure and government Web services, but meanwhile, the digital economy presents a variety of complex policy issues that can lead to unintended consequences for consumers. These kinds of legal and regulatory vagaries are a global issue and can have unique consequences for urban refugees and displaced people.

When we look at the technology policies of the Colombian government, we see an overall strategy that has put the country ahead of its peers in overall digitalization of government services. The government has put an impressive amount of planning and coordination into its digital inclusion efforts. What is missing at the policy level is a focus on digital inclusion for urban displaced people, especially those displaced from outside Colombia. We will see this theme repeated in the other two case studies, but Colombia is unique in this regard because many of the respondents are internally displaced people who would be covered by many of the existing technology regulations, and government policies regarding Venezuelan urban displaced people are rather welcoming. Here, many of the regulatory structures around technology access that negatively impact urban displaced people do so by omission rather than commission.

Official identification, such as a national ID or a passport, is often a prerequisite for accessing mobile phone services and, by extension, the internet. This is the case in Colombia, where you need some form of ID to set up a mobile phone account. For an internally displaced person the identification rules should be less of a constraint than for a foreign urban displaced person, but many citizens do not have access to ID. For poorer citizens, especially those who have been forcibly displaced, obtaining an official ID can be a challenge. For a foreign migrant who has been displaced across a border, as is the case with many Venezuelan urban displaced people in Colombia, obtaining the correct visa or resident card can be functionally impossible. If someone has crossed a border without a passport, which many Venezuelans have done, applying for protection status or a resident permit becomes extraordinarily complex – one generally needs a passport as the starting point for further migration-related registration. For people displaced across a border, the process of gaining access to the identification documents necessary to set up a formal mobile phone account can feel Kafkaesque. In spite of this, many migrants eventually gain access to both a mobile phone and an internet connection after settling in Bogotá.

Two technology policies that are unique to Colombia that could have a unique negative impact on cross-border migrants are Decree 2015/2025 and Decree 2124. Decree 2015/2025 was implemented in 2015 in response to the large black market in Colombia for stolen smartphones. The law makes it harder for people to mail mobile phones into Colombia from other countries and to bring phones across the border from another country. Decree 2124 supplements

Decree 2015/2025 by setting rules for registering foreign mobile phones with a local mobile network operator (MNO) using the phone's international mobile station equipment identity (IMEI) number. If someone does this within fifteen days, the phone can then be used on Colombian mobile phone networks; if not, the phone will not work in Colombia. For a displaced person from a country like Venezuela, these laws inadvertently add a barrier to ICT and internet access. It means that a relative living in, say, the United States cannot mail you a device, and if you cross the border with a phone purchased in Venezuela you have to find time to register it with a carrier. Given the conditions people are leaving behind, and the challenges they face after arriving in Colombia, this law can be costly – fail to register your phone on time and it gets blacklisted by local MNOs. If that happens, you then have to acquire a new phone, which can be costly if done through an official shop and risky if you purchase a black market phone (since that phone could also end up blacklisted).

Colombia's technology sector is ahead of its peers with regard to infrastructure and e-government. So is its public policy around technology use and access. However, like many countries it is struggling to develop consistent regulatory standards for app-based companies like Uber and to balance the rules around identification with the reality that poorer citizens and refugees risk being excluded by omission from accessing ICTs and the internet. The regulatory issues that arise between governments and firms like Uber may appear to take place at a level above the daily lives of urban refugees, but for many, access to Uber (or Grab, in Malaysia) can be the difference between being ripped off by a taxi driver and having a set price for a journey. For urban displaced people in Bogotá the more mundane issue of having the correct ID to gain access to ICTs and the internet is the primary issue. Urban theory can help us understand how, in a space where technology policy inadvertently creates hurdles to digital inclusion, a longer period of residence in the same neighbourhood can create social networks for working around these hurdles.

DIGITALIZATION IN THE LIVES OF URBAN DISPLACED PEOPLE

In line with the historical demographics of large-scale migration, the population we focused on during the survey included predominantly poor urban displaced people from within Colombia and from

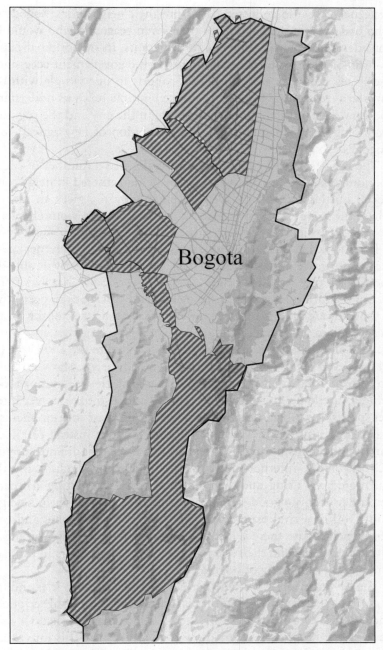

Figure 6.3 Approximations of where data were collected in Bogotá (striped spaces indicate general locations)

Venezuela. We also collected data from their neighbours: Bogotános who had lived in the city longer than seven years and who would be considered long-term residents, not migrants. In our original paper (Martin-Shields et al. 2022), we focused on e-government access and use issues, comparing the displaced cohorts in our sample with the long-term residents. However, the mixed sample helps us understand too how different people experience life in the city and the role that technology plays in supporting the integration of new arrivals into Bogotá's urban society.

The process of collecting the data highlighted a number of socio-economic issues that arise when data is being gathered in neighbourhoods hosting urban displaced people. Figure 6.3 gives an idea of where the survey work took place; as noted in the previous chapter, a number of issues arose when we tried to find migrants to interview.

If we look back at table 6.1, we get a sense of how internet speed maps onto geography and social strata. Usaquen has nearly double the mobile internet download speed (6.03 Mbps) of San Cristobal, Engativa, and Fontibon (3.23 Mbps, 3.08 Mbps, and 3.05 Mbps respectively). If we compare mobile internet speed to the social strata of the localities, Usaquen is in strata 6, while San Cristobal, Engativa, and Fontibon are all in strata 3. Kennedy (strata 2), Tunjuelito (2), and Usme (1) all have even lower mobile internet download speeds. Many variables go into how fast mobile internet is; that said, the neighbourhoods refugees are likely to arrive in are poorer and also have slower internet speeds. It is worth noting that when I took these measurements, I was roaming using my German Telekom account instead of a local carrier and was using an early-generation iPhone that did not support 4G LTE mobile internet speeds. Thinking autoethnographically, the hardware I was using, and the internet speeds I was getting via roaming, are probably a good estimate of what the average user in a neighbourhood of arrival experiences. Thus, from a geographic and economic perspective there is likely to be a digital divide between urban displaced people and their long-term resident neighbours in the eastern and city core areas of Bogotá.

The key question is not whether people have access to ICTs and the internet – the data from Colombia on mobile phone subscriptions and internet access in figures 6.1 and 6.2 tell us that people do indeed have access. What we want to know is how this access fits into urban refugees' daily lives. In the survey, this was addressed by asking people why they had moved to Bogotá. Two key historical drivers of urban migration in Colombia have been work seeking and displacement as a result of rural violence. When respondents reported their primary reason for moving to Bogotá, I was rather surprised at the totals – among the Colombian and Venezuelan respondents who answered the question ($n = 321$), 234 cited work or economic reasons, whereas 61 were drawn by family or social ties. Only 26 mentioned seeking safety from violence. These numbers could be a function of only asking for the primary reason for moving to Bogotá; it is possible that people moved mainly for work but that the need to do so had roots in earlier displacement due to violence. Alternatively, without access to the IDP registration database it could have just been that we were unlikely to find respondents who were officially IDPs in the eyes of the state. Among the Venezuelan respondents, the numbers make sense; the key reason to flee Venezuela in the last few years has been that country's economic collapse. The people there face violence and insecurity, but the economy is the overwhelming reason they cross into Colombia.

These numbers tell us a story of moving that is in line with the economic side of urban theory encountered in the work of Jane Jacobs, Edward Glaeser, and Doug Saunders. Cities are hubs of economic activity and opportunity, even for poor urban displaced people who arrive in slums or irregular urban developments. There is also a social side we can evaluate, in that 19 percent of the respondents to this question answered that they had family or social network reasons to come to Bogotá. We have an idea of which areas of the city people arrive in, and the social strata of those areas, as well as some information about the speed of mobile phone–based internet and data. This gives us a sociogeographic basis for understanding the responses we received about the use of technology in migrants' daily lives.

As a starting point, we asked people which online platforms they use. The options included big names like Facebook, WhatsApp, and Twitter as well as apps that are specific to the Colombian context. The vast majority of respondents used WhatsApp, followed by Facebook. Other apps and online tools were used far less, and e-government services were used very little among the sample. The results for e-government will be covered later; for now I will focus on WhatsApp and Facebook since they were the most prominent technologies for respondents and are designed to facilitate the kinds of information sharing that can meet social and economic needs. When we asked people why they use these technologies, we gave them the opportunity to respond with three options. We found that they used social media and digital technology largely to stay in contact with local friends or to maintain contact with friends and family elsewhere. Many of those who ranked staying in contact with local friends as the most important digital activity said that the second most important reason was to stay in contact with family and friends elsewhere. The third most important online activity focused more on work opportunities, and here, a small number of respondents mentioned e-government. These results require some interpretation since they are only descriptive, and displacement theory can help with this.

Even though job seeking was the dominant reason for coming to Bogotá, digital behaviour was focused first on maintaining translocal social networks. For respondents the most important thing they could do with digital technology was maintain contact with networks in Bogotá or with social networks from home. This is perhaps no surprise, but it should be laid out clearly – the use of social media and messaging technology for things like job seeking *follows* developing networks of people one knows well enough to share things with like information about jobs. For many urban displaced people, things like online job boards are not going to be where they find work. Jobs are likely to come via networks of other urban displaced people or people who live in the vicinity. This means that social online behaviour is not necessarily merely social; the act of building a wide network of friends who can be reached via WhatsApp is itself a way of seeking work opportunities. Thus, while the goal of moving to Bogotá was to find a better job or economic opportunity, the means for achieving that goal rest partly on the social use of digital technologies. This means that access to ICTs and internet can have positive effects on economic outcomes. Yet as we saw in earlier figures, living in a poor neighbourhood likely means having a slower mobile internet connection. Worse, if you are a cross-border urban displaced person your phone may not work or you may not have the ID to set up a Colombian mobile phone subscription. That said, the nature of the city itself may play a mitigating role against digital exclusion. There was an interesting statistical relationship between the length of time a migrant had lived in a neighbourhood and the probability that they would be able to access ICTs and the internet (Martin-Shields et al. 2022).

Urban displaced people on arriving in Bogotá had significantly lower probability of access to ICTs and the internet. But we found that after urban displaced people had stayed in the same neighbourhood for at least twelve months, they were just as likely as their long-term resident counterparts to have ICT and internet access. After eighteen months in the same neighbourhood, internal urban displaced people had a higher probability of using ICTs and the internet than their long-term neighbours. Our core question was whether ICT and internet access was a sufficient condition for urban displaced people to then make the step to using municipal e-government services. It turned out not to be, which was a little bit surprising – we did not expect the difference between long-term residents and urban displaced people to be so stark in this regard. Our work focused on the ways that uncoordinated technology and migration policies created a scenario in which urban displaced people lacked access to the necessary documentation to actually use formal e-government services. But I would also argue that explanations can be found in urban theory as to why urban displaced people do not turn to e-government.

Why would an urban displaced person use technology after arriving in a new neighbourhood? The most basic reason could be to make the space around them legible – with a smartphone and GoogleMaps I can see how my house connects to the city block and how my city block connects me to the wider physical city space. For an urban displaced person who did not grow up in the neighbourhood of arrival, this can be a useful way to start getting to know the city's terrain. However, Martin-Shields and colleagues' (2022) data showed that urban displaced people's probability of using digital technology and internet continued increasing long after they would have figured out how to navigate the city. Referring back to Jacobs, the answer to this question of continued digital integration could be that neighbourhoods are inherently social networks. As a newly arrived urban displaced person learns their way around the physical space of a neighbourhood, they get to know the characters who inhabit it. Jacobs talked about the importance of sidewalks as spaces for building social networks among the characters in a neighbourhood. While we still have physical sidewalks, stoops, and storefronts, digital technology creates a range of new opportunities to connect to the neighbourhood's characters – digital sidewalks, so to speak.

How could Jacobs's description of a neighbourhood help us understand an urban refugee's digital urban integration? For a newly arrived urban displaced person in Bogotá, the initially low probability of using digital technology is likely, at basis, a supply problem. Perhaps the phone they brought with them cannot be registered with a local carrier, so it takes a month or so to get a new one. Once an urban displaced person has a working phone, though, that person is likely to have a wide translocal network of family and friends to stay in contact with, so the probability that they will use digital technology and the internet more than their long-term-resident neighbours quickly goes up. Over time, an urban displaced person gets to know the characters and institutions in the neighbourhood, and these connections allow them to play a greater role in that neighbourhood's social, administrative, and economic life. This is likely to be facilitated through tools like WhatsApp, which further increase their probability of using digital technologies.

This trend quantitatively reflects Andrew Wong's (2009) Urban Footprint model of technology use among urban migrants. A mobile phone is not just a communication tool; it is a connection to urban society. At the start, it is a connection to home, and perhaps a tool for navigating – its footprint in daily life is narrow but important. But over time, owning a mobile phone not only keeps the owner connected to translocal networks but also signals to neighbourhood characters that the owner has the tools to become involved in local activities that require mobile connectivity. This leads to a broadening daily digital footprint, so that the likelihood that an urban migrant will use digital technology increases. The interaction between urban displaced people's socialization into an urban community and the growth of a digital footprint means that in the context of Bogotá, digitalization plays a key role in helping build the social networks that undergird access to work and economic opportunities.

THE INTERACTION BETWEEN DIGITALIZATION AND URBAN INTEGRATION

In Bogotá there is evidence that a mobile phone is not just a node connecting people via telecommunications infrastructure. Owning a mobile phone is a means of maintaining distant networks and building new local ones. If we follow the logic of Wong's Urban Footprint model, a mobile phone starts to take on social importance by signalling that the owner is engaged in activities and networks that require such a device. These are individual-level factors, though – how does urban refugees' and displaced people's digital footprint affect the trajectory of urban development? In Chapter 2 I proposed four scenarios for how digital technological change would impact how urban migrants affect the socio-economic development of growing cities: "North End" (digitalization reinforces and creates new socio-economic networks within neighbourhoods), "Lonely Hustle" (digitalization creates highly atomized jobs and decreases social integration), "Jobless Panopticon" (digitalization does not create new jobs but increases the ways in which neighbours and authorities surveil one another), and "Rust Belt" (there are no jobs, and the urban population is disconnected and shrinking).

When we take together the historical development of the city, the current neighbourhoods that urban displaced people move to, and the ways that technology fits into urban displaced people's lives, "North End" is a good fit for the potential direction of urban migration and city development in Bogotá. The starting point for this argument is based on the historical arc of neighbourhood-level development; the areas where urban displaced people are arriving today have a mixed history of middle-class occupation and homesteading. One hundred years ago a neighbourhood like Bosa would have been an unincorporated, irregular development on the outskirts of the city core. Over time, a mix of poor migrants from the city core moving out to Bosa, and middle-class *bogotános* seeking land, created a neighbourhood that had a life of its own before being incorporated into the growing city. The story was similar in the areas where we collected data – what were initially semi-rural satellite towns and settlements outside the city core, such as Usme, Ciudad Bolívar, and Suba, have been incorporated over time. If we go back to the mid-twentieth century and look at the networks of people displaced to these areas when they were still on the city's edge, we see in Flinn's research from the late 1960s that new arrivals were arriving in areas where they had existing family and friend networks.

Using information about the historical physical development of Bogotá in combination with the empirical data on urban migrants through the mid- to late twentieth century, we can see why hardware like mobile phones and digital technologies like WhatsApp can play a key role in the life of neighbourhoods of arrival. Economic opportunity and escape from violence are intertwined aspects of urban displacement, with economic opportunity being the leading factor. Flinn described urban displaced people arriving in Bogotá in the 1960s with the tools of their trade and perhaps a change of clothes. Among the Colombian respondents in our survey who had arrived recently, it was interesting that family and friend connections were not as important in their migration decision-making process. For the Venezuelans, family connections were even less critical. How does digitalization help us understand this change over the past fifty years? In the pre-digital era one moved where there were some pre-existing networks to help one find housing, settle in, and find work. While social networks still matter for urban displaced people, technologies like WhatsApp mean that an urban displaced person's or refugee's social or familial network is simultaneously near and distant. For example, a newly arrived urban displaced person may not personally know anyone in Bosa, but a family member in a neighbouring region might provide them with a contact there via WhatsApp after they arrive.

What makes Bogotá a "North End" instead of a "Jobless Panopticon," though, is that neighbourhoods like Bosa, Kennedy, and Usme, despite being relatively poor, had their own urban societies before they were absorbed into the city as "official" localities. There was farming and industry, and the mid-twentieth-century networks of friends and family that connected urban displaced people to one another laid a foundation for translocal digital networks to help newly arrived urban displaced people integrate into the neighbourhood. Cities are not a *tabula rasa* onto which digitalization inscribes new social networks – WhatsApp without the history of urbanization and demographic change experienced by localities like Bosa, Kennedy, and Usme would just be a digital artifact without purpose. However, WhatsApp combined with the history of displacement and urbanization of these localities means that urban displaced people can connect with a much wider range of people that would have been possible in an analogue world.

It is not just the pre-existing layers of urban society that make Bogotá a "North End." A key difference from Kuala Lumpur and Nairobi is that the Colombian and Venezuelan refugees we surveyed all could live and work legally in Bogotá. The Colombian government has made an effort to welcome Venezuelans who have been displaced across the border into Colombia. While previously noted Kafkaesque issues arise when dealing with the bureaucratic paperwork required to claim a resident visa, the current Colombian government's policy toward Venezuelans has been generally welcoming. In Bogotá, urban displaced people are allowed to find work, and this freedom can be compounded through access to digital technologies.

This final point raises a question: In cities where urban refugees have no rights to work or seek asylum, does digitalization create new spaces to create "North Ends" outside the constraints of official policy? Or do exclusionary migration policies mean that urban refugees are only able to engage in the social and administrative aspects of digitalization, creating the "Jobless Panopticon" scenario of no work opportunities but greater ability to surveil one another? Kuala Lumpur and Nairobi are two cities where refugee policy makes integration into urban society difficult and where populations often do not share a common language or nationality. How does digitization affect how urban refugees integrate into these cities when the refugee population is heterogeneous and the politics are decidedly less accommodating?

7

Kuala Lumpur: Time, Distance, and Legal Exclusion

Moving from Bogotá to Kuala Lumpur, we will see a large shift in the policies that shape the lives of urban refugees. The previous chapter noted that in general terms, the Colombian government's policy toward Venezuelan displaced people has been rather welcoming. In Malaysia, the opposite is true; there is no official refugee policy, and while the Malaysian government allows the UNHCR to provide services to refugees, the current interior minister has made it clear that the government views refugees as "illegal immigrants with UNHCR cards" (Anis 2020). Despite this hostility, refugees from Southeast Asia, Central Asia, and as far away as East Africa and the Middle East have established communities in Kuala Lumpur with the help of the UNHCR and a limited number of NGOs.

The city itself feels vast, with high-rise buildings spreading across valleys and hills in what can seem like an ever-expanding urban landscape. Central Kuala Lumpur extends from the Petronas Towers in the city centre, outward to the mountains and forests in surrounding Selangor state on the horizon. I remember driving from Bangsar, a neighbourhood southwest of central Kuala Lumpur, out to Klang, a city that is part of the Kuala Lumpur conurbation. We were driving west on the freeway toward Klang, on the Klang River, which flows into the Strait of Malacca. Massive apartment blocks dot the landscape, visible from kilometres away. On our way out of the city, we drove over a mountain pass, and on the other side was more high-rise, high density urban landscape as far as the horizon. I remember being struck by just how far refugee communities in greater Kuala Lumpur have to travel to reach the UNHCR office, almost solely by car or road vehicle, since subway and light rail service is limited in Kuala Lumpur. Compared to Bogotá, which struck me as a walkable continuity, Kuala Lumpur at first felt disorienting and hard to grasp spatially. I had a similar feeling when I started my work in Nairobi, and as a researcher, in order to see how the communities we were working with created an order of their own, I had to recalibrate my expectations of how urban space should be organized.

Malaysia can be described as a "quiet" refugee-hosting country. It is not a principal recipient of humanitarian aid; in the policy discourse around refugee hosting, Bangladesh probably receives more attention from the international humanitarian and refugee response community. Regardless, Malaysia still hosts around 185,000 refugees, and the Kuala Lumpur conurbation, which includes parts of surrounding Selangor state, hosts around 70,100 of them (UNHCR Malaysia 2022). Most of these urban refugees come from Myanmar, and they represent a cross-section of minority groups, the largest of which are currently the Rohingya, who are being persecuted and terrorized by the Myanmar government. These refugees live in Kuala Lumpur with neither legal status nor pathways to durable solutions. Indeed, unlike in Colombia, where the government has developed policies to register and aid internally and cross-border displaced people, Malaysia has actively avoided formalizing any aspect of refugee hosting. It is not a signatory to the 1951 Convention or the 1966 Protocol, and its legislative framework contains no legal category for refugees. It allows the UNHCR to operate in Malaysia but does not provide it with any funding – essentially, all refugee protection processes in Malaysia are outsourced to the UNHCR and donors. Refugees live in ethnic or national enclaves in Kuala Lumpur, and while the UNHCR provides them with internationally recognized registration as refugees, they have no legal status under Malaysia's immigration laws. This essentially has forced urban refugees in Kuala Lumpur into a state of self-reliance; they must source everything from within their own communities, from housing to health care to education.

With regard to technology, Kuala Lumpur is advanced and well connected. Mobile internet is widely available, and regional apps like Grab (an Uber competitor developed in Singapore) can be used to hail cabs and ride-sharing services. Mobile internet in urban areas is fast and relatively affordable, and, as with the other cases, mobile internet access far outstrips home broadband services in rates of use. This is unsurprising; it reflects a trend that is especially pronounced in low- and middle-income countries, and it reminds us of the mobile phone's centrality as a sociotechnical device in the lives of urban refugees. While internet technologies are quite well established as part of the urban landscape, we found that in Kuala Lumpur the regulatory space had uniquely pernicious effects on refugees' access to internet services. Acquiring a mobile phone handset is not hard – almost every refugee who was interviewed had one. But because refugees in Malaysia have no legal status, and thus no form of legally recognized ID, a legal wall blocks many mobile phone–based apps and online services that could be helpful to them.

Technology as a component of urban refugees' lives in Kuala Lumpur seemed to manifest itself in perceptions of distance and time. As noted earlier, the city is vast, and the enclaves where the various refugee communities live are on the edges of the city or farther afield in surrounding Selangor state. The UNHCR's office is in central Kuala Lumpur, in the Bukit Petaling district near the National Palace, yet many of the refugee communities are in Ampang and Gombak, 11 and 22 kilometres away respectively. The travel time that entails can be measured in hours, depending on traffic or public transit connections. The internet should have reduced or eliminated that time, and refugees were frustrated that it had not. In many ways, the things that refugees wished for in terms of integrating into life in Kuala Lumpur were amenable to internet and mobile phone–based solutions.

The intersecting complexities of legal and social exclusion, sociotechnological behaviour, and the nature of the city itself meant that digital technology did not reduce the challenges of urban self-sufficiency faced by most refugees in Kuala Lumpur. However, in interviews with refugees there were also examples of creativity and innovation in how they used technology to make ends meet. There were also deeply affecting stories of how digital channels of communication became avenues of "returning from the dead," in the sense of creating digital lives unbounded by the geography of Kuala Lumpur and the laws and restrictions imposed on them in Malaysia.

BRIEF HISTORY:
KUALA LUMPUR AND URBAN DISPLACEMENT

Kuala Lumpur was founded in 1857 as a tin-mining colony at the confluence of the Gombak and Klang Rivers (the name Kuala Lumpur translates as "muddy confluence") (Gullick 1955; Ooi 2004). Above that confluence, it was not possible to move equipment and people by water, which made the village of Kuala Lumpur the jump-off point for the Chinese workers who continued on to Ampang and Gombak to mine tin. The Malay chiefs from the Klang region worked with Chinese businessmen in Malacca to raise the funds for the tin-mining venture, and within a few years they were successfully exporting tin. The town of Kuala Lumpur started to grow as a trading centre, and miners settled in increasing numbers in Ampang and Gombak. As the tin-mining operations expanded, a market square developed, and roads were built that linked Kuala Lumpur to Gombak and Ampang. Gombak and Ampang themselves evolved into formal settlements as miners stayed, preparing the ground for what would grow into Greater Kuala Lumpur.

Up to the late 1800s Kuala Lumpur was administered largely by Malay and Chinese leaders. With the expansion of tin mining and other business ventures, British colonial involvement in Kuala Lumpur intensified. After fires and floods in 1879 and 1881 destroyed the Kuala Lumpur settlement, Britain's colonial resident in Selangor, Frank Swettenham, declared that new buildings were to be built of brick and tile and that the streets were to be widened. Chinese businessmen set up brickworks in the neighbourhood now called Brickfields, and many of the buildings that replaced the existing wood-and-thatch structures were designed in the regionally unique shophouse style: a second-level balcony over a covered, arched walkway. During his time as resident, Swettenham also oversaw the building of a rail line from Kuala Lumpur to Klang, the nearby port. The road and rail expansion spurred the growth of Kuala Lumpur, whose population grew from 4,500 in 1884 to 20,000 in 1890. The city developed a formal city council, and in 1896 Kuala Lumpur became the capital of the newly formed Federated Malay States (Lee 1990).

Against this background of growth, there were layers of violence. The British administration, which brought building codes and railways to the city, also brought the brutality of colonialism. In the early stages, as tin mines started to turn a profit and the settlements of Kuala Lumpur, Ampang, and Gombak grew, local gangs from the settlements fought repeatedly for control of the most productive mines (Ooi 2004). The development of Kuala Lumpur revolved around control of capital and extractive activities, with Malay political leaders, the Chinese business community, and the British colonial authorities all involved. In the early 1900s, the rubber industry in Selangor state surrounding Kuala Lumpur brought multinational firms to the city, accelerating its growth and political importance as a federal city. With this growth came pushback from workers. After the Second World War, during the Malayan Emergency (1948–60), British colonial forces fought a guerrilla war against a communist insurgency. One part of the British forces' counter-insurgency strategy, referred to as the Briggs Plan,[1] involved setting up "New Villages," essentially relocation settlements around the country, to which around 500,000 ethnically Chinese Malayans were interned.

The British intended to use these settlements to break up social networks among communist insurgents and rural sympathizers. The impact of the New Villages on the development of Kuala Lumpur, and on urban planning in Malaysia more generally, can be felt to this day. Based on Baillargeon's (2021) maps, the three largest New Villages in Greater Kuala Lumpur held between 8,000 and 13,000 relocated people each. In what is now Greater Kuala Lumpur, around 69,800 inland Chinese residents were forcibly displaced into around twenty-five New Villages.

This recent history of structured displacement, including the violence that was part of the extractive industry that established Kuala Lumpur, continues to impact Malaysia's politics and urban culture. The New Villages around Kuala Lumpur were all newly constructed (Baillargeon 2021), and as such they followed planning guidelines applied to all New Village settlements (Goh 2022). Many of these planning guidelines have been integrated over time into the planning practices of many municipalities and planning authorities across the Malay Peninsula (Goh 2022); in this way, the legacy of colonial violence and counter-insurgency has been "baked into" contemporary urban planning. Many of the original New Villages themselves remain intact, with people living in them and maintaining them as historical spaces. However, the use of plans for forced resettlement areas in today's municipal or city planning processes raises questions about the health and social connectivity of contemporary urban spaces. People were not supposed to leave the New Villages, and while over time the use of fencing and barbed wire was reduced, the idea of isolating the population in a built environment remained.

This historical background helped me understand why, as we conducted our research in the Ampang, Gombak, and Klang areas of Greater Kuala Lumpur, these neighbourhoods that were part of Kuala Lumpur's contiguous conurbation still felt isolated. My feelings of isolation are inherently subjective; even so, they helped me understand why time and distance kept emerging as themes during interviews with refugees in Kuala Lumpur. Ampang, Gombak, and Klang, which I will describe in detail below, are indeed contiguous to Greater Kuala Lumpur – roads and rail link them to the city centre, and on maps there are no physical borders, like mountains or waterways, that would separate them from the city. Another feature of these districts that I found interesting when doing the research for this case study is that refugees were not part of the historical narrative of Greater Kuala Lumpur. In a way, one has to make some inferential leaps to bring together the historical strands of urban planning and displacement in Malaysia, and those interwoven histories of planning and displacement help us understand the role of urban refugees in the development of contemporary Kuala Lumpur.

Ampang today is split into two parts: Ampang Hilir is within the city boundaries of the Federal Territory of Kuala Lumpur; Ampang Jaya, farther west, is in Selangor state and borders on the Federal Territory. Leaving aside the administrative division between the two parts of Ampang, if one were to drive through it would feel like a single unit of urban space. During the Malayan Emergency, one of the largest New Villages was built in Ampang, housing 8,000 forcibly relocated ethnic Chinese; a second New Village called Kampong Pandan was just to the south of Ampang New Village and held 1,275 forcibly relocated people (Baillargeon 2021). One legacy of these New Villages is the influence of Chinese culture. Ampang is known for celebrations like the Nine Emperor Gods festival, celebrated in the ninth month of the Chinese lunar calendar. Physically, Ampang is a mix of planned housing estates and low- and mid-rise commercial buildings, with street food markets in the spaces between buildings. The refugee communities in Ampang are spread throughout the district, with community centres in anonymous office or commercial buildings.

North of Ampang is Gombak, which, similarly, straddles the border between the Federal Territory of Kuala Lumpur and surrounding Selangor state. Historically it shared Ampang's developmental trajectory as a tin-mining camp that evolved into a town and was absorbed over time into the Greater Kuala Lumpur conurbation. It is a largely residential district and includes tourist sites like the Batu Caves, as well as educational institutions like the International Islamic University of Malaysia. The refugee community in Gombak is housed in row house developments and high-rise apartment buildings. The neighbourhood felt to me rather suburban compared to Ampang; there was far less mixed-use commercial real estate, and the roads linking the clusters of row houses were smaller.

The third area where interviews took place was Klang, a port city that was once the capital of Selangor state. The legacy of British colonial administration is strong in Klang; the main rail line connecting Klang to Kuala Lumpur was built in 1886, when Swettenham was still the colonial resident for Selangor. The port was named after Swettenham until independence; it is now named Port Klang. Like Ampang, Klang had a large New Village, home to 8,000 forcibly relocated people (Baillargeon 2021). The city centre features mid-rise commercial buildings; sprawled around it are mixed-use commercial buildings and high-density housing. As in Ampang, the interviews for this study were conducted mainly in an anonymous area of the city, a mix of weathered commercial low-rise buildings and row houses.

The history and legacy of colonial and political projects like the New Villages, and the absorption of the planning principles that were part of the Briggs Plan, helped me understand the sense of isolation that pervaded Ampang and Klang in particular. The UNHCR offices in the centre of Kuala Lumpur were far from the places in Ampang, Gombak, and Klang where refugees lived – a journey of anywhere from 11 to 30 kilometres. Reflecting on the strategy of isolation inherent to New Village planning provided some perspective on why these areas of the city felt *distant*. Part of this could be attributed to the sprawling nature of outer Kuala Lumpur, where the buildings all looked similar and large roads and highways cut through developments. Another feature of Kuala Lumpur's urban landscape is how car-centric it is. Public transportation options for urban refugees living in Ampang, Gombak, and Klang were extremely limited, which seemed to add to the sense of distance to the city centre. The sense of distance and isolation that pervaded the outer areas of the city, legacies of planning built around extraction and colonial violence, made itself felt in interviews with refugees as we talked about the ways internet technologies influenced perceptions of time, distance, and legal exclusion in daily urban life.

TECHNOLOGY IN KUALA LUMPUR

Kuala Lumpur, like Malaysia more generally, has a well-established computing and internet industry, as well as a robust national high-speed mobile phone network. Four major firms comprise the com-

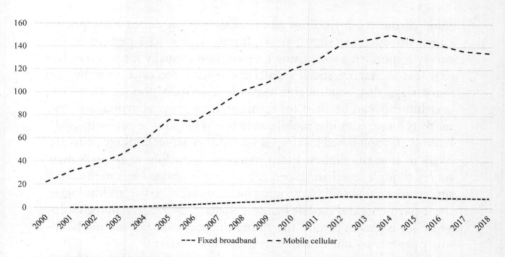

Figure 7.1 Fixed broadband versus mobile cellular subscriptions per 100 inhabitants in Malaysia
Source: ITU (2020).

petitive mobile telecommunications market (there are a few smaller ones), and Malaysia is implementing a strategy of increasing digitalization, especially in the financial and payments industries. Data from Malaysia's national regulator, the Malaysian Communications and Multimedia Commission (MCMC), indicate that around 45 percent of premises have fixed broadband, with a higher concentration in Greater Kuala Lumpur (MCMC 2022).[2] That statistic refers only to buildings with the infrastructure to have fixed broadband internet – the rate of actual subscriptions for fixed broadband, compared with mobile broadband, tells a different story.

Like many middle-income countries, Malaysia has a significantly higher number of mobile internet subscriptions per hundred inhabitants. In 2022, according to MCMC data, the absolute numbers of fixed broadband subscriptions totalled 3.9 million nationwide; by comparison, mobile broadband subscriptions totalled *41.9 million* in a total population of 32.7 million. Nationwide, and in Kuala Lumpur, the main mode of accessing the internet is by mobile phone. Against this background, it makes sense that so much of the internet industry is developing applications and tools for mobile phones, particularly smartphones.

To unpack how this difference in the mode of connecting to the internet influences the market for internet services, we can look at some of the main findings from MCMC's most recent Handphone Users' Survey 2021 (MCMC 2021). It tells us that 94.8 percent of the survey respondents were using a smartphone, mostly for social activities. Text messaging, social media, and voice/video calls were the primary ways that respondents used their mobile phones. However, smartphones can be used for far more than these activities, and the markets for services like mobile wallets and banking, e-payments, ride hailing, and app-based tasking[3] is where internet technology firms are likely to find the highest profit margins. According to MCMC's own survey, though, less than 50 percent of mobile phone users in the 2021 survey were interested in using, or had the ability to use, technologies like e-payments and mobile banking. Regardless, Malaysian technology policy is geared toward increasing the prevalence of mobile banking, e-payments, and smartphone-based task services.

Mobile banking and e-payments are a growing part of the internet economy in Malaysia. For our purposes, there are three products that matter: internet banking, mobile banking, and e-wallets/payments. These make up around 85 percent of the financial technology market in Malaysia by transaction volume (Fintech News Malaysia 2022). The following definitions are common as opposed to technical, but enough to understand the practical differences. Internet banking involves accessing bank accounts and transaction services through a browser, either through a computer, a tablet, or a smartphone. Mobile banking is essentially a subcategory of internet banking, but done using a smartphone app. E-wallets and payments are non-banking financial services; a user can set up an e-wallet as a space to store cash digitally and make online payments without a bank account.[4] This ecosystem of financial technologies represents an important component of the Malaysian digital economy, especially since there is currently a push by the government to move toward a cashless economy. E-wallets are especially interesting as consumer products because they are usually one component of an app that ostensibly exists in order to provide other services, such as ride hailing.

Ride hailing apps are a key part of urban digital infrastructure in Kuala Lumpur. While Uber is the largest digital ride-hailing app in the world, Grab is the most popular in Southeast Asia. Most ride-hailing apps have grown to include logistics and delivery services; for example, Uber has a service called UberEats that can be used to order food for delivery. Grab has taken this further, creating something of a super-app that functions primarily as a ride-hailing tool, with integrated food ordering, e-finance services, and courier services (Suruga

2022; Grab 2022). What makes Grab uniquely influential in the Southeast Asian market is that the user experience is tailored to regional and national social and cultural preferences. For example, people can pay for rides using cash instead of integrated credit card or e-wallet payments, which makes this app accessible to lower-income or unbanked customers. In a city as sprawling and car-centric as Kuala Lumpur, Grab is a solution to accessing transportation options in lower-traffic areas of the city farther from the centre.

Up to now, my focus has been on private sector technologies, but Malaysia and Kuala Lumpur also provide residents with e-government tools for managing citizen-to-government activities. The Malaysian Administrative, Modernisation and Management Planning Unit in the Prime Minister's Department has been in charge of the various iterations of national e-government and innovation strategies going back to 1996 (UNESCAP 2022). The current national e-government strategy's citizen-oriented services include providing multipurpose national "smart" ID cards, ensuring that all schools have internet and computing facilities, and providing national telehealth and online health services (UNESCAP 2022). At the city level, which is our level of interest, Kuala Lumpur has a dedicated e-government portal for residents.[5] That website includes specific links for municipal services such as garbage and street maintenance, paying and filing taxes, registering pets, and renting municipal sports and social facilities. There are also links to mobile-phone-app-based services that can be accessed via smartphone. The UN E-Government Knowledgebase (2022), which calculates comparative scores for the quality of municipal e-government services in 193 cities globally, currently ranks Kuala Lumpur at 70, with Kuala Lumpur's strengths being a robust institutional framework for e-government and effective use of available technologies. Overall, public perceptions and satisfaction with Malaysian e-government services are positive, particularly among the urban poor (Yap et al. 2020; Shuib, Yadegaridehkordi, and Ainin 2019).

Refugees are not part of the policy-planning process since they have no legal status in Malaysia, but they still represent a market for telecommunication and internet services. Thus, they are also going to be using smartphones for making calls, sending texts, and accessing social media, just like their Malaysian peers. However, they lack the identification documentation necessary to set up basics like a mobile phone account. To acquire a local SIM card and set up a pre- or postpaid mobile phone account, a non-Malaysian resident needs a passport, work permit, or student ID card (MCMC 2022). Most of the refugees in Kuala Lumpur do not have any of these; the majority do not have passports, and since the Malaysian government does not recognize refugees as legal residents, they do not have work permits. Refugees do have UNHCR registration cards, but these are not government-issued ID cards and generally are not accepted as ID for setting up mobile phone accounts. UNHCR Malaysia (2022) makes this abundantly clear on its local website: a UNHCR ID card merely signals that the person has registered and been granted refugee status; it does not confer legal residency or work status in Malaysia. This has the further effect of excluding refugees from services like Grab, which requires as part of registering as a new user a selfie-photo and a photo of either a passport bio-data page or a Malaysian national ID card. However, through interviews with urban refugees in Kuala Lumpur, we will come to see how digitalization is part of their lives even though they live in precarious legal and social conditions.

DIGITALIZATION IN THE LIVES OF REFUGEES

In the previous chapter, digitalization in the lives of urban displaced people in Bogotá represented a process of integration. Venezuelans arrived and used digital technologies to make sense of the city and build social and economic connections. Urban refugees in Malaysia, by contrast, are often building entire parallel urban societies in Kuala Lumpur. This is due to the legal framework governing their lives. Venezuelans in Colombia have had the right to full legal residence status since 2021, whereas refugees in Malaysia continue to live in a country that does not recognize "refugee" as a legal category. They do not have predictable access to health services, cannot access social services and public education, and are unable to set up bank accounts or work legally.

In effect, digitalization in the lives of urban refugees in Kuala Lumpur represents something akin to creating a parallel urban society, one that exists in the same physical space as Malaysians but not in the same administrative or legal space. Refugees are setting up a parallel urban society, and that entails establishing access to health services, finding labour opportunities, creating social networks that ensure protection and safety, and supporting different types of community education systems. During the interviews with refugees in Kuala Lumpur it became clear that digital technologies played a

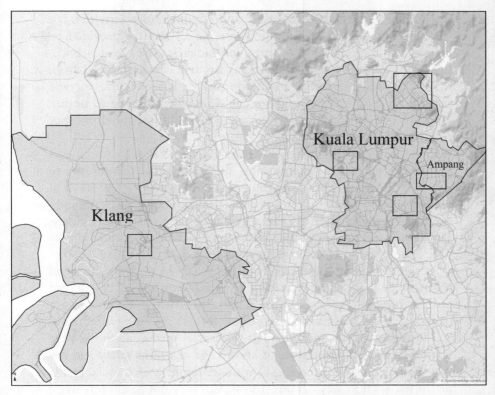

Figure 7.2 Approximations of where data were collected in Kuala Lumpur (boxes indicate general locations)

role in all these processes, but that role was not always a helpful one. In order to understand how urban refugees' digital lives fit into Kuala Lumpur's urban development more broadly, and which of the theoretical scenarios from Chapter 2 are likely to emerge, it is critical to examine how the lack of legal rights and status magnifies confusion and digital misinformation. When one is constantly having to weigh the costs of time and distance when going to the doctor, or to work, or when trying to update records at the UNHCR office, a lack of reliable information presents a serious problem. Figure 7.2 shows the general areas where the urban refugees who were interviewed live; they are often far from services, with limited options for transportation.

The five areas of life in the city that refugees talked about having to develop within their own communities were safety and security, health care, job seeking, education, and administrative activities. For legal residents of Kuala Lumpur, these are all services provided by the city and national governments. For refugees, these are all services that must be self-organized, since urban refugees are barred from Malaysian public services. Particularly striking was how idiosyncratic and intimate digital technologies could be when it came to health, safety, and building social networks, and how bluntly unhelpful they could be in an emergency.

Safety and security is where I will start, since a key draw for cities is the chance to live in a community, and within that community to find a measure of safety and connection. There were a few levels at which the interview questions dealt with this. The first was the individual level, which focused on individual online safety and privacy: Did people feel safe using the internet and social media, and did they have a sense of how to ensure their safety online?

At the individual level, only a minority of respondents discussed having knowledge of cybersecurity, privacy, and online safety (e.g., not posting photos on Facebook or sharing photos on WhatsApp, not using Facebook Messenger "as it doesn't feel safe": Rohingya female 2, 10 November 2019), and most felt that social media platforms were secure. The lack of interest in, or knowledge of, online safety and privacy is particularly concerning, as younger refugees used social media platforms, such as WeChat and TikTok, but may not have been aware of the risks posed by being active on them (organization 4, 15 November 2019). Staff from community organizations felt that refugees' understanding of cybersecurity was limited. For example, in the context of sexual and gender-based violence (SGBV) cases, many survivors who had left their partners were reportedly unaware of the "track my phone" app or of the threat of being outed on social media platforms by members of their own community (organization 4, 15 November 2019). Contrary to expectations, it was surprising how little individual respondents seemed to care about digital security and privacy. These individual-level issues were secondary to them in terms of safety in urban spaces. Under conditions where the normal apparatuses of public safety do not provide safety, and indeed are a direct threat to safety, visibility within the community is one of the key ways that urban refugees achieve a measure of security.

At the community level, organizations in Kuala Lumpur used ICTs to foster refugee protection in a variety of ways. One was using WhatsApp groups to alert members about immigration raids or a police presence in an area. Another was to advocate for community members' expedited registration at the UNHCR, as well as email the UNHCR lists of community members who had been detained. SGBV response was one area where communities and NGOs consistently used digital technologies to support refugee self-reliance. An NGO working with survivors of SGBV operated a hotline where people could report cases. This same organization disseminated MP3s in the Rohingya language to provide awareness on SGBV in Rohingya communities and received a generally positive response: people liked being able to listen to its content in their own time, and some shared the file with friends and family (interview, organization 4, 15 November 2019). In this way, ICTs were used to both educate individuals and help communities recognize issues of SGBV, while also increasing access to support services.

What we heard in interviews, which aligns with Grabska's (2006) and Pascucci's (2017) findings, is that refugee- and community-led organizations can be central to fostering self-reliance through protection activities. However, there are limits: some community organizations, like the Chin organization, were very effective at using ICTs to document abuses by police and human traffickers so that refugees could include them in interviews with the UNHCR (interview, Chin community leader, 8 November 2019). Their ability to extend this capacity to support neighbouring communities was limited, however. In practice, refugee community–organized safety and protection activities could not be extended to protecting refugees' rights or affording legal protections, since there is no national legislation that provides any legal rights or protection to refugees in Malaysia.

At the state level, the UNHCR's Malaysia office has attempted to leverage digital technologies to prevent harassment of refugees by police. Because no legislation in Malaysia defines refugees' immigration status, police often arrest refugees under the pretence that their UNHCR documents are fake and then require someone from the UNHCR to come to immigration detention and confirm that the arrested refugee is, indeed, registered with the UNHCR (interview, Pakistani male 1, 6 November 2019). The local UNHCR office developed an app, in collaboration with the Malaysian government, that police could use to scan QR codes on UNHCR registration cards to verify their authenticity. Few respondents knew about this app, and among those who did, enthusiasm was lacking: police often just arrested people anyway, since the UNHCR card itself was not a legal form of identification under Malaysian law (interview, Pakistani male

1, 6 November 2019; interview, Chin community leader, 8 November 2020). The UNHCR ID cards' lack of legal standing was the root problem; for refugees in Malaysia, UNHCR registration had no legal standing, so demonstrating a UNHCR card's "realness" had no binding effect on whether police arrested a refugee for being in Malaysia. A more recent ID system, the Tracking Refugees Information System (TRIS) has been rolled out by the Malaysia Home Ministry but does not confer any legal status either and is perceived as merely a means to surveil refugees living in Malaysia (Qarssifi 2022).

This lack of visibility to the state, and exposure to arrest and detention, has downstream effects on health care. Refugees were caught in a legal vacuum regarding access to emergency health care. The mix of misinformation that refugees had to wade through online created the basis for terrible outcomes. One respondent recounted that he and his wife were unaware that they would be allowed access to birth and postnatal medical treatment in Malaysia; thus, they decided to smuggle themselves back into Thailand for her to give birth (interview Myanmar Muslim male 1, 16 November 2019). There were complications during the birth, and while they were being smuggled back into Malaysia, the baby died. Had reliable information explaining that he and his wife could access emergency services in Kuala Lumpur been available, they would not have made the journey to Thailand. Institutions like the UNHCR may see a website as a means to disseminate information efficiently to a large audience, but the sheer volume of information can lead to confusion and tragic outcomes. Essentially, a high volume of information on a website does not necessarily create the conditions for self-reliance.

Beyond these kinds of very acute situations, the refugee communities in Kuala Lumpur had to deal with a mix of information about where and how they could access health care, as well as the practicalities of actually receiving it when they were entitled to do so. There were mobile doctors who would come to neighbourhoods where refugees lived on a semi-predictable schedule, and refugee community organizations would share these doctors' schedules with their members on digital channels. This meant that refugees in various neighbourhoods of Kuala Lumpur at least had access to check-ups, even if emergency care in the formal medical system was hard to come by.

The domains of safety and security, and health care access, are heavily influenced by the laws and policies of the Malaysian state. To shift gears a little, we also looked at urban behaviours such as job seeking. Refugees could not access the formal job market, but just as in many other places, they were able to find work in the informal sector. There were inherent risks in this, and some community groups used digital technologies to mitigate those risks. The Chin community organization in Kuala Lumpur ran job boards on its Facebook group, curated by its leadership. Employers reached out to that organization's leaders, who verified job details and the employer's reliability before posting the ad online (interview, Chin community leader, 8 November 2019). These online job boards were the only examples of community organizations formally filtering job opportunities to make sure refugees were treated fairly at work; this surprised us, given the legal and workplace safety risks that refugees face in Malaysia. Indeed, many respondents shared experiences of employers refusing to pay them for work they had completed (interview, Chin male 4, 8 November 2019; Rohingya male focus group discussion, 13 November 2019; Myanmar Muslim male, 16 November 2019).

Where the law does not protect refugees who are working, refugee communities themselves try to at least filter and manage the risk. Digitalization makes irregular work marginally safer but is not a replacement for full access to legal protections. A similar pattern arose when the discussion turned to education within the refugee communities, which they organized on their own, faced as they were with legal barriers preventing refugees from accessing the Malaysian school system.

Respondents from the Pakistani community reported using YouTube in classrooms and accessing English-language websites in order to teach students English. The coordinator for community schools in the Pakistani refugee community described using Google Drive to manage records across different schools. This same community used e-books and downloaded worksheets for their students (interview, Pakistani male 2, 6 November 2019). Overall, though, it seemed that ICTs in the classroom were not a central concern for respondents. As one respondent put it, "you can have good education without computers; you just need good teachers" (interview, Pakistani male 1, 6 November 2019). Note, however, that the Pakistani interviewees included a computer scientist and a trained medical doctor, both of whom led the process of digitizing the management of school activities. For communities that lacked skilled individuals, schools were often "only simple ... we don't have technology" (interview, Chin female 2, 8 November 2019).

Digital solutions for learning and teaching existed outside classroom structures. For example, one Somali respondent who was a professional baker had the idea of starting a YouTube channel to advertise a community bakery and show others how to set up bakeries in their host countries or cities (interview, Somali male 3, 7 November 2019). This was only one example of using a digital channel to teach others a trade; many respondents noted that YouTube was a useful resource for learning how to do things. But this is not formal education, for it does not come with recognized credentials.

The principal theme that emerged as we spoke with refugees about education and visited their community schools had nothing to do with technology: the respondents' greatest concerns were that refugees were barred from Malaysian government schools, colleges, and universities and that community schools could not provide credentials that host governments would recognize. Thus, ICT solutions had only limited potential in terms of supporting the educational domain. In a similar way that refugees turned to ICTs and the internet to make informal work less risky, communities used digital technologies in education to mimic an education system. Digital technologies allowed refugees to continue learning, but that learning was disconnected from the documentation that would allow refugees to use it as full members of Kuala Lumpur's urban society.

It is in the realm of documentation and administrative visibility that we begin to see the influence of digital technologies and humanitarian organizations in the lives of urban refugees in Kuala Lumpur. The Malaysian state plays no administrative role in the lives of urban refugees (except to occasionally detain and harass them), with the result that a challenging interface sometimes develops online between the UNHCR, a handful of NGOs, and the refugee community organizations. Everyone, it seems, is trying to use ICTs and digital technologies to bridge the gaps that arise from a lack of funding and resources at all levels. These imperfect solutions often leave everyone feeling acutely aware of how much demand there is for services and how hard it is to meet that demand with digital tools when the underlying legal and financial resources are not there to make it possible.

All the organizational and NGO staff we interviewed used ICTs to some degree for communicating with refugee communities. The UNHCR had set up WhatsApp groups with community leaders, and an NGO working with survivors of sexual and gender-based violence (SGBV) often contacted clients through WhatsApp. But when communicating with the larger refugee community on administrative issues such as confirming appointments with the main office, the UNHCR resorted mainly to phone calls. Those calls were often made during the workday, when, respondents explained, they were not allowed to answer them (some reported that their phones were confiscated by employers during work hours). Thus, appointments went unconfirmed, with the result that those who made the journey to the UNHCR office were often told to reschedule. These journeys were time consuming, and respondents mentioned that an app to confirm appointments outside work hours would be a significant help. As one respondent noted: "They take our email and phone number, but they only ever call. They should use this [email] contact data" (interview, Pakistani male 2, 6 November 2019).

The UNHCR also operated a website that provided general information on resettlement, voluntary repatriation, education, health services, and how to update a phone number. An email address was also available for refugees to submit queries to the UNHCR; this email account was managed manually, however, so that emails were forwarded to the relevant unit. UNHCR staff acknowledged that not all refugees were familiar with email services and that they relied instead on local organizations or friends to assist them with emailing the UNHCR (UNHCR, interview 5, 5 November 2019). The lack of response from the UNHCR, including missed emails and calls, was cited by refugee interviewees as a frustration and as restricting their administrative self-reliance. One refugee said she felt stuck in "limbo," since she was unable to ascertain where her resettlement case stood in the review process (interview, Pakistani female 1, 7 November 2020). Respondents said they would feel reassured and empowered if they were allowed access to information regarding the progress of their cases; this could be an app or Web platform that gave them access to their biodata and a summary of their resettlement status.

Refugee communities in Kuala Lumpur relied on their community organizations' strong digital networks to deal with the administrative domain. These organizations had well-established WhatsApp groups managed by community leaders in different neighbourhoods. Information (e.g., where health services were located, or when community schools would open) was communicated by refugee community focal points through community Facebook pages. In the Chin community, Facebook Messenger was the main forum of communication between the community organization and community members (interview, Chin community leader, 8 November 2020). In other communities, WhatsApp was the predominant form of communication. On both platforms, voice memos were often sent to ensure that people who could not read could at least listen to the information. Using these channels, community organizations played a key role in rebroadcasting and sharing updates from the UNHCR office.

In a context where all who are involved – refugees, the UNHCR, and NGOs – are trying to make ends meet, digital technologies can only do so much. It was striking: the city offered everything refugees needed, yet the political and legal structures that governed their lives and the limited degree to which the UNHCR and NGOs could aid them meant that digital technologies were at best a Band-Aid covering bigger problems. In the most acute scenarios, outcomes spawned from refugees' legal exclusion could be tragic.

THE INTERACTION BETWEEN DIGITALIZATION AND URBAN INTEGRATION

This case study is using the concepts of time and distance and law to link the role of technology in the lives of urban refugees to how they affect the trajectory of the city's development. Those concepts arose directly in interviews, for example, when it was noted how long a trip to the UNHCR took, or when a respondent wished there was a quick way to check her asylum status remotely, or when examples were provided of (mis)information creating confusion and increasing the time needed to make a decision about something. The physical environs of Kuala Lumpur themselves magnify the challenges posed by time and distance. In practical terms, it takes a long time to travel from the city's periphery to its centre; there is also the perceptual sense of isolation that I mentioned earlier. The legacy impacts of the New Villages on urban planning and social exclusion are difficult to demonstrate but should not be dismissed when we try to understand how marginalized communities fit into the wider urban society of Kuala Lumpur.

The results of this case point to two different theoretical scenarios, one manifesting at the urban refugee community level and the other at the wider Kuala Lumpur city level. The first is the North End scenario, where urban societies self-manage and propagate without significant financial capital or inputs from city planners. In each community where interviews took place, this was the case. Communities attended to their own needs, finding resources (human and otherwise) within themselves to continue to survive (see also the Mixed Migration Centre's 2020 report on migrants and refugees in Kuala Lumpur). The Pakistani refugee community had medical doctors and IT professionals among its ranks who provided community services, including running the community schools. The Somali community had a baker who not only produced bread commercially but also used YouTube to show others how to set up and run a bakery. Around these people there were further activities; for example, a Somali youth centre shared a building with the bakery, which made that site a hub for community organizing and socializing. Digital channels were key to these kinds of urban refugee social spaces' growth and inclusion.

The second level, the wider Kuala Lumpur city level, reflected the Lonely Hustle scenario. While an individual urban refugee in Kuala Lumpur was part of a community, the refugee communities themselves were atomized, and abstracted away from Malaysian urban society in Kuala Lumpur. Their skills, ingenuity, and non-Malaysian perspectives were not being added to the mix of Kuala Lumpur's wider urban society. And the refugee communities themselves were cut off from the city's resources, which often meant they were replicating all the services in the city with limited material and financial support. Refugee communities can use digital technologies to try to paper over the gaps in resources, but in the end, they still exist as atomized groups that must survive on their own.

The Kuala Lumpur case demonstrates the risk that digital technology will create a two-tiered urban society. Refugees have access to technology, and within their communities they can create something approaching a North End scenario. However, they do not shape the city in which they live, and that, perhaps, is to the detriment of Kuala Lumpur. Historically, where there has been space for displaced people to engage in the politics and society of a city of arrival, they have often been part of social progress. We can look back at examples like the young Jewish women who brought their experience of labour organizing in Europe to New York City and were central to organizing strikes and reforming the garment industry. In Kuala Lumpur, refugees could play similar roles. For example, James Bawi Thang Bik is an activist and organizer who represents the Alliance of Chin Refugees in Malaysia. He uses digital technology in his work with the alliance to organize job boards, collect information about missing people, and help other refugees gather and organize information so that they can apply for asylum with the UNHCR. These skills, however, are stovepiped within the urban refugee community – James's activism and the progress it generates have not shaped the wider urban society of Kuala Lumpur.

When we move on the third case study, Nairobi, Kenya, we will find some themes that carry over from Kuala Lumpur. The idea of distance or isolation also arises in Nairobi, where urban refugees also live in ethnic or country-of-origin enclaves that are often outside the city core. The legacy of urban securitization is another theme that carries over; in Malaysia there were the New Villages, while in Nairobi the shadow of the security services and the buildings they used shape how people who live in Nairobi relate to the city (Nyabola 2017). We also see in Kuala Lumpur and Nairobi two experiences of colonialism. Planning and capital played dominant roles in both cities, and independence, which came much later, shaped both cities' trajectories in ways that are very different from what we find in Bogotá. The legacies of urban planning and securitization have been similar in Kuala Lumpur and Nairobi. The latter city, though, shows us how urban refugee communities can engage in politics and economic life when there *is* a legal framework in place that recognizes their status (however tenuous that framework may be). In the following chapter, we will start to see how digital technology can influence the development of the host city when there are legal avenues for refugees to involve themselves in the host city's urban society.

8

Nairobi:
Shifting Politics in a Digital Metropolis

Coming into Nairobi by air is one of the best ways to introduce yourself to the city and to get a sense of its shape and energy. Long-haul flights from Europe usually arrive in the evening, and the landing pattern often involves flying southwards to the Ngong Hills and then turning east for the final approach, where the suburbs start. During the descent, one can see the city out of the left side of the airplane, the suburbs and residential sprawl of the Kawangware area of the city giving way to low-rise, higher-density buildings in the Kilimani neighbourhood, and then the brightly lit high-rises of Upper Hill and the Central Business District (CBD). It is a striking visual at night because directly below the airplane is Nairobi National Park, a large wildlife reserve that stops abruptly at the Southern Bypass highway – unlit darkness and then the sharp line where the city starts. Large freeways like the Southern Bypass, the Nairobi Expressway, and Langata Road, notorious for their traffic jams, glow like golden veins running through the city. It is a high-energy place; over drinks one evening a colleague said he thought Nairobi was the most "neoliberal city in the world."[1] There is a long history of coming to Nairobi for work, seeking entrepreneurial opportunity, and supporting family back home. As Mas and Radcliffe (2011) note, this was a significant reason for the success of the M-Pesa mobile phone–based cash transfer service that was established in 2008. The service's marketing catchphrase, "Send Money Home," has historical cultural-economic meaning for urban workers in Kenya. Nairobi is a city of movement, whether that means domestic migration for work or refugees seeking safety in urban enclaves.

Sited on a high plain where the Nairobi River and its tributaries flow into the Athi River on what is now the east side of the city, Nairobi started out as a railway depot under the British East Africa colonial government in the late 1800s. At the time, Mombasa was the colonial administrative capital, and the site where Nairobi currently sits was a convenient place to set up a switch yard for trains running between Mombasa on the coast and Kisumu on Lake Victoria. It was temperate, had a good water supply, and was east of the steep Limuru Escarpment above the Great Rift Valley. By the early 1900s the city was growing quickly, and the colonial government moved the capital of British East Africa from Mombasa to Nairobi in 1907. This was also the start of the colonial segregation of the city: Indian and African residents could only live in specific parts of the city, a legacy that still shapes Nairobi's neighbourhood-level demography today. As Owuor and Mbatia (2008) explain, Nairobi is an archetypical colonial city. The British expressly established it as a transit hub, and built it on land that had not yet been urbanized. Nairobi as we now know it came into existence as part of a colonial logic.

The legacy of being a colonial urban centre meant that the city was shaped by exclusion, racial restrictions on residency, and the violence of segregation (Owuor and Mbatia 2008; Mundia 2017; Martin and Bezemer 2019). As with Kuala Lumpur, these legacies are important if we are to understand how the city today hosts urban refugees. As the city grew, White colonial residents built homes on the west side of the city, uphill, in the drier areas. Indian railway workers lived in planned developments that had been set aside for them, while in what is now the eastern and southeastern parts of the city, housing compounds were set up for Black bachelor labourers coming to the city to work. These were firm boundaries, set along racial lines and magnified by the exclusion of Black African families from the city. Initially, the Black areas of the city were solely for men who were there to work. This changed with independence, and Black Kenyan politicians, planners, architects, and civil society leaders played key roles in shaping Nairobi as an African city pushing beyond its synthetic colonial past. Landmark buildings like the Kenyatta International Convention Centre are part of a skyline that reflects the 1960s politics of Pan-Africanism and the energy of postcolonial independence (Woudstra 2020; Uduku 2016).

When we look at the role of contemporary urban refugees in Nairobi's urban society, these legacies help us understand the disconnected nature of the city's quarters, the role of state violence in poor neighbourhoods and slums, and the negotiations around rights and participation for communities that exist in legal grey areas. In the post-independence period the dictatorship of Daniel arap Moi built administrative buildings in Nairobi that served routine citizen needs but were also sites of state violence against perceived enemies. As Nanjala Nyabola (2017) explained in her retrospective on the Nyayo House and Nyati House buildings in downtown Nairobi, the acts of torture and state-sanctioned violence that took place in those buildings imbued the areas around them with a sense of dread. The buildings became synonymous with the power of the state during the Moi dictatorship to enact violence against citizens, and in many ways the intersection of state violence, socio-economic class, and geography remains central to Nairobi's urban politics. These legacies of violence are still part of urban life, especially in marginalized neighbourhoods and slums, where there is both fear of and support for the use of violence by state security entities (Wairuri 2022; van Stapele 2016, 2019; Elfversson and Höglund 2019).

However, contested politics, especially between the state's security politics and a civil society that is pushing for more openness, have created space for otherwise marginalized communities to play a role in the city's development. Unlike Malaysia, Kenya has a national refugee law and provides asylum seekers with protection. This protection and aid is supposed to be administered in camps, and refugees living in urban areas exist in a constantly shifting legal space. The laws and rules that dictate when and why refugees can live in urban areas change regularly. Refugee communities in Nairobi know this, and with the help of NGOs and the UNHCR they have organized their own community networks, which advocate for urban political and economic inclusion. Understanding where technology fits into these processes thus requires some background regarding the ways that urban refugeehood has evolved in Nairobi since independence in the 1960s.

BRIEF HISTORY: NAIROBI AND URBAN DISPLACEMENT

For decades, Kenya has received refugees and asylum seekers from neighbouring countries; currently they number almost 500,000 "people of concern" (UNHCR 2022). Nairobi is a case in point: the city's population currently stands at 3.5 million and is still growing, giving home to a diverse population of Kenyans citizens, migrants, and refugees. The majority of refugees are from Somalia (54 percent), followed by South Sudan (25 percent), the Democratic Republic of Congo (DRC) (9 percent), and Ethiopia (6 percent). Kenya follows a strict encampment policy, with most refugees residing in the Dadaab and Kakuma camps; however, official estimates are that more than 71,000 refugees live in Kenya's urban areas (mostly in Nairobi). However, there is a lack of accurate data on displaced populations living in urban areas; estimates are that it may be as many as 100,000. The majority of registered refugees in Nairobi are from Somalia, followed by the DRC and Ethiopia. (All figures here are from UNHCR 2022.) One can only take this as part of the picture, given that the ethnic distribution of unregistered refugees may have a different composition than that of registered refugees. Displacement flows are a mixture of different groups, ranging from highly skilled refugees who skip camps in search of better economic opportunities in cities to refugees or displaced people with unregistered status who settle in ethnic urban enclaves. The former often choose a life in the city in order to escape from from the limited livelihood opportunities in the refugee camps. Refugees residing in Nairobi tend to head for specific neighbourhoods, where social networks play a major role in their settling in. Examples are Eastleigh, which is traditionally a Somali enclave, and Kayole, which mostly accommodates refugees from the DRC and the Great Lakes region (Pavanello, Elhawary, and Pantuliano 2018).

Kenya has been hosting refugees since colonial times. Shadle's (2019) analysis of the British colonial office's response to hosting refugees fleeing Italy's invasion of Ethiopia between 1935 and 1940 shows how the competing logics of security and humanitarianism create spaces of minimal safety for refugees, while also magnifying arguments over the costs and security concerns the hosting state faces. As Shadle explains, competing politics were at play when it came to hosting refugees from Ethiopia in what is now Kenya. Concepts like a "legitimate" threat to life were central to deciding who would be allowed into Kenya to access asylum, with London and the administrators in Nairobi taking a conservative line. Colonial officers at the borders had to make decisions using a different ethical and political calculus, and found arguments for allowing women and children to seek asylum alongside those who faced death for defecting from the Italian colonial army. The tensions between distant politics that were shaped by concerns about security and costs, and the ethics and practicalities of managing large numbers of people seeking safety and security, are still felt in Kenyan refugee politics. This is especially true in Nairobi, where the Kenyan government, the UNHCR, aid donors, NGOs, and urban refugees navigate legal complexities, social precarity, and the practicalities of seeking refuge in a large city.

The tensions I just listed certainly influence how refugees themselves choose to live in Nairobi. Most of them remain invisible to the state, often by choice, for to live in Nairobi is to exist in a legal grey area due to the country's encampment policy. After masses of Somali refugees arrived in the 1990s, Kenya's refugee policy changed and, with this, its until then favourable approach toward local integration. While previously, refugees (mostly from Uganda) were allowed to work, to access education, and to move freely around the country, in the 1990s the country started down a path towards strict encampment policies (Abuya 2007). This created a policy environment that makes integration – a key ingredient for a cohesive society – complex and challenging even for urban refugees with official documentation. One would expect that only those refugees with sufficient resources would live outside the camps, since their access to humanitarian services is not guaranteed outside the camp structures (Banki 2004). Formal integration through naturalization is virtually impossible. Due to lack of information, changing laws and policies, and arbitrary enforcement, urban refugees are often unclear about their own rights and status or which procedures they are supposed to follow. Moreover, urban refugees who lack a national identity card face the constant risk of being sent to one of the refugee camps. Additionally, administrative procedures to obtain documentation and complete refugee status determination are often delayed, sometimes for many years (Norwegian Refugee Council 2017).

Without a national identity card, urban refugees struggle with restricted access to services that require one, such as health care and banking services. At times they cannot even enter public buildings. Lack of documentation can also result in harassment by police and demands for bribes. Free movement in the city and open participation in society are heavily restricted in these ways. Parents who are unable to present documentation or a birth certificate are often unable to enrol their children in school (Njeri 2015). And even when their children are allowed to access the national school system, refugees continue to experience exclusion and discrimination. This is particularly true for Somali refugees, who are often perceived as a security threat (Ikanda 2020). Somali refugees and Kenyan Somalis have been marginalized and discriminated against in Kenya for decades, and rising xenophobia in Kenya has exacerbated this (Lind, Mutahi, and Oosterom 2017; Wambua-Soi 2012).

For displaced persons, the barriers to obtaining a work permit are high, and this prevents them from entering the formal employment sector no matter how well educated they are and from improving their income situation. Seventy percent of Nairobians work in the informal sector, and ethnic exclusion and marginalization are evident there as well (Bidandi 2018). Some firms, including Uber, are open to them, but the problem is that urban refugees in Kenya are unlikely to have things like a driver's licence, access to a car, or a bank account or e-wallet with which to accept payments. Thus, while native Kenyans can use new technologies to provide on-demand app-based services like Uber, refugees cannot.

There is legal space for NGOs and international organizations to provide urban refugees with job opportunities and avenues for financial inclusion. The problem with these options is that refugees still depend on the development and humanitarian sectors to facilitate them. Urban refugees can take jobs with groups like Samasource, which hires refugees (for a pittance) to do menial computer-based tasks, and with the help of aid and humanitarian agencies, they can access loans and financial services through financial technology firms located in high-income countries. But they encounter a number of drawbacks when they rely on aid agencies and the private sector for work and financial opportunities, for they do not enjoy the labour and banking rights afforded to Kenyans. A particular example is the role of financial technology (fintech) in providing refugees with, or excluding them from, banking services. As Baghat and Roderick (2020) explain, fintech solutions are often the only source of capital for refugees in Kenya, and this has resulted in a system where private capital from the Global North intervenes in livelihood support for refugees, favouring those deemed most entrepreneurial and most likely to repay loans. This creates a policy and legal lacuna between the potential ways that urban refugees in Kenya can be self-sufficient and the potential for innovative technologies to facilitate this. Without laws that enshrine urban refugees' rights to work and be financially included, and with a residency status that makes living in Nairobi at best only quasi-legal, there will always be a gap between urban refugees' potential to contribute to urban society and the technology to enable this. This is unfortunate, because there is a great deal of energy and innovation in Nairobi's technology sector, as we will see in the next section.

TECHNOLOGY IN NAIROBI

Since the early 2000s, the narrative in media and policy circles has been that Kenya is an important hub of Africa's technology sector. Mobile phones have been part of daily life in Kenya since the early 2000s, and their ubiquity and the population's comfort using them did a great deal to drive social technologies like Ushahidi as well as the rapid expansion of mobile money technology. Social innovation and mobile money have been foundational components in Kenya's burgeoning technology sector. In 2010 the iHub, a co-working space and tech start-up incubator, became a focal point for the still-nascent internet-based technology economy in Nairobi (Manske 2015). While there had been flashes of innovation that built on Kenya's robust mobile internet infrastructure, such as Ushahidi (see below), the iHub and other local incubators played a key role in developing both talent and financing (Manske 2015). Supporting private and social sector technological innovation is the Kenya National Innovation Agency (KeNIA), a state corporation that operates under the auspices of the Ministry of Education. KeNIA's principal aim is to support the educational, scientific, and research ecosystem that underpins the technology economy (KeNIA 2022). Kenya has achieved success with social innovations for preventing election violence and supporting civil society and has developed policies to support local tech entrepreneurs, but challenges remain (Nitsche 2019). What has helped drive the technology sector in Nairobi despite those challenges is reliable internet and telecommunications infrastructure.

I cannot cover every example of social innovation technology that got its start in Nairobi, so I will focus on what is perhaps the best-known piece of software: Ushahidi, which was created in 2007. "Ushahidi" means "testimony" in Swahili, and the team that created the software did so in response to the election violence that escalated in 2007 and 2008 (Rotich 2017). Reporters were unable to access voting districts due to the violence, so Ushahidi's software development team opted to focus on gathering crowdsourcing information via text messaging; it then geolocated testimonies provided by the public onto a digital map that the public could access on the internet. The Ushahidi software allowed administrators to categorize reports,

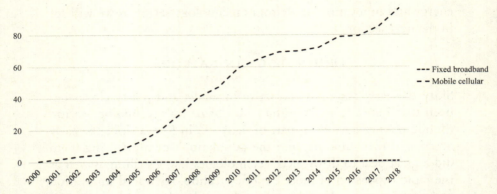

Figure 8.1 Fixed broadband versus mobile cellular subscriptions per 100 inhabitants in Kenya
Source: ITU (2020).

include the information from the text messages, and indicate on the map where the incidents had taken place. Ushahidi has always been open source and is designed to interface with mobile phone–based systems like SMS that are broadly used. Since 2008, organizations have been using it to crowdsource data on events such as the 2010 Haiti earthquake, to track potential violence during the 2013 Kenyan election, and to track violence during the early stages of the civil war in Libya (Cinnamon 2014). Ushahidi, which is still headquartered in Nairobi, is an example of local Kenyan technology innovation that has been used by civil society and humanitarian actors globally.

Continuing with the theme of maps and crowdsourcing, Map Kibera is a social technology project launched in 2009 that uses OpenStreetMap software to map the Kibera slum on the south side of Nairobi.[2] Kibera is one of the largest urban slums in Africa, and up through the early 2000s there were no official maps of it (Map Kibera 2022). Using OpenStreetMap to support community mapping, wherein residents of the slum actively contribute data to the map, the Map Kibera foundation has created maps that list social services, provide street plans, and serve as visual archives for data the community deems important. The Map Kibera foundation has also created community maps in other slums in Nairobi, helping render visible the infrastructure issues and social services these communities need. In effect, Map Kibera is an empowerment organization that uses a mix of internet technologies to help communities identify infrastructure and social issues and advocate with the Nairobi city government to address these. Map Kibera and Ushahidi, both developed in Nairobi, are social innovations that have captured the interest of development and humanitarian organizations. They have also served as exemplars for civil society actors in other countries who are doing social innovation work.

The second foundational technology, one that made Kenya a leader in both private sector and economic development circles, is mobile money and financial technology (fintech). I mentioned M-Pesa in the first paragraph of this chapter. M-Pesa is a mobile money service that was started by the Safaricom mobile phone company in Kenya in 2008. This product reshaped financial inclusion in Kenya and changed how Kenyans transfer money and pay for products. Safaricom subscribers start by setting up an M-Pesa account, onto which credit can be loaded. M-Pesa functions through a network of cash-in and cash-out agents around the country, who facilitate SMS-text-based transactions. A customer who wishes to transfer money finds an M-Pesa agent and gives the agent cash and their M-Pesa account details. The agent then credits the cash to the customer's account; the customer can then send credit to someone via SMS text message. The recipient of the text message then goes to a local M-Pesa agent with the relevant information, and that agent completes the transaction; the credit is deducted from the sender's account and converted into cash by the receiving M-Pesa agent. M-Pesa started as a mechanism for transferring money between individuals; since then, it has become so pervasive that almost any payment can now be made using it. For example, when I paid for my permit to do this research, I did so through the National Commission for Science Technology and Innovation's (NACOSTI) M-Pesa account.

While M-Pesa and Safaricom were the first to introduce this technology in Kenya, other mobile network operators have followed suit, setting up their own mobile money services. Airtel has Airtel Money, and Telkom has a product called T-Kash; both of them operate on the same principle as M-Pesa. For a long time these systems were not interoperable, but recent regulatory updates should enable Airtel Money and T-Kash customers to pay merchants who use M-Pesa and allow M-Pesa users to make payments to Airtel and Telkom accounts. What does all this mean for the average Kenyan? Jack and Suri (2010) found that while it was initially wealthy Kenyans who already had bank accounts who used M-Pesa, over time it has been adopted by less affluent customers. There has indeed been a significant increase in these people setting up bank accounts and engaging with the formal financial sector. Ng'weno (2010) also notes that uptake of M-Pesa and mobile money technology among lower-income Kenyans has allowed families to weather economic shocks better, since money can be moved quickly to where it is needed. This has meant faster access to health services and being able to pay school fees quickly and on time. While the advent of mobile money has generally been a net good, there remain issues about the high fees for transferring money. M-Pesa is the dominant platform, and smaller services like Airtel and Telkom rely on the M-Pesa infrastructure for processing transfers and payments (Augustine 2022), with subscribers and businesses bearing the consequences. This kind of near-monopoly remains an issue for regulators to solve (Ombok 2022).

While mobile money has been one of the most notable successes in the Kenyan technology sector, there are other sectors where digital innovation is taking place. One challenge has been finding ways to consolidate the emerging technology scene in Nairobi so that funders and multinational firms can locate talent and new products. The iHub, a technology and start-up incubator and workspace, was founded in 2010 as a space where technologists, developers, and investors could come together in Nairobi (Nitsche 2019; Shapshak 2016). The iHub has expanded over the years, providing event space, partnerships for connecting local technology talent with global technology firms that operate in Nairobi, and programs supporting social innovations such as hackathons with a focus on refugee self-reliance. The iHub's model, which has been replicated in other Kenyan and African cities, is an example of locally led efforts to consolidate national technology sectors (Dahir 2017). While it has been successful, it can only scale up so much, and the Kenyan government along with donors and investors has been pushing forward with a planned "technology" city, Konza Technopolis, to be built just south of Nairobi.

Konza Technopolis is a multi-stakeholder endeavour. The goal is to build a digital city. This project is part of the Kenyan government's Vision 2030 economic development portfolio, which focuses on building a science and technology economy (Konza Technopolis 2023). Partners in the project include the private sector, bilateral donors such as South Korea, and UN-HABITAT, which focuses on urban planning. Johari (2015) found, though, that the vision for the city, and the ensuing plans, largely exclude the communities that already exist where the city is to be built. It remains unclear whether a technology city will have a positive impact on the communities already there. As Van den Broeck (2017) points out, the practicalities of building a city are less important than the narratives around its potential and the uncertainties that arise when envisioning a future technological city. The surrounding communities, the government, and the partners pushing this project forward are doing so based on different visions for Konza Technopolis's potential (Van Noorloos, Avianto, and Opiyo 2019). What matters is whose vision will come to pass as the city is built; at the moment that vision seems to be one that will benefit investors, political elites, and international stakeholders more than the average Kenyan.

Technology in Nairobi has reached a point where deep tensions have developed between "growth" and benefits for the wider society. The iHub and software firms like Ushahidi are examples of Kenyan-led technology that supports social and economic inclusion. The iHub is a private enterprise, but it also has a clear mission to support public goods by growing Nairobi's digital economy. The introduction of M-Pesa and mobile money did a great deal to expand financial inclusion to poor and middle-income Kenyans, as well as to displaced people and refugees living in Nairobi. However, when we scale up to the level of building Konza Technopolis, or ask which start-up founders have the best access to venture capital, we quickly find that the urban poor and working class are likely to be left behind. This has implications for how urban refugees in Nairobi use digital technologies, as well as for the degree to which digitalization will improve social and economic outcomes for urban refugee communities.

DIGITALIZATION IN THE LIVES OF REFUGEES

In Nairobi, digital behaviour and activities in urban refugee communities took shape in two ways. One was expressly around community organizing, political engagement, and common resource management. Because urban refugees in Nairobi live in a legal grey zone, having status under Kenya law as refugees but not expressly allowed to live in urban areas, a significant amount of community organizing has been taking place in order to maximize inclusion in urban society while minimizing the risks of surveillance and attention from state security services. The other level is individual and focuses on how social and familial networks are maintained using digital technologies and how individuals can find ways to contribute to communities through volunteerism and social activities. The results regarding how technology has enabled refugees to find volunteer and social activities in their neighbourhoods showed up in the analysis of survey data on technology use and social cohesion (Martin-Shields and Kuhnt 2022). There was an interesting link between individual and community levels of digital technology use: social media in particular play an important role in helping individuals find a community-level role to play, and urban refugee communities use digital technologies to organize politically and socially. I will focus mainly on the interview data collected from the Somali and Congolese respondents, since these are the largest national groups of urban refugees in Nairobi, and refer to survey data collected across all the national groups when talking in general terms.

I will start by describing the community organizational level, since it was urban refugee community organizations that developed the social apparatus for protecting newly arrived refugees and providing them with pathways into Nairobi's urban society. To understand the interview data collected in different urban refugee communities conceptually, we can refer to the concept of moderation in information spaces. Grimmelmann (2015, 55–79) provides us with a "grammar of moderation," which differentiates between "techniques," "distinctions," and "community characteristics." "Techniques" are the verbs that describe moderation, such as excluding people, putting prices on access, and setting norms for posting and sharing. Distinctions are adverbs, describing whether Techniques are automatic or manual, centralized or distributed, and so on. Community Characteristics include the size of the user base and the identity of the users. I use this "grammar of moderation" to categorize and understand how the Somali and Congolese refugee communities in Nairobi moderate and govern the use of collective digital communication channels in a hybrid governance context. Moderation in this case represents a type of community governance – rules are set for what can be stored and shared, and access to community digital channels can be granted or revoked based on how moderators enforce digital community rules.

Once online, digital moderation within the communities follows path dependencies based on overall community governance strategies. The Congolese community, as discussed, is spread across two neighbourhoods and is less centralized than the Somali community. As Pavanello, Elhawary, and Pantuliano (2010) point out, the Congolese – and other Great Lakes region refugees – can often blend into their neighbourhoods to avoid unwanted attention. My team and I saw this first-hand; if one were to visit Kawangwari or Umoja it would be difficult to distinguish Congolese refugees from their Kenyan neighbours. Many speak Swahili, and the community tends to be able to integrate into the informal economy. The organizing hubs that most respondents talked about were local churches – most settlement processes, including getting access to a mobile phone and SIM card, were organized through churches or with Kenyan neighbours who could be trusted (DRC interview 4, 19 March 2019). This type of decentralized organizing through informal mechanisms like churches is how collective digital governance takes place in the Congolese community.

The Congolese community leaders and mobilizers thus played far more of a "gatekeeper" role than their Somali counterparts. Privacy and legal protection were key components of the moderation that was practised in the Congolese community. A number of respondents talked about using WhatsApp to communicate with family and friends and to tap into community news and information. People would borrow a community leader's smartphone if important news or information was being shared on "official" WhatsApp or Facebook groups (DRC interview 1, 19 March 2019). While social digital communication took place quite readily between individual Congolese and their families and friends, something that came up in all interviews was the importance of doing any kind of administrative task face-to-face. Refugees went to NGOs in person, and interactions with authorities that were mediated by community leaders were done in person. The lack of digital archiving, and the community expectation that collective activities would stay offline, sharply distinguished the Congolese community from the Somali one. Tying this evidence back to Grimmelmann's grammar of moderation, we can say that norms around privacy and decentralization shape online moderation; the Congolese community tends to shepherd sensitive topics offline and into in-person spaces.

For the Somali community the strategy for surviving in Nairobi, and by extension managing digital channels of communication, could be described as power in numbers. Like the Congolese, the Somali community had community organizers and mobilizers, but unlike the Congolese, these people often worked on visible committees. While WhatsApp was a general platform for all types of communication, the messaging app *imo* was the preferred platform for intra-community communication and organizing. As one interviewee noted, large numbers of Somalis in Kenya and abroad use it, so it was easy to have Somali-language discussions (Somali interview 7, 18 March 2019). It is interesting how language helped set community moderation norms. Seven of our respondents talked about how important it was to start the day listening to the news on BBC Radio Somali. From there, any useful news would be passed along to moderated WhatsApp and *imo* groups.

One thing we observed in the Somali community that seemed unique to the digital norms and moderation strategies they employed was the use of social media platforms as digital archives of their political activities and organizing. Leurs (2017) offers a theoretical way of understanding mobile phones and multimedia as tools for migrants and marginalized communities to archive and broadcast data and information about their experiences at the margins. The media that migrants curate, archive, and share on their phones becomes part of a narrative for negotiating space in an otherwise exclusionary political context. We saw a version of this during a meeting that a Somali community leader held while preparing members of his community for interviews (personal communication, 10 March 2019). His name was Mohamed,[3] and he had been in Kenya long enough to raise a family and acquire permanent resident status for his children. We met in the late afternoon at the Kilimanjaro Food Court in Eastleigh[4] and were soon joined by one of the Somali enumerators from a survey team we were working with.

The conversation itself was mainly about organizing the issues faced by the community in Eastleigh. But while we talked, the role of digital moderation emerged as a background theme. Mohamed explained how he and other Somali community leaders magnified their voices by organizing formal events to promote Somali refugees' needs and highlight their contributions to the city of Nairobi. From a digital moderation perspective, it interested us that his smartphone was essentially a digital photo archive of community events, Somali business and cultural association meetings, and workshops with the UNHCR and representatives from Kenya's Refugee Affairs Secretariat. He showed us which WhatsApp groups were being used for different types of organizing and how photos and videos of events were shared. It was a very well-curated set of digital channels, and, following on Leurs's description of archives as tools for shaping narratives, it made the community look not only economically strong (one only needs to visit Eastleigh to see this) but also highly organized politically. It was clear that these channels were centrally moderated and were being used exclusively by those who were part of the community leadership milieu. Comparing these images and content to what would be stored on the mobile phone of a Congolese community member brings the strategy side of moderation into focus. The Congolese were atomized and private in their digital moderation, whereas the Somali images were curated to be make sure the Somali community was *seen*. Moderation in this case focused on creating the digital narrative that the Somali community was politically and economically large and active. Put simply, if you can't blend in, then look as big as you can.

These community organizations and apparatuses rely, of course, on the individual engagement, so understanding how individual urban refugees use digital technology is also important. What is interesting here is the way that digital technology helps urban refugees maintain translocal connections to family and friends while simultaneously creating channels for refugees to find community and volunteer organizations in Nairobi after they settle there. Somali and Congolese urban refugees all used digital technologies to maintain distant relationships, but making new local friends was something people did offline. This finding maps fairly well onto how urban refugees in Malaysia and Colombia, and people generally, use these technologies. Interesting differences in individual digital behaviour among these communities emerge in how they build in-group networks and relationships with Kenyan neighbours.

The Somali urban refugee community in Nairobi is tightly knit, and indeed one challenge that arose during the survey work in Eastleigh was finding Kenyan nationals who lived in the neighbourhood. This indicated that Somalis who built social relationships with Kenyans often did so offline in places or contexts outside Eastleigh. One respondent (interview, Somali 2, 20 March 2019) explained how she developed friendships with Kenyans at the National Council of Churches Kenya (NCCK) refugee response services centre. She described how she initially went there to find services for herself. Then over time she got to know Kenyans who were seeking social services at the NCCK health centre, and she built relationships with them during her visits there. Another respondent (interview, Somali 3, 20 March 2019) explained that her daily activities were around the house, so the Kenyans she was friends with were mostly women who were doing domestic labour in the neighbourhood. It was not until one of the interviewees (interview, Somali 5, 20 March 2019) talked about being settled in long enough to start looking for stable work that the issue of digital technology arose. Somalis would meet Kenyans offering work in the informal economy; then, after establishing rapport, any ongoing contact was done via text message.

The Congolese may have found it easier to develop friendships with Kenyans since they resided in more heterogeneous neighbourhoods than the Somalis, but the pattern of getting to know people face-to-face and then transitioning to digital channels for maintaining relationships was similar. For the Congolese as well as the Somalis, WhatsApp and similar technologies were initially more for maintaining contacts with family and friend networks outside Kenya. Building friendships and individual connections remained in the realm of face-to-face. What Martin-Shields and Kuhnt's (2022) survey data on digital technology and social cohesion in refugee-hosting neighbourhoods showed was that digital technology began to have a significant impact once refugees started seeking out opportunities for community participation and volunteering. In a way this makes sense; one would not necessarily go looking for strangers on Facebook or Twitter to become friends with, but they would seek out community organizations' Facebook pages to find out how to join them.

As urban refugees' urban footprints grow, they reach a point where they involve themselves in community matters. This brings us back to how community activities are moderated and coordinated through online digital channels. The grey legal status that urban refugees face in Nairobi means that as individuals they have little power. They rely on their neighbours and trusted host-community members to use mobile money services for them, get them mobile phone SIM cards, and so on. They still have some measure of legal status, though; they are refugees according to Kenyan law, and while that may not confer residency and permission to work, they still have some rights under that law. Exerting those rights can take the form of political activism or setting up community organizations that serve both refugee and host-community needs, both of which are more easily accessible to new volunteers through social media and the internet. As these activities aggregate at the level of organizing across urban refugee communities, moderation of online activities starts to kick in as national communities balance the risk of being visible to the Kenyan state with the benefits of coordinating the collective interests of all the urban refugee communities in Nairobi.

THE INTERACTION BETWEEN DIGITALIZATION AND URBAN INTEGRATION

Urban refugees in Nairobi inhabit a liminal space; compared to urban displaced people in Bogotá, they have fewer legal rights, while compared to urban refugees in Kuala Lumpur they have more opportunities to build a life in the legal grey areas left to them by Kenya's refugee laws. Within that space, they can use digital technologies to become part of Nairobi's urban society. They cannot take much part in Kenya's digital economy, and many of the online e-government services that Kenyan nationals can use are unavailable to urban refugees. The UNHCR and NGO-organized digital services are a stopgap; urban refugees continue to be excluded from local services and markets and by extension are unable to participate fully in urban society. Being legally excluded from commercial services does not mean that urban refugees in Nairobi do not use those services; indeed, many urban refugees find ways to use those technologies with the help of Kenyan neighbours or through refugees who have found ways to get around exclusionary regulations. Finally, because urban refugees do have some measure of legal status, social media channels are indeed practical ways to organize socially and politically. Urban refugees can use digital technologies to advocate for their rights as well as their value to urban society; in a purely analogue world, they would find this much harder.

In camp settings, refugees in Kenya receive all their services and support from the UNHCR, NGOs, and aid donors. In Nairobi, though, where refugees are technically not supposed to reside, the humanitarian and aid community is more constrained in what it can provide. If refugee laws were more liberal and allowed urban refugees to obtain residency status and work permits, the lack of direct humanitarian services would not be such a serious problem. But because Kenyan law is so restrictive, they are excluded from the traditional labour market and even from app-based options like driving for Uber. They also cannot use local municipal e-government portals and tools, so in many ways they are digitally locked out of the formal operations of the city in which they live. There are, however, informal, civil society, and NGO efforts that support urban refugees' digital inclusion. Map Kibera works in areas where urban refugees live and by extension makes these neighbourhoods and slums more legible to both residents and the city administration. Techfugees, an international network of volunteer technologists, software developers, and members of local refugee communities, has been working in Kenya to develop digital health, education, and administrative solutions for urban refugees. The informal networks that refugees have set up within their communities are also critical, since they provide a means to circumvent restrictions on M-Pesa use by urban refugees.

In many ways, the economic and financial key to accessing Nairobi is through M-Pesa and mobile money. As I mentioned earlier, M-Pesa has become a principal means for making payments and other financial transactions within the city – everything from paying bills to visiting the Nairobi Arboretum. Urban refugees who can use M-Pesa can thus access the city in ways that those who only use cash cannot, especially as some services have started accepting payments solely through M-Pesa. An M-Pesa account also makes sending and receiving money easier, thus improving access to formal financial services. It is noteworthy that communities like the Somalis in Nairobi have developed hybrid pathways to using mobile money, thereby linking themselves to the formal economy through investments in property and goods. M-Pesa and systems like it are a means to link informal cash systems with formal investments that community members have made in the Eastleigh neighbourhood. M-Pesa has also added value for communities like the Congolese, who live in more heterogeneous neighbourhoods in smaller groups. It has made it easier for them to pay their daily expenses and to be paid for formal and informal work, and it has reduced the risks associated with the constant need for cash. While there are serious concerns about things like the exorbitant fees charged for cash transfers, and while regulations still lock many refugees out of M-Pesa and other types of mobile money, this technology still provides tangible benefits for urban refugees making their way in Nairobi.

The fact that there is a legal grey area that gives *some* rights to refugees has created an environment in which they can advocate for further inclusion. In both Nairobi and Kuala Lumpur there are refugee-led organizations representing different national groups, but in Nairobi, uniquely, these groups have organized internally and collectively online. The existence of some rights, however minimal, has opened the door for advocacy and for a robust network of NGOs, international organizations, and bilateral donors that provides urban refugees with an apparatus for engaging politically in Nairobi. This is in sharp contrast to Kuala Lumpur, where the UNHCR office operates on a tight budget and there is little donor interest in refugees. Urban refugees in Kenya can use the politics of aid and the minimal rights they hold to their advantage, to organize and advocate for themselves in digital spaces; whereas the lack of aid and absolute lack of rights in Malaysia makes it harder and less marginally beneficial for urban refugees there to engage overtly in local urban politics.

These three case studies, representing three very different geographies, political contexts, and legal frameworks, offer interesting divergences and overlaps. To bring them into conceptual discussion with one another and with the historical examples from the first section, the next chapter breaks down the comparative elements of the cases and histories using the four future scenarios introduced in chapter 2. I will evaluate the three cases through the lens of each scenario. This will allow us to see where there are similarities and differences across cases. The historical element will also be useful in understanding what attributes of historical cities facing technological change are reflected in the contemporary cases, as well as where differences between the past and present can help point to likely future outcomes. The goal is to lay out empirically and conceptually grounded scenarios that can be used to guide future empirical and theoretical research on how digitalization facilitates or frustrates urban refugees' efforts to join and actively participate in urban society in cities of arrival.

9

Digitalization and Urban Displacement: Future Scenarios

Across the three case studies, and in the historical analysis from Part 1, there are empirical data that paint a complex picture of how digital technological change will shape the role played by urban refugees in the development of host cities in the Global South. Indeed, all three cases contained elements that would fit into the different scenarios. Given how relatively new digital technological change is, the snapshots of data from the case studies are instructive, but they require historical scaffolding to tell a fuller story. Thus, the historical arc from the first section framed technologies in the context of urban displacement as either serving industrial or surveillance purposes, both of which were, and still are, inherent parts of displaced peoples' lived urban experience. This chapter analyzes the three contemporary descriptive case studies and historical analysis through the lens of the four theoretically derived scenarios presented in chapter 2. This will help us understand which attributes of the cases and history fit across scenarios, and which are unique to one case or historical example, and to inductively derive a general future vision of how digital technologies will shape the role of urban refugees in the development of cities in the Global South. As a reminder, here are brief descriptions of the scenarios:

1 "North End," named after Boston's North End, was described by Jane Jacobs (1961, 8–13) as the kind of bustling and lively urban space that represents cities that are at their most organically vibrant. Although it was widely regarded as a slum in the 1950s and 1960s, it possessed the social networks and skills to revitalize itself. This is the direction Saunders sees slums taking in the twenty-first century. While far from perfect, the areas of cities

that poor migrants move to serve as entry points where they can find a place in urban society. Digitalization offers new ways for poor migrants to establish social networks, which can lead to finding housing, social support mechanisms, and initial jobs.

2 "Jobless Panopticon" describes jobless city growth combined with the expansion of digital networks. The Panopticon is an architectural approach to prison building, first conceptualized by Jeremy Bentham in the late eighteenth century and later cited by Foucault (1977) as a mechanism for maintaining surveillance and control. In such a prison, the prisoners can always be observed, but they cannot see the observers. Because they never know for sure whether they are being observed, they behave as if they are always under observation. In this scenario, digitalization does not bring formal jobs, but it does bring the opportunity for people to network, and stay in contact with one another, and for communities and the state to monitor urban refugees' activities. The idea of a Panopticon is not inherently "bad," although passive surveillance can stifle freedom if it is deployed for that purpose. Instead of fostering a "bad/good" dichotomy, what digital technology does on an unmatched scale is create generally accepted modes of behaviour within communities. Indeed, social digital networks in slums and arrival neighbourhoods can keep track of who comes and goes as a means to increase safety.

3 "Lonely Hustle" refers to a city where urban refugees may find formalized work through digital means such as driving for Uber or Grab, or doing menial computing tasks like training machine-learning software, and are highly socially atomized through this work. The sense of community through work, and the requisite opportunities to innovate or combine skills, do not manifest themselves in this scenario. Jacobs would critique this scenario as representing a *planner's* city, that is, a thoroughly planned city in which there is no regard for the natural ways that urban spaces develop to encourage social networks and internal economic regeneration. The digital perspective on this kind of planning could be the modern smart city, where computing and digital connectivity aim to maximize the efficiency of how the city operates, possibly at the cost of making it a poor place for people to live.

4 "Rust Belt," named after the central northern urban industrial region of the United States that used to produce steel, is a city

where digitalization is not creating jobs (and may be costing them) and the population is not using digital technology to build any kind of urban society. Those who can leave are doing so, leaving behind cities with depleted fiscal capacity, brain drain, and limited resources to meet the needs of those who cannot leave. From a development perspective, this is a "bad" scenario. There is outward migration as people are forced to seek livelihoods elsewhere, as well as forced immobility for those who cannot leave but want to. There is probably not much that technological change can do to improve this situation.

Since these scenarios are based on urban theory, they allow us to bring the arguments about the nature of cities back into the picture. While the empirical data are useful for understanding trends or comparative differences among cases and across time, engaging urban theory within the scenario analyses provides a conceptual frame to support inductive reasoning. Unpacking how urban spaces and planning affect social behaviour and political organizing, both by urban refugees and by the host state, is necessary if we are to understand how technological change shapes human urban society. Without urban spaces, it would have been difficult for the Industrial Revolution to consolidate urban manufacturing the way it did, or for Black Americans to have the existing networks of information sharing and surveillance necessary to move from the South to the North during the Great Migration. The scenarios provide an apparatus for bringing together the at times disparate empirical, historical, and theoretical components of this book in a cohesive way that allows for complexity and variation in how technology fits into the localized aspects of urban refugees' lives.

NORTH END

Jane Jacobs (1961) and Edward Glaeser (2011) represent a tradition of scholarship that highlights the importance of cities as sites of opportunity as well as drivers of social and economic innovation and political evolution. Jacobs's work is echoed in Doug Saunders's (2010) analysis of cities in the Global South as both challenging places for refugees and migrants and hubs of opportunity for building new lives. Before getting into the analysis, it is important to remind readers that this is not an effort to romanticize slums and tenements. It can be easy to look back on working-class neighbourhoods and slums through rose-coloured lenses and find reasons why they were culturally, economically, and politically important to the developmental arcs of cities in high-income countries. We know what happened, and we can see how contemporary high-income cities' positive attributes evolved over decades out of poor neighbourhoods that were the first stops for displaced people on their arrival. In the case studies we can see how the neighbourhoods of arrival are self-regenerating and how historical examples link to these processes today. Digital technological change plays an important role in how regeneration takes place, as well as how urban refugee communities manage resources through formal and informal means and find ways to shape the cities and urban communities that exist around them.

Since the North End of Boston in the 1960s is what this scenario is named after, it is important to bear in mind that it too was a hub of immigration and immigrant communities. During the 1800s and into the early to mid-1900s, Irish, Jewish, and Italian immigrants settled in the neighbourhood; there was also a small community of free Black residents, and it was the location of Boston's first Black church (Goldfeld 2009; Sammarco 2007). Technological change helped set in motion the development of urban spaces for people displaced from either rural settings or their countries of origin. These communities created neighbourhood spaces that were often poor and that developed in haphazard ways, often outpacing sanitation and transportation infrastructure and generally fitting the common definition of a slum. However, what slums lacked in administrative planning they made up for in safety and community (see Jacobs's [1961, 29–74] chapters on the importance of sidewalks to the health of urban societies). I will focus here on the experience of Jewish communities in industrial Manchester and turn-of-the-century New York. As we saw in Chapter 3, Jews were a unique community in that they faced distrust, antisemitism, and xenophobia across time and geography. Cities provided Jews with a physical and social space to safely practise their faith and to contribute to urban society. This was particularly true in New York City, where young Jewish women were key labour organizers in the garment industry.

In historical terms, Manchester and New York City as places of arrival for displaced people were organized around industrial technological change that brought labourers into close contact. Digital technological change in the lives of urban refugees, especially technological change around internet software and devices, can bring people "together" beyond physical space. Does this inherently mean that North Ends will cease to exist? Not necessarily! The team in Bogotá with whom I ran the survey featured in that case study found that time spent in a neighbourhood had a significant impact on how the internet was accessed and used, especially via mobile phone (Martin-Shields et al. 2022). I described this in a blog post about the research as creating digital sidewalks (Martin-Shields 2020), in a nod to Wong's (2009) analysis of mobile phone use reflecting the size of a displaced person's urban footprint. In Bogotá, a newly arrived Venezuelan refugee would have had translocal networks of family and friends, but Bogotá would be a new social and economic space. Urban refugees need a reason to use the internet, and it takes time to get to know a city and neighbourhood after arriving; as one stays longer, opportunities for socializing and working increase, and so does the likelihood that one will use the internet to facilitate these. In the case of Bogotá, a comparatively welcoming environment for urban refugees compared to Nairobi and Kuala Lumpur, digital technologies smooth the way for urban displaced people to build connections with the host urban society.

In Nairobi, where urban refugees cannot integrate into host urban society with the same legal ease as in Bogotá, there is a similar phenomenon: robust community networks are built without the help or input of city authorities. In interviews, respondents from the Congolese and Somali communities noted that time and face-to-face contact were necessary for building individual and community relationships; these were then magnified online (Eppler et al. 2020). As noted in the Nairobi case study, the strategies for building and regenerating community networks were very different between the Congolese and Somali communities; but in both, digital technologies became significant after urban refugees had reached a point where they wanted to volunteer or contribute to activities at the community or neighbourhood level (Martin-Shields and Kuhnt 2022). Urban refugees in Nairobi do not have all the rights of residents, but even in the legal grey area they inhabit, they are still able to work with NGOs at setting up community organizations that connect community members to services and economic opportunities. Social media and chat software like WhatsApp make it easier for urban refugees in Nairobi to seek out opportunities for volunteer and community action, and as more and more of them participate digitally, the scope of online community organizing grows, which makes it still easier for new urban refugees to take part.

In Kuala Lumpur, the most legally closed city among my three case studies, regeneration through participation in community organizing is the only pathway along which digitalization uniquely affects urban refugees. Because of the paucity of support services, NGOs, and humanitarian aid, there are almost no donor-funded or internationally supported economic and financial inclusion programs. This is quite different from Nairobi, where aid and humanitarian organizations can support refugee-specific economic activities, and from Bogotá, where urban displaced people from Venezuela can now receive residency status and work permits. Because of the limited help that UNHCR Malaysia is able to provide, refugee-led organizations end up being tasked with helping urban refugees find jobs, education, housing, and health services. The best example of how digitalization can magnify the role of refugee-led organizations in such a legally constrained context was found in the Chin community. In an interview (8 November 2019), James Bawi Thang Bik, a Chin community focal point, described how the Alliance of Chin Refugees in Malaysia used Facebook as a quasi-community job board and WhatsApp and *imo* as messaging and archival tools for collecting evidence that refugees were being abused. The Chin organization's administrative and social infrastructure ran on social media – Facebook served as a community news service and archive, and Chin refugees used their smartphones to stream Christian sermons in their native language, which helped keep them spiritually healthy.

The North End of Boston as an example of urban self-regeneration in Jacobs's recounting included both physical and social processes. Through community networks, houses and buildings were repaired and infrastructure needs were met. It was a healthy urban society, one that was informal, that defied planning diktats, and that made sure the neighbourhood and its inhabitants survived and to varying degrees flourished. Technology's role in creating this kind of urban society – one heavily reliant on the arrival of displaced people – started on the industrial side in Manchester as people came seeking work and over time became an urban society. Technological change in the New York garment industry decentralized many labour processes but also created spaces for displaced people to advocate for their rights. Digital technological change for urban refugees, especially in contemporary cities in Global South, fosters new concepts of regeneration that are not necessarily bound to the physical neighbourhood where people settle. As we see in Nairobi and Kuala Lumpur, this often means archiving the experience of the community, thus building social continuity so that even if a community is displaced within a city of arrival the knowledge of how it functions economically, socially, and politically is archived in a digital space for those who arrive in the future.

JOBLESS PANOPTICON

Somewhere between Mike Davis's (2006) vision of permanent urban slums cut off from the financial capital that drives city growth and David Kilcullen's (2013) argument that growing cities will be centres of securitization in response to violence is a scenario in which digital technological change creates political unrest and the permanent exclusion of urban refugees from the processes of urban development. Note that there is always work to be done in cities, but the change from the nineteenth century over time to the twenty-first century has more to do with the nature of urban jobs. In Manchester the growth was in factory labour, which by the turn of the nineteenth century in New York City was shifting to a factory/sweatshop hybrid, and in the United States at least to a hollowing out of urban industrial cores during the 1970s and 1980s as industrial production moved out of city centres. Since the 1980s, cities in the Global North, including Manchester and New York City, have been reinvigorated – people have returned, property prices have gone up (and up, and up), and urban centres have become hubs of digital, creative, and financial industries. Cities like Nairobi, Bogotá, and to a lesser degree Kuala Lumpur are today being challenged to build robust economies without the legacy effects of two hundred years of manufacturing-based urban growth. In a digital world, how will the future's urban refugees fit into cities where manufacturing and industrialization are not the core drivers of job creation?

The idea of jobless urban growth – more accurately, a type of urbanization where formal work opportunities are limited and urban refugees/the urban poor rely on the small-scale informal economy to earn money – predates Mike Davis's work. Michael Todaro, whose work shaped so much of how development economics as a field understands rural-to-urban migration, was writing about this in 1997. Regarding urban development in Sub-Saharan Africa, he focused on the intersecting issues of planning and the split between formal and informal labour (Todaro 1997). Given how hard it is to find work in the formal economy, the informal small-scale economy is where urban refugees in the Global South are often forced to go. The historical lens can provide some perspective on the long arcs of technological change, urbanization, work, and surveillance. In the pre-industrial period, Manchester itself was not a metropolitan centre; it was only one town in a broader network of rural towns in Lancashire and Cheshire that were known for artisan cotton spinning. Pre-industrialization, the economy of what is now Manchester was largely a semi-formal artisan one. The factory was a key technological change that "formalized" the urban workforce. By the turn of the nineteenth century in New York, the technological and social structures of the garment industry were already bringing the labour of urban displaced people back into a formal/informal hybrid through contracted sweatshops. Labour organizing pushed back against abusive, dangerous working conditions, reinforcing workers' rights and workplace safety. Thus, even by the time the Rust Belt era had fully settled in across the US north and midwest, there was a fundament and tradition of urban industry and infrastructure as a basis for reinvigorating American cities.

Kuala Lumpur has perhaps the strongest laws restricting access to formal labour markets for urban refugees, so surveillance is the way that technology most often manifests itself in urban refugees' daily lives. While the ability to find work draws urban refugees to Kuala Lumpur, in interviews with refugees the themes of social connection and safety routinely came up. Digital technology was key to building community networks of protection and information sharing, as well as to linking the community to the UNHCR's Kuala Lumpur office. I will focus on a striking response from an interviewee in the Myanmar Muslim community (16 November 2019) about how community surveillance helped "bring people back from the dead." That was how the interpreter translated her answer, and I asked the respondent to elaborate. The response was based on a question about how the interviewee had gotten to Kuala Lumpur, and whether social media or her mobile phone had played a facilitating role. She said that both technologies played a role and that everyone used them in some way during their journey. She then expanded on her comment about coming back from the dead:

After the border crossing, her son had been separated from the group by the traffickers who had brought them across the border from Thailand. They sent her onward to Kuala Lumpur, and she already had WhatsApp contact data for family who were waiting for her there. Then the traffickers took her son's phone and he disappeared with the traffickers into the forest. Without a phone, or any way to know where he was, she described him as being dead – when someone disappeared without their phone it was not uncommon to never see them again. Six months later, this respondent recounted, she had received a WhatsApp message from a friend in the community saying that someone had arrived in the city and had asked if anyone knew where she was. The person was her son, who had spent six months incommunicado doing forced labour on a plantation. When he was released he hitchhiked to Penang, a city about five hours north of Kuala Lumpur, got hold of a mobile phone, and followed a trail of information on Facebook about how to find the Myanmar Muslim community organization in Kuala Lumpur. Once he found the community organization's physical office, WhatsApp messages were sent to community groups explaining who he was and who he was looking for. One of those messages reached his mom; with one WhatsApp message he was back from the dead. In Kuala Lumpur, digital technology was not creating new labour opportunities for urban refugees; instead it was keeping them visible to one another in a context in which the state refused to see or protect them.

In Nairobi, the idea of urban refugees using digital technology to be visible resonates as a theme, but given the more open (albeit still restrictive) legal conditions facing urban refugees, the nature and intent of visibility is different. Interviewees in Nairobi who were urban refugees said that digital technology made social and political organizing easier. As in Kuala Lumpur, most urban refugees in Nairobi live in peripheral areas of the city, and this meant that social media and messaging apps were key for reducing the organizational costs of living in different corners of a large city. Indeed, social and political organizing was important to the various urban refugee communities, since the choice to live in Nairobi placed them in a precarious legal situation. Nairobi offered more freedom and connection to the wider world than life in Kakuma or Dadaab refugee camp, but Kenyan law says that refugees should not reside outside the camps. Because of the laws that recognized asylum seekers and refugees, though, there was more space in Nairobi than in Kuala Lumpur for the UNHCR, NGOs, and donors to provide support to urban refugees. However, where Mike Davis saw the economic exclusion of urban refugees (and of the urban poor more broadly), in cities like Nairobi digital technology has created new reasons to come to a city and then work to shape it.

Except in the Somali community, which was running an internationally networked economy in Eastleigh, jobs were often not the primary thing urban refugees discussed in interviews when we asked how they used digital technologies. For them, digital technological change was facilitating new ways to magnify their political and social intent. It also helped them overcome the challenges of having to organize from different urban peripheries. Note that Mike Davis's book on slums and economic exclusion was published in 2006, at a time when living in a slum like Kibera meant far greater isolation from the rest of Nairobi and from other marginalized communities. While they have not radically changed the nature of work and economic inclusion for urban refugees in Nairobi, digital technologies do offer a powerful tool there for collectively organizing to push for changes to the laws that place labour and financial inclusion out of reach for many urban refugees.

Do we have a "jobless panopticon" in these case studies? Certainly not jobless; the urban refugees whom we surveyed and interviewed did indeed work, but this work was not tied to digital technological change. What we do see is that technological change is serving less and less as a driver of urban labour opportunity for displaced people. Manchester and cities like it from the late 1700s to the mid-1800s were filled by people seeking jobs. However, by the mid-1800s there was a growing labour movement seeking both better working conditions and full suffrage – that is, involvement in urban society was no longer just about coming to a city for a job. By 1900 in New York City, technological change in the garment industry had altered the social structures of labour so that spaces of work were also where people lived and organized themselves politically. Identity – for example, being a woman from the Eastern European Jewish community – played as great a role as work opportunities in making New York City a city of arrival for displaced people. By the time of the Great Migration, the role of work as a draw to cities shared importance with the opportunity to participate fully in urban society politically and socially. Certainly, the opportunity to work under fair conditions was part of the calculus for Black Americans leaving the Jim Crow South, but the development of neighbourhoods like Harlem is indicative that cities offered the chance to create fully realized Black urban societies – something that was impossible in the South.

The case studies indicate that as digital technological change continues, work is no longer the sole motivation for urban refugees to move to cities. Indeed, digital technology has amplified the non-work aspects of life for urban refugees in Kuala Lumpur and Nairobi. For urban refugees in Kuala Lumpur, digital technology allows the various communities to organize and coordinate in parallel to the state. In Kuala Lumpur, an urban space in which the Malaysian state provides them with nothing, refugees can use digital technology to help their loved ones "return from the dead." It is also how communities organize social services. There is work in the city that would be unavailable in a rural setting, but more importantly there is a density of social and identity networks that provide safety and a sense of community in a country where all other avenues for integration are walled off. In Nairobi, where there is more space for interacting with the state, refugees use digital technologies to seek out involvement in community organizations and to advocate for a greater role in the life of Nairobi. This is not without risk; the Kenyan state has proven that it is willing to tolerate violence towards people politically considered "other" (van Stapele 2016, 2019), and the Malaysian government has its own history of using state violence against urban refugees when it is politically expedient to do so (Article 19 2022). This is not the first time that technology has changed social and labour structures and thus the politics of identity and class. The 1819 Peterloo Massacre of workers in Manchester, violent crackdowns on striking garment workers in 1909 in New York City, and race riots in US cities during the 1960s all took place in response to displaced people pushing for a fair and equitable space in urban society. It could well be that in the digital era, the social organizing and political activism that *followed* industrial technological changes in previous eras' labour structures now *presages* large changes in the digital labour system.

LONELY HUSTLE

This scenario most clearly reflects Mike Davis's vision of socioeconomic exclusion; it also runs contrary to Saunders's view that growing cities in the Global South remain places of possibility in an increasingly digital world. I noted in the previous section that Davis's work, which was rooted in a critical view of capitalism, would not have been able to account for how digital technological change affected social and political organizing among groups like urban refugees.

However, this type of organizing is taking place outside the context of labour or work. When we look back at technological change during industrialization in Manchester or the growth of the garment industry in New York City, we find that the technological changes brought large numbers of people together under shared social and labour conditions. Over time, labour and union movements built momentum, often having been organized by urban displaced people. Industrial technological change from the late 1700s to the early 1900s helped set the conditions that created a class-conscious, politically active labour movement by bringing large numbers of workers into factories and densely populated tenements. Digital technology that directly creates labour opportunities, particularly app-based gig work platforms like Uber and Task Rabbit, have the opposite effect: they atomize workers and in the process freeze out urban populations that are too poor to acquire things like driver's licences and formal bank accounts, or that are legally excluded from acquiring them. In this section, I will lean on the idea that technologies have politics and that these politics affect how the job-producing benefits of digital technological change are distributed.

Already in the late eighteenth century in the villages surrounding what is now Greater Manchester, the lonely hustle is evident in the distributed networks of artisans who were spinning cotton. Production was atomized, yet there were established communities around that mode of production, in the form of artisan workshops. Industrialization and the technological changes that led to factories and rapid urbanization disrupted the artisan structure of community. Emma Griffin's (2014) collection of personal histories from industrializing England often highlights the physical and social displacement people faced: children leaving home to work, young men and women leaving villages to work in rapidly growing cities, and the loneliness and trauma that often came with being poor or working class in early nineteenth-century England. For an urban worker, work in a factory could abruptly end, leading to work on the canal loading docks or in a different factory in a different city. For the first generations of urban displaced people in Manchester and other industrializing cities, technological change meant a lonely hustle (and often a dangerous one, given workplace safety standards). By the time Eastern European Jews began arriving in New York City, there was an established urban society. Young women like Theresa Malkiel, one of the Shirtwaist Strikers who took on the garment industry in 1909, were arriving not in rapidly expanding cities but in established urban centres that hosted a variety of urban societies. The development of the sewing machine atomized labour away from the factory, but workers stayed in the city, and this meant that contract garment workers, even though they were working in a decentralized production system, were still in close enough social proximity to organize in ways that artisan spinners and the first factory workers in Manchester could not. In the 1900s the hustle of working in New York's garment industry was still exploitive and dangerous, but it was also less lonely.

The invention and scaling of the sewing machine helps us understand how digital technology atomizes labour. Today, the social impacts of platform economies may look more like the transition from factory-based industrialization to distributed networks of contractors. Platforms like Uber make each individual a contractor while removing the physical closeness of the work space; how can drivers who are tasked individually by an internet-based app on their smartphones organize themselves? Mark Graham (2020) argues that the urban space is precisely where organization, regulation, and localization can change the power dynamics between platform workers and the technology firms that own those platforms. What does this mean for urban refugees in the Global South? In Nairobi, where Uber expanded rapidly, national laws barred urban refugees from accessing the licences, permits, and identification to earn money as drivers.[1] When the Kenyan government moved to regulate Uber and other ride-hailing platforms, Uber sued, claiming that requiring potential users to have a national personal identification number was discriminatory (Njanja 2022). It remains a hypothetical scenario, but if Uber were to win in court, and the burden to have a national personal identification number (PIN) were removed, would urban refugees sign up to drive for a transport platform? Could agencies like the UNHCR and NGOs working with refugees in Kenya set up initiatives directly with technology firms like Uber to include urban refugees as drivers? This type of arrangement would not be unheard of in Kenya; the Norwegian and Danish Refugee Councils have already funded and coordinated with SamaSource, a US-based outsourcing firm, to provide refugees in Kenya with internet-based tasks paying $1 to $2 per hour (ITC News 2018; Terdiman 2009).

Are inclusive labour rights and access to identification sufficient to bring refugees into the local digital economy? The evidence from Bogotá indicates that while social media are useful for job seeking, the digital space itself is not where urban refugees find work. Since the survey was completed in November 2018, the Temporary Protection Status (TPS) for Venezuelans who arrived after 2016 and before January 2021 has come into effect (Trompetero 2022). This program offers ten years of resident status, including access to health care and schools, as well as work permits and the opportunity to convert to permanent residency and apply for Colombian citizenship. However, because of the high rate of informal labour among Colombian citizens, opportunities for Venezuelans to enter the labour market are limited, and platform economies are unlikely to provide enough jobs even after Venezuelans gain the right to reside and work in Bogotá. The result is that urban refugees are looking for the same types of informal work already available to them but doing so with the help of WhatsApp groups and social media. The recent large numbers of Venezuelans traversing the Darien Gap between Colombia and Panama (Turkewitz 2022) indicate that even with the legal right to find work, and with a relatively robust digital sector, digitalization does not provide the economic foundation on which Venezuelan urban refugees will build urban societies in cities like Bogotá.

In Nairobi, Bogotá, and even Kuala Lumpur, urban refugees do find work, often in the informal sector. However, the digital sector, including platform economies like Uber that provide avenues for digitally mediated gig work, is for legal, practical, and financial reasons largely inaccessible to urban refugees. What I saw and heard in interviews was that far from being a lonely hustle, social media and messaging apps like WhatsApp helped urban refugees stay in contact with one another and vet and share opportunities for work. If this is mostly in the informal sector, even at a large scale like the economy of Eastleigh in Nairobi, it indicates that digital technological change is going to shape the role of urban refugees in the development of cities in the Global South through social or political rather than economic and labour processes.

RUST BELT

It is interesting that none of the case studies offered evidence that digitalization was weakening the draw of urban spaces for refugees. However, in light of what we see in the "Jobless Panopticon" and "Lonely Hustle" scenarios, what *could* be changing is the relationship between physical presence in a city and participation in that city's greater urban society. Some of this is driven by the local laws that govern and exclude urban refugees; but it could also be attributed to what migration scholars refer to as translocality. For digitally networked refugees who are by omission or commission excluded from local public and urban life, the city they physically inhabit is replaced by a wider community unbounded by geography. Unlike the American Rust Belt cities that experienced physical population loss and economic degrowth from the 1970s to early 2000s (Hartley 2013), urban refugees in Bogotá, Nairobi, and Kuala Lumpur could choose not to engage in local urban society in favour of engaging digitally with more meaningful translocal political or social networks in other cities.

The cases of Manchester in the early industrial period and New York City at the turn of the nineteenth century show how industrial technological change brought displaced people into the greater urban society of the city of arrival. Displaced people in Manchester were working in weaving factories or on the canal docks, settling in growing working-class sections of the city, and over time starting families and engaging in the early stages of labour activism and urban politics. In New York City, the booming garment industry created a demand for sweatshops, and later clothing factories, which served as both work and social entry points for Eastern European and Russian Jews who had fled pogroms in their home countries. Technological change created a physical gathering place in the city that evolved into an urban society, creating strong enough bonds among communities of displaced people that they were able to engage in confrontational labour activism and politics. The role of displaced people in shaping the politics, economies, and social structures of Manchester and New York City was rooted in spaces where labour took place, and industrial technology was key to creating the growth of these spaces.

The Great Migration is an example of a physical place being replaced by translocal networks as well as by the organizational and surveillance technologies necessary to let that happen. The Black experience in the mid-twentieth-century United States was one of official and unofficial segregation. While Black Americans did not face the official segregation and political terror of the Jim Crow South in northern cities, the legacy effects of redlining, public works projects built on top of Black neighbourhoods in cities like New York City, the unofficial exclusion of Black Americans from access to public goods like recreation areas (see Caro 1974 for more on the racialized planning of New York City infrastructure), and exclusion from higher-earning jobs in sectors like the garment industry meant that they still faced racial exclusion in the urban North. However, as explained in Chapter 3, the networks that made it possible to move North were themselves a technology. They linked Black Americans in the South to Black urban communities in cities like New York, Chicago, and Detroit, and they served to set up the journey and provide support to Black Americans on arrival in new cities. While there are elements of "place" in the experience of displacement during the Great Migration period – for example, neighbourhoods like Harlem served as hubs of Black urban culture – analogue networking technologies connected people who had shared experiences of racism, political violence, and economic exclusion. Harlem, as an example, is an important part of the history and development of New York City, but its existence is also indicative of the Black community's history of racial exclusion from the industrial, political, and social fabric of the city.

Perhaps the closest analogue for Harlem in the case studies is Eastleigh, the neighbourhood in Nairobi that is the economic and social hub of the Somali community. Like Harlem, Eastleigh plays a central role in the social, economic, and political functioning of Nairobi, but it is also a space that is a function of the racialized and securitized exclusion of both Somali refugees and ethnic Somali Kenyans. Eastleigh contributes up to 25 percent of Nairobi's GDP (Kebaso 2020), and its urban society also represents a node in a global community of Somalis who share familial connections, lived experiences of displacement, and the securitized politics and narratives about terrorism that shadow Somali communities in Nairobi and elsewhere (East African 2017). Eastleigh contributes heavily to Nairobi's economy, yet it is a separate urban society. To the degree that the Kenyan authorities and Somali community leaders have to deal with each other, they do, but beyond the borders of Eastleigh the influence of Somali urban refugees on Nairobi's urban society is limited. Through interviews with urban refugees from this community, we learned that the importance of the diaspora, and connections to family in Europe, North America, other parts of Kenya, and at home in Somalia, as facilitated by Facebook, Instagram, and WhatsApp, had as much if not more salience to Somali urban society than being physically resident in Nairobi.

Kuala Lumpur offered a starker example of translocality creating separate categories: there was life in the physical city, and there was participation in digitally mediated global communities. As in Nairobi, interviewees from the Somali community in Kuala Lumpur described the importance of international familial and economic networks, with digital tools like WhatsApp, *imo*, and Facebook making it possible to maintain these networks. I also observed that refugees in Kuala Lumpur created online "selves" on platforms like Instagram. During interviews in the Somali community in the Gombak area of the city, three young women from the community were with us at the row house that served as a community centre. They were dressed traditionally, with their heads covered. They exchanged greetings with me but otherwise we did not interact; over the course of the interviews they left the community centre. When I left the building and walked down the street, which had a large green space opposite the row houses, I saw a group of young women in Western clothes taking selfies. As I passed, they said hello and invited my colleague and me over; it was the same group of young women from the community centre, but now they were updating their Instagram profiles. It was not a formal interview, but when I asked about how they used Instagram, they explained how it was a space where they could build identities outside the constraints of life in Kuala Lumpur and the Somali community (interaction took place on 7 November 2019).

This was not the only example in Malaysia of young women using digital communities to establish translocal or merely self-organized online networks. During a focus group discussion with women from the Rohingya community, in a humorously subtle way, the fifteen- to eighteen-year-old daughters who had come with the mothers let us know they did indeed have active online lives. My female colleague and an interpreter were leading the discussion while I sat to the side and made notes. Facing my colleague sitting in a row were the women we were interviewing; the daughters were sitting behind the row of women (their moms) outside their field of vision, also facing my colleague and me. When we asked, "Do your children use social media or the internet?," the mothers uniformly and confidently responded that they did not, and that it would distract from their prayer time and activities at the mosque. While the mothers were saying this, the daughters all smiled and gave one another conspiratorial looks, then looked straight at me and very subtly nodded to indicate that they were indeed using the internet and social media (focus group took place on 13 November 2019). The interaction was a humorous insight into the universal way that teenagers rebel, as well as a moment of private exchange that enriched what we were learning in the official interview with the mothers. We never found out what channels the teenagers were using;

there was no way to talk to them (our protocols did not allow us to interview minors), but it was enough to know that these teenagers had online lives that were meaningful to them and that existed outside the scope of their city and the community of which they were part.

Digital technological change in urban refugee contexts does not seem to create a feedback loop of decreasing labour opportunities and people moving out of cities. On the contrary, cities remain critical places of arrival for urban refugees. Cities provide a space for individual self-determination that camp settings do not; moreover, the density of support services, community organizations, social connections, and economic opportunities is unmatched in rural settings. And all of these things can be accessed legally – or illegally, in settings where urban refugees are not legally recognized – and do not require urban refugees to be part of the urban society of the city in which they physically reside. Indeed, being part of the local urban society, and having the opportunity to shape the politics and social aspects of a city to improve the quality of life for citizens, is out of reach for the majority of urban refugees in Nairobi and Kuala Lumpur, and only recently has it become legally possible for urban displaced people in Bogotá through the Temporary Special Protection (TPS) decree. For urban refugees who lack the right to participate in the political and social life of the host city, digital channels offer an opportunity to build a digital, translocal society in which they can participate in the unbordered politics and social processes that affect them. Yet those same channels fail to harness the social, economic, and political ambition that refugees bring with them to a new city. Cities like Manchester and New York were hubs of innovation, labour organizing, and cultural growth because urban displaced people not only physically resided in them but also contributed to their urban societies. Laws and policies that force refugees to live out the social and cultural parts of urban life online risk losing out on the transformative impact that urban refugees can have on urban society.

THE DIGITAL FUTURE FOR URBAN REFUGEES AND THE CITIES THEY CALL HOME

When we imagine a digital future for urban refugees and what that future holds for how they shape the cities in which they live, politics is the inescapable variable that indicates which of the scenarios we can expect to play out. Urban theory and histories of displacement help create a theoretical and empirical framework for understanding *what* happens when displaced people in urban spaces interact with industrial and surveillance technologies. *Why* different scenarios have a greater future likelihood is a function of the contested politics of human mobility that play out between urban society and the state. The openness (or lack thereof) of borders, the state's perceptions of security, the demands of capital for labour (and labour's ability to maintain class solidarity) – these all shape both how and how much urban refugees, through technology-mediated processes, influence the development of host cities. The reverse is also true – technological change shapes politics and interests, as when industrialization meant Manchester could be the global hub of cotton spinning, and when social networks and migration clubs made moving north a strong possibility for Black Americans. In both these cases, the politics of the time reflexively changed and adapted.

This contestation holds true in the contemporary world. When the Kenyan state cracked down on the digitally connected, translocal Somali community in Nairobi, that community's economic response was swift (Manson 2012). When banks saw millions of dollars leaving Nairobi, the contested politics of urban displacement in the digital world came into focus. Digital technologies, including social media and networked banking, shaped how the Kenyan state, the Somali refugee community in Nairobi, and capital all exercised their political interests. Without the digital connectivity to a global diaspora community, it would have been difficult for the Somalis to move money out of Nairobi, and the state would have found it easier to crack down without having to reckon with the interests of capital. Not every community uses size and capital to shape its role in the development of Nairobi – the Congolese, for example, navigate life's legal and economic challenges by blending in and living in heterogeneous neighbourhoods around the city. These strategies are shaped by context: the Somalis have capital and international networks that the Congolese do not, but the Congolese do not face intense othering and security politics from the Kenyan state the way the Somalis do. For urban refugees in Nairobi, digital technological change creates new avenues for collective local organizing – for example, sharing resources between refugee communities – while magnifying the ability of each community to implement its own survival strategy in the legal grey area that urban refugees occupy in Kenya.

When urban refugees cannot shape the political or social environment of the city in which they live, digital technology creates the opportunity to disengage from the host city in part or in total. What was so striking in Malaysia was how digital technology allowed refugees to build lives that were unconstrained by the geographic and legal limitations placed on them by the Malaysian government. It is important to say up front: this is not an optimal outcome! Urban refugees in Malaysia would have a much better quality of life, and the city itself would benefit, if refugee policy there promoted social and economic inclusion. However, there were moments in the interviews when refugees mentioned using digital technologies to meet their daily needs that are instructive here for imagining a future in which life in both physical and digital spaces will be harmonized in creative ways. This could manifest itself in work life; as one Pakistani interviewee explained, he could run an e-commerce business in the United States from Kuala Lumpur because he happened to have a US Social Security number and a small business registered in Florida from the time he studied there years before (interview, 6 November 2019). Education is another factor that arose in all the communities where we did interviews: there were computers in community schools, and good teachers, but the Malaysian state would not let refugees sit for their A- and O-Level exams. Why could a third-party country not allow registered refugees to sit their A- and O-Levels remotely? Laws and regulations that remain grounded in an analogue world of physical borders often stifle the creativity and innovation that digital technological change can provide for urban refugees.

But at the end of the day, is policy change enough in combination with digital technological change to make cities of arrival spaces of opportunity for urban refugees? The evidence from Bogotá since the survey in 2018 through the implementation of the TPS indicates that there is much more to the economics and sociology of urban refugees finding a place in urban society than just inclusive laws and technological innovation. Over the long historical arc of urbanization and urban displacement, I discussed two broad types of technology: industrial and surveillance technologies. When we look at the draw to cities in the 1800s and early 1900s, we find that industrial technology played a key role in setting the conditions for settling in cities: it created demand for labour. Industrial technology is also very tangible. A sewing machine is metal; it can be manipulated with one's hands, and when someone finishes using it there is a physical product. The development of urban centres as amalgamations of labour-intensive technologized manufacturing and physical spaces of arrival and opportunity for displaced people points to the conclusion that digital technological change should introduce a new wave of labour opportunity for urban refugees in the Global South's rapidly growing cities.

However, the data tell us that labour and work are only part of the story when it comes to digital technological change in the lives of urban refugees, and perhaps not the most important part of the story. Digitalization has fundamentally changed the nature of urban refugee societies from a networking and surveillance perspective. Surveillance technologies, including public demographic data, social networks like migration clubs, and ever-developing border crossing documentation, developed alongside tangible industrial technologies. The effects these technologies had on urban displaced people's daily lives in the 1800s through the mid-1900s are harder to see; social networks between displaced people existed over long distances and were managed using paper or analogue wire services. Turn-of-the-nineteenth-century labour organizers had to meet in person to plan strikes, and Black Americans wanting to move to the North often relied on church networks and surface mail to organize their trips. Now urban refugees politically organize in Nairobi using WhatsApp, making the long distances between refugee enclaves less of a problem. Urban refugees in Kuala Lumpur remain in one another's lives via video calls and voice memos, and community leaders can collect and archive digital records on smartphones to help newly arrived refugees register with the UNHCR.

Two hundred years ago, industrialization changed the structure of society in Europe and the United States by establishing a dynamic in which labour was the basis for social and political organizing for urban displaced people. Digitalization, and the ways that internet technologies enable large-scale organizing and surveillance, are combining to flip this process. Urban refugees in today's growing cities in the Global South are organizing in terms of the experience and identity of refugeehood; digitalization has removed the intermediary space of the factory floor or the sweatshop, creating direct channels for refugees to organize, network, and contest the politics of urban displacement globally.

10

The Future: Digitalization, Displacement, and New Urban Societies

At the end of the preceding chapter, we arrived at the argument that digital technology represents a new type of organizing apparatus for urban refugees. In cities like Bogotá, Kuala Lumpur, and Nairobi, urban refugees discussed coming to these cities because of the economic prospects, which is in line with long-standing theories of urban migration (e.g., Harris and Todaro 1970). However, digital technological change has introduced new ways that urban refugees can organize, engage in politics, and build urban lives both online and offline. The organizing, social networking, and class politics that used to centre on factory floors or working-class tenements housing urban displaced people can now take place online. This raises some important questions. What happens to the developmental arc of an urban society when urban refugees and displaced people organize around the identity of "refugee" instead of, say, organizing as members of the general proletariat? How will the physical urban space evolve if digital technological change does not lead to physical changes to the urban environment? This is no small thing: factories created the need for high-density housing, high-density housing created the need for water and electrical infrastructure, and so on. What happens to urban planning if urban refugees and the urban poor are no longer making physical settlement decisions based on proximity to places of work?

These questions are not meant to indicate that the changes a digital future will bring are "bad." Quite the opposite! There are new avenues for research, and new spaces for the economic development and humanitarian policy communities to rethink long-held assumptions about urbanization and forced displacement, as well as insights that can help citizens and policy-makers in the Global North understand how digital technological change is shaping high-income cities in new ways. What has been so fascinating from my perspective as a researcher has been the opportunity to engage on the topic of technological change and displacement across a variety of contexts and historical vantage points in doing this research. I have reflected on results in the data that help me understand the place where I grew up (the American South) in new ways and that help make sense of the unease everyone feels during systemic changes in economies and society.

NEW RESEARCH DIRECTIONS: TECHNOLOGY, URBANIZATION, ECONOMICS, AND HUMAN MOBILITY

This book's audience is primarily academics and researchers, so I will start this conclusion with a deeper look at possible future directions for research based on the data and analysis. In developing a conceptual framework and empirical strategy, I drew upon literature and research from urban studies, migration and refugee research, science, technology, and society, development economics, and economic history. It was fascinating to spend time exploring these fields on their own terms and seeing how the touch points between them helped me understand what I was seeing in the data and case studies. I will focus on the touch points between fields as the richest directions for future research on urban refugees and technological change, especially because those touch points are also the spaces where development and humanitarian practitioners work and, perhaps, where they can turn the book's scientific findings into action.

I did not draw heavily on political science literature in this book, focusing more on concepts rooted in sociology and development economics. One of the main conclusions in Chapter 9 is that digital technology changes the social and political organizing space of urban refugees as they arrive in a new city. Digital organizing is not done in spaces of physical labour, rather it takes place on digital messaging and social media platforms. It became clear from the interviews that participation in digital networking was based on national identity, or the identity of being an urban refugee, or both. Two strands of political science offer new avenues for understanding how urban refugee identity in digital organizing, as opposed to identity with the general urban working class, could affect the development of urban societies in the Global South. Jesse Acevedo and Covadonga Mesegeur's (2022) work on the historical effects of national identity formation in Mexico, which included the violent exclusion of Asian immigrants, can be linked over time to contemporary prejudice directed towards migrants. Andreas Steinmeyr (2021) examined how exposure to refugees can break down prejudices; among Austrians who spent extended periods in personal contact with refugees, the likelihood of voting for far-right, anti-immigration parties decreased. Social media can magnify these patterns; Bail and colleagues (2018) show how online exposure to different political views can increase polarization, while McGregor's (2018) work on digital personalized politics showed how voters change their voting heuristics when they rely on social media for information about candidates. If digital social networks are formed around the identity of "urban refugee" and there are reduced opportunities for contact between the refugee and host communities, will a risk emerge that urban societies become more politically polarized and exclusive?

This brings us to a second future line of research. Saunders (2010) and Glaeser (2011) discuss the importance of cultural and knowledge exchange as part of the ongoing process of the regeneration of urban societies. Opportunity is often framed from the perspective of better economic opportunities for migrants and displaced people, and it is the mix of new ideas and new identities that undergirds this. Can this be maintained, though, if urban refugees, by preference or by policy, are excluded from the social and cultural life of a city and in response nurture their cultural and social needs online? If we take Jacobs's (1961) and Massey's (2005) intellectual tradition of urban development and the health of cities as our starting point, then refugees living out their cultural and social lives online instead of as part of the host urban society will have deleterious effects on the advancement of the host city. But how much truth is there in this? Digitally hosted and mediated urban societies are hardly new, and for cities like Bogotá, Nairobi, and Kuala Lumpur, which have different historical and economic trajectories than their northern peers, digital social and cultural organizing could create rich new forms of urban refugee inclusion.

The third direction for research focuses on the city and capital rather than on urban refugees directly. The results from this line of research could tell us a great deal about how the new forms of digital refugee inclusion could manifest themselves. Mark Graham (2020) has done some of the most innovative work on platform economies in the Global

South, using the tools of political and economic geography to understand how digital economies affect economic prospects and inclusion. Something important we see in his work is the way that platform firms, which exist both in physical geography and in non-physical cyberspace, contest labour law, regulation, and market governance with national governments. Governments are struggling to figure out how to regulate platform firms and social media companies and are starting to do so more aggressively. Indeed, if we just take the example of Uber, the ride-sharing firm, two case study cities from this book are in countries that either have driven Uber temporarily from the market through regulation (Colombia) or are going to court over the issue of how these firms are to be regulated and classified (Kenya). This creates a fascinating space for urban refugees to engage with the digital economy, since the power relations between the firm and the state are not entirely aligned. Historically, capital and the state tended to align in opposition to labour, with the labour movement often being represented by urban displaced people. This leads to an interesting question: if, in the digital era, capital and the state become oppositional, does this create space for urban refugee societies that are organizing online and in physical urban enclaves to play off that opposition for their own benefit? We do not know yet, but critical political and economic geography approaches could help us understand how economic, regulatory, and political contestation is changing the context in which urban refugees organize.

ECONOMIC DEVELOPMENT AID AND THE DEVELOPMENTAL ARC OF CITIES

These academic questions are useful not only for expanding knowledge but also for supporting innovation in economic development and cooperation in urban settings. The economic development policy community plays a key role in setting the policy agenda around urbanization and economic development, and this, of course, has a significant impact on urban refugees. Large organizations like the World Bank and the European Union (EU), as well as bilateral development agencies, remain intensely involved in funding initiatives on urban development, migration and displacement, and digitalization. Digitalization and the future of digital work is another area that economic development agencies are involved in, although unlike humanitarian agencies their focus is often not on refugees specifically. The findings in this book help bring development aid work on urbanization, migration and displacement, and digitalization into closer discussion.

A key component of economic development theories of urban migration and displacement is the prospect of work and better wages in cities relative to rural settings. This is the basic assumption behind the Harris–Todaro (1970) model, one of the most important twenty-first-century models of urban migration in developing country contexts. This informs, although perhaps it should not, the logic of recent development policies focused on reducing irregular migration and displacement in the Global South. If cities are the places people move to for better jobs and wages, then supporting more jobs and better wages in the countryside will reduce people's desire to migrate. One example of this logic being used in policy action is the EU Trust Fund for Africa (EUTF), which has a specific component on job creation and economic inclusion that ties into preventing irregular migration and displacement (European Union 2022). But does this hold up in a modern urban, African economy? Harris and Todaro in 1970 were careful to note that their model accounted for the expectation of higher urban wages compared to known rural wages, not the guarantee of formal sector work. Blattman and Dercon (2018) found that efforts to create formal factory labour in Ethiopia did not lead to long-term employment and that survey respondents often preferred informal labour. Furthermore, the concept of the migration hump tells us that once a country moves from lower- to middle-income status, people living there are increasingly likely to migrate (Martin-Shields, Schraven, and Angenendt 2017; Clemens 2014). The evidence indicates that as we move deeper into the digital era, jobs and work may not play the same role in bringing people to cities, and keeping them there, as was the case in the industrialization period.

Development agencies and actors thus may need to think of technology and work in the lives of urban refugees in ways that are not rooted in a factory-based idea of urban displaced people settling into cities. Part of this is because digital technological change is unlikely to reproduce the volume of formal jobs that factory manufacturing did in the 1800s and early to mid-1900s. This change could force the field of development aid to look beyond jobs and wages as the main reasons for coming to a city, or staying there. Even in Manchester and New York City during their periods of rapid population growth, there were many reasons to come to a city. For work, yes, but also because of cultural and national connections, the opportunity to reimagine one's identity, and access to public services unavailable in places of origin. Digital technologies magnify these factors; jobs are important, but in a world where new technologies make it easier to build social networks and reimagine identities, cities offer far more than just work.

For generalist development agencies, urban refugees are probably too specific a population to build global policy around. However, the findings in the case studies, and what we see in the historical analysis, indicate that urban refugees are not the only people moving to cities who are doing so for reasons beyond work and wages. Engaging with the multiplicity of reasons people from different walks in life move to cities, and the role of digital technology in enabling their mobility, could help policy-makers identify heretofore underresourced services and aspects of city administration that could improve long-run prospects for urban refugees.

HUMANITARIAN AGENCIES AND DIGITAL TECHNOLOGY

Another group of practitioners who were instrumental in doing the research and data collection for this book, and who could make use of the results in a practical way, is the humanitarian community. While generalist development agencies may take the findings in this book and apply them in less concrete ways, there are direct applications of the findings for humanitarian practice. One policy area that affects urban refugees is the global shift away from encampments and towards self-reliance as residents in host countries. Digitalization will play a key role in this, as we saw in the Malaysia case, where refugees were doing significant amounts of self-organizing online. What mix of policy, political, and social changes will be needed to unlock the potential of ICTs and digital technologies in the humanitarian policy and practice space?

For urban refugees, self-reliance is likely to be the direction that humanitarian agencies focus on in the coming years. After an initial period where agencies like the UNHCR provide direct aid, the goal of self-reliance policies is for refugees to settle into cities or rural communities and be financially and administratively independent. How well this works in practice is an open question, and the degree to which digital technologies can support these processes is mixed. In the Malaysia case, where there were no legal pathways for urban refugees to access the city's services, ICTs and digital technologies could do little more than create parallel services within the refugee communities. Evan Easton-Calabria (2022) has been a leading voice in rethinking what refugee self-reliance and development mean from economic, social, and political perspectives and unpacking how the concept of self-reliance has evolved over time. Looking to the future, the role of secondary cities will grow when it comes to hosting urban refugees, and host countries will need to think about how resources flow to cities to support this. There will also need to be greater harmonization among refugee laws, immigration laws, and digital technology regulation so that regulatory gaps of the sort that appeared in Bogotá do not become the norm.

To achieve all this, institutions and agencies that provide humanitarian services to refugees will have to rethink how they do digitalization and innovation. Luckily, the UNHCR has already pushed forward in this space; its Innovation Service has expanded how it defines innovation to encompass institutional change within the agency and has begun to think about innovation in terms beyond technological artifacts. This is highlighted by reports such as Dragana Kaurin's (2020) "Space and imagination: Rethinking Refugees' Digital Access," a UNHCR Innovation Service–commissioned analysis of the spatial and architectural characteristics of refugee digital inclusion. And this is not simply about seeing the spaces that refugees live in; the UNHCR's Innovation Service is also running internal programs for UNHCR staff on digitalization and innovation across the global agency. Institutional innovation, in terms of how it sees the communities it works with and how it sees its own operations in the digital world, is only part of the story.

Humanitarian agencies have long stayed out of politics and avoided playing an advocacy role when comes to national laws and policies. This makes sense, to a degree; the UNHCR's national offices are not government agencies, and its staff are not elected lawmakers. That said, when governments wish to operate in good faith and find solutions to increase refugee inclusion, digital or otherwise, the expertise available in agencies like the UNHCR and the International Organization for Migration (IOM), and in NGOs like the Norwegian Refugee Council (NRC), can be directed towards helping create coherent whole-of-government refugee policy. In Bogotá, the problem was not that refugees lacked rights, or that they lacked access to ICTs and the internet. It was that the laws regulating residency and the ability to buy a SIM card or mobile phone failed to align, with the result that refugees were unable to easily get residence permits or a mobile phone.

The research in this book shows that refugee communities are exceedingly adaptive and will find creative ways to use digital technologies in daily life. They rarely need an international organization to create a new app or website for them. What they often do need is humanitarian organizations that are willing to engage with host-country governments in creating inclusive regulatory and legal environments in which refugees can be truly self-reliant and use technologies to act as full members of their host city's urban society.

WHAT THIS MEANS FOR THE EVERYDAY PERSON

When I started this book, I wanted to provide new directions for research and new insights for humanitarian policy and practice. But I also wanted to illuminate the ways in which digital technology in cities was fostering change in non-refugee contexts as well. Essentially, I wanted to make what I had learned from the contemporary experience of urban displacement and digital technological change accessible to an audience that might not be experiencing physical displacement but could still be feeling the unsettling changes arising from the digital world. I mentioned at the start of this chapter that doing this research helped me understand where I grew up, in the American South, and my personal history with cities, migration, and the socio-economic ladder. Engaging with histories of displacement and how those histories can inform today's theories of urban displacement was a chance for me to rethink how I go about providing policy advice in my daily work.

For someone living in the Global North who does not work in research or in humanitarian or development policy, the ways that urban refugees in Bogotá, Kuala Lumpur, and Nairobi are using digital technologies to get a foothold in the cities of their arrival may seem too abstract or far off to have any lessons. Yet we see lessons every day when we think about it. In the first year of the COVID pandemic, grandchildren could only talk to grandparents on FaceTime – relationships were maintained across space in ways that were not bound to physical location. It was disrupting, and it was a chance for people to think for the first time about how they would maintain intimate relationships across space if they were forced to leave home and settle in a new city. It is an unsettling proposition to think of such forced distance in a relationship, yet to varying degrees it became universal during the pandemic.

What do forced distance, the creation of translocal social and political networks, and the potential disconnect between physically residing in a city and engaging in community all mean for the future of cities of arrival in the Global North and Global South? While urban refugees in the Global South may face these questions in the most acute ways, digital technological change is also reshaping how we work, live, and build community in cities in the Global North. Because of the internet, the remote worker living in rural California now has something in common with a Pakistani refugee in Kuala Lumpur who is remotely running an e-commerce business in the US. How will urban societies reshape themselves in the digital era, as more people are on the move? History offers some perspective on what will happen, but we are not passive riders. We do not have to repeat the violent contested politics of displacement during the industrial period in order to build an inclusive digital society today. We can start now by recognizing how new constellations of contestation and sociopolitics around labour, human rights, and social inclusion are emerging. These will shape the future of cities in ways that will break down many of the legacy differences between cities in the Global South and the Global North, creating new opportunities for negotiating a more just world for people seeking safety and opportunity in the twenty-first century's digital metropolises.

Notes

CHAPTER ONE

1. While I focus on a European and North American migratory history, this is not done to exclude other regions. For example, the nineteenth and twentieth centuries featured mass movements of people in South and East Asia (McKeown 2004).
2. For more on the debates around the framing and narratives of modern migration, particularly from a critical perspective, readers can refer to Gerard Boucher's (2009) review article in *Third World Quarterly*, and Anna Boucher and Justin Gest's (2015) more recent article on the emerging problems with existing categorizations of migration classifications.
3. For an in-depth exploration of how large-scale urban infrastructure projects during the 1950s and 1960s not only destroyed urban neighbourhoods but also intentionally destroyed working-class and majority African American neighbourhoods, Robert Caro's (1974) historical biography of Robert Moses, the head of New York City's Tri-borough Authority, is indispensable.
4. The term "internally displaced person" (IDP) first entered into the broader policy debate in the early 1990s.

CHAPTER TWO

1. Quotes taken from the 2003 edition, translated by Robert Bononno and published in Minneapolis by the University of Minnesota Press.
2. Women also played a major role in driving rural and agricultural labour politics. Dolores Huerta has been a leader in agricultural labour organizing for decades and continues that work today, in her nineties.

3 Translocality is the idea that in a world with high levels of human mobility, social and familial networks are not embedded in single neighbourhoods or cities, but exist across geographies and are facilitated using various media. Greiner and Sakdapolrak (2013) cover the concept and theory of translocality in more detail.
4 I use the word "atomize" to describe the breakdown of communities and social networks – atomization in physical science is the breakdown of a substance into its constituent atoms. In the social sense, it is when a community breaks down into smaller units that no longer have social connections with one another. At its most extreme it can mean that individuals in a community no longer share social bonds.

CHAPTER FOUR

1 Palantir is a global data firm that got its start as a data and analysis software firm supporting clients from the global intelligence and military communities: https://www.palantir.com.
2 For example, in the late 1700s and early 1800s when industrialization was taking off, modern Germany did not exist; it was not until 1871 that the various German-speaking kingdoms, duchies, principalities, and free cities were merged into a single nation-state. Thus, there would not have been an administrative concept of German "national" citizenship.
3 At this point, the only people eligible for naturalization were White people and people of African descent.
4 Judith Kohlenberger's (2022) work on the paradoxes of asylum seeking is one of the best resources for understanding why being an urban refugee is so politically and sociologically complex, and is highly recommended for its handling of the sociological and conceptual complexity of asylum and refugee politics.
5 It is important to note that it was not just institutional lag and statutory problems that prevented more Jews from Germany, Austria, and Eastern Europe from getting immigration visas. The toxic mix of xenophobia, antisemitism, and isolationism in many of the Allied countries prior to the outbreak of the Second World War largely accounted for why many governments did not increase or eliminate entry quotas for Jews fleeing Nazi persecution. Law is not an objective system separate from politics after all.

# Notes to pages 93–141

CHAPTER FIVE

1. The survey was done in 2018, so this cohort would have moved to Bogotá in 2011 or later.
2. More on the SpeedTest app can be found here: https://www.speedtest.net/apps.

CHAPTER SIX

1. An Mbit is a volume of data that passes through a server or over a mobile phone connection, representing 1,000,000 bytes of information.

CHAPTER SEVEN

1. This counter-insurgency plan was named after General Harold Briggs, the British officer in charge of military operations during the Malayan Emergency.
2. Based on map data from MCMC, Greater Kuala Lumpur has somewhere between 50 and 55 percent of premises with fixed broadband access (MCMC 2022). This is just an estimate based on the shading of a map of Malaysia's states and federal territories available on the MCMC data dashboard.
3. Apps like TaskRabbit (https://www.taskrabbit.com) allow users to make requests for one-time short duration tasks, such as repair services, delivery, and transportation.
4. The mechanics of putting cash into an e-wallet vary. In Malaysia that can be done via bank transfer, giving cash to an agent, or receiving credit from someone via text message. In Kenya, the M-Pesa system uses a network of agents who take cash, note the amount, and then enter a code into a mobile phone. The code tells the M-Pesa computer system how much equivalent value in e-money to credit to a customer's M-Pesa e-wallet.
5. https://www.dbkl.gov.my/?lang=ms.

CHAPTER EIGHT

1. This was not part of an interview, and I do not remember exactly the day this conversation took place. It was sometime during the second week of February 2019, shortly after I arrived to do the research for this

chapter. It was a perfect crystallization of the simultaneous sense of opportunity and stress that I felt from everyone around me living in Nairobi.
2   OpenStreetMap is an open-source online map that users can add visual layers and indicators to, creating a community-designed geographic representation of a city or neighbourhood.
3   I only use his first name for privacy and safety reasons.
4   This restaurant is in the heart of Eastleigh, on the traffic circle of First Avenue and General Waruingi Street. While we were eating, a number of men who seemed to also be from the community leadership milieu passed by and chatted with us.

CHAPTER NINE

1   It is important to note that Uber's expansion into the Kenyan market involved a great deal of predatory pricing, aggressive tactics for signing up drivers, and abusive contracting practices (Sperber 2020).

References

1 World Connected. 2020. "Case Study: Kioscos Vive Digital." http://1worldconnected.org/case-study/kioscos-vive-digital.
Abuya, Edwin Odhiambo 2007. "Past Reflections, Future Insights: African Asylum Law and Policy in Historical Perspective." *International Journal of Refugee Law* 19(1): 51–95.
Acevedo, Jesse, and Covadonga Meseguer. 2022. "National Identity and Anti-Immigrant Sentiment: Experimental Evidence from Mexico." *Migration Studies* 10(4): 608–30.
Acosta, Luis Jaime. 2020. "Uber Returns to Colombia Less than a Month after Exit." Reuters, 20 February 2020.
Adeola, Romola. 2020. *Development-Induced Displacement and Human Rights in Africa: The Kampala Convention*. London: Routledge.
Alam, Khorshed, and Sophia Imran. 2015. "The Digital Divide and Social Inclusion among Refugee Migrants: A Case in Regional Australia." *Information Technology and People* 28(2): 344–65.
Albino, Vito, Umberto Berardi, and Rosa Maria Dangelico. 2015. "Smart Cities: Definitions, Dimensions, Performance, and Initiatives." *Journal of Urban Technology* 22(1): 3–21.
Alencar, Amanda. 2018. "Refugee Integration and Social Media: A Local and Experiential Perspective." *Information, Communication, and Society* 21(11): 1588–1603.
Alencar, Amanda, and Julia Camargo. 2023. "Spatial Imaginaries of Digital Refugee Livelihoods." *Journal of Humanitarian Affairs* 4(3). https://doi.org/10.7227/JHA.093.
Alevizou, Giota. 2020. "Civic Media and Placemaking: (Re)Claiming Urban and Migrant Rights across Digital and Physical Spaces." In *The SAGE Handbook of Media and Migration*, edited by Kevin Smets, Koen Leurs,

Myria Georgiou, Saskia Witteborn, and Radhika Gajjala, 489–502. London: Sage.

Anis, Mazwin Nik. 2020. "Rohingya Refugees Have No Right or Basis to Make Demands, Says Home Minister." *The Star*, 30 April 2020.

Article 19. 2022. "Malaysia: End Hateful Rhetoric against Rohingya Refugees." *Article 19* (blog). https://www.article19.org/resources/malaysia-end-hateful-rhetoric-against-rohingya-refugees.

Asabere, Stephen Boahen, Ransford Acheampong, George Ashiagbor, Sandra Carola Beckers, Markus Keck, Stefen Erasmi, Jochen Schanze, and Daniela Sauer. 2020. "Urbanization, Land Use Transformation, and Spatio-Environmental Impacts: Analyses of Trends and Implications in Major Metropolitan Regions of Ghana." *Land Use Policy* 96 (104707). https://doi.org/10.1016/j.landusepol.2020.104707.

Augustine, Abraham. 2022. "Mobile Money Interoperability in Kenya Has Its Work Cut Out." *TechCabal* (blog). https://techcabal.com/2022/07/22/mobile-money-interoperability-in-kenya-has-its-work-cut-out.

Aysa-Lastra, Maria. 2011. "Integration of Internally Displaced Persons in Urban Labour Markets: A Case Study of the IDP Population in Soacha, Colombia." *Journal of Refugee Studies* 24(2): 277–303.

Bail, Christopher, Lisa Argyle, Taylor Brown, John Bumpus, Haohan Chen, M.B. Fallin Hunzaker, Jaemin Lee, Marcus Mann, Friedolin Merhout, and Alexander Volfovsky. 2018. "Exposure to Opposing Views on Social Media Can Increase Political Polarization." *PNAS* 115(37): 9216–221.

Baillargeon, David. 2021. "Spaces of Occupation: Colonial Enclosure and Confinement in British Malaya." *Journal of Historical Geography* 73: 24–35.

Banki, Susan. 2004. "Refugee Integration in the Intermediate Term: A Study of Nepal, Pakistan, and Kenya." UNHCR (Geneva).

Beauchemin, Cris, and Bruno Schourmaker. 2005. "Migration to Cities in Burkina Faso: Does the Level of Development in Sending Areas Matter?" *World Development* 33(7): 1129–52.

Bhagat, Ali, and Leanne Roderick. 2020. "Banking on Refugees: Racialized Expropriation in the Fintech Era." *Environment and Planning A: Economy and Space* 52(8): 1498–515.

Bhattacharya, Prabir C. 2002. "Rural-to-Urban Migration in LDCS: A Test of Two Rival Models." *Journal of International Development* 14(7): 951–72.

Bidandi, Fred. 2018. "Understanding Refugee Durable Solutions by International Players: Does Dialogue Form a Missing Link?" *Cogent Social Sciences* 4(1). https://doi.org/10.1080/23311886.2018.1510724.

Birn, A.E. 1997. "Six Seconds per Eyelid: The Medical Inspection of Immigrants at Ellis Island 1892–1914." *Dynamis* 17: 281–316.

Blattman, Christopher, and Stefan Dercon. 2018. "The Impacts of Industrial and Entrepreneurial Work on Income and Health: Experimental Evidence from Ethiopia." *American Economic Journal: Applied Economics* 10(3): 1–38.

Boucher, Anne, and Justin Gest. 2015. "Migration Studies at a Crossroads: A Critique of Immigration Regime Typologies." *Migration Studies* 3(2): 182–98.

Boucher, Gerard. 2009. "A Critique of Global Policy Discourses on Managing International Migration." *Third World Quarterly* 29(7): 1461–71.

Braun, Trevor, Benjamin C.M. Fung, Farkhund Iqbal, and Babar Shah. 2018. "Security and Privacy Challenges in Smart Cities." *Sustainable Cities and Society* 39: 499–507.

British Library, The. 2014. "Manchester in the 19th Century." https://www.bl.uk/romantics-and-victorians/articles/manchester-in-the-19th-century.

Brunner, Karl. 1939. *Manual de Urbanismo (Bogotá, 1939)*. Edited by Arturo Almondoz. New York: Routledge.

Cabalquinto, Earvin. 2018. "'We're Not Only Here but We're There in Spirit': Asymmetrical Mobile Intimacy and the Transnational Filipino Family." *Mobile Media and Communication* 6(1): 37–52.

Calderón-Mejía, Valentina, and Ana María Ibáñez. 2016. "Labour Market Effects of Migration-Related Supply Shocks: Evidence from Internal Refugees in Colombia." *Journal of Economic Geography* 16(3): 695–713.

Caro, Robert. 1974. *The Power Broker*. New York: A.A. Knopf.

Castro, José Miguel Alba. 2013. "El plano Bogotá Futuro. Primer intento de modernización urbana." *Anuario Colombiano de Historia Social y de la Cultura* 40(2): 179–208.

Cecco, Leyland. 2019. "'Surveillance Capitalism': Critic Urges Toronto to Abandon Smart City Project." *The Guardian*, 6 June 2019.

Cecelski, David, and Timothy Tyson, eds. 1998. *Democracy Betrayed: The Wilmington Race Riot of 1898 and Its Legacy*. Chapel Hill: University of North Carolina Press.

Chambers, J.D. 1953. "Enclosure and Labour Supply in the Industrial Revolution." *Economic History Review* 5(3): 319–43.

Chavis, John. 1964. "The Artifact and the Study of History." *Curator: The Museum Journal* 7(2): 156–63.

Chouliaraki, Lilie, and Myria Georgiou. 2019. "The Digital Border: Mobility beyond Territorial and Symbolic Divides." *European Journal of Communication* 34(6): 594–605.

Cinnamon, Jonathan. 2014. "Deconstructing the Binaries of Spatial Data

Production: Towards Hybridity." *Canadian Geographer/Le Géographe canadien* 59. https://doi.org/10.1111/cag.12119.

Clemens, Michael. 2014. "Does Development Reduce Migration?" IZA Discussion Paper no. 8592. Bonn: IZA.

Cohn, D'Vera. 2015. "How U.S. Immigration Laws and Rules Have Changed through History." Pew Research Center. https://www.pewresearch.org/fact-tank/2015/09/30/how-u-s-immigration-laws-and-rules-have-changed-through-history.

Cortes, Sandra Patricia Ortiz. 2009. "Karl Brunner: Un retazo en la ciudad." Facultad de Ciencias Sociales, Carrera de Historia, Pontifica Universidad Javaeriana. https://repository.javeriana.edu.co/bitstream/handle/10554/6605/tesis133.pdf.

Dahir, Abdi Latif. 2017. "Kenya's Newest Tech Hubs Are Sprouting Outside Its 'Silicon Savannah' in Nairobi." *Quartz*, 23 August 2017.

Davis, Mike. 2006. *Planet of Slums*. London: Verso.

Déglise, Carole L., Suzanne Suggs, and Peter Odermatt. 2012. "SMS for Disease Control in Developing Countries: A Systematic Review of Mobile Health Applications." *Journal of Telemedicine and Telecare* 18(5): 273–81.

Dekker, Rianne, Godfried Engbersen, Jeanine Klaver, and Hanna Vonk. 2018. "Smart Refugees: How Syrian Asylum Migrants Use Social Media Information in Migration Decision-Making." *Social Media and Society*. https://doi.org/10.1177/2056305118764439.

de la Roche, Roberta Senechal. 1996. "Collective Violence as Social Control." *Sociological Forum* 11(1): 97–128.

de Wet, Chris, ed. 2006. *Development-Induced Displacement: Problems, Policies, and People*. New York: Berghahn Books.

Dye, Christopher, and Melinda Mills. 2021. "COVID-19 Vaccination Passports." *Science* 371(6535): 1184. https://doi.org/10.1126/science.abi52.

East African. 2017. "Eastleigh: Kenya's Global Somali Hub." *The East African*, 6 May.

Eastman Company. n.d. "Our History." https://www.eastmancuts.com/about/history.

Easton-Calabria, Evan. 2022. *Refugees, Self-Reliance, Development: A Critical History*. Bristol: Bristol University Press.

Elfversson, Emma, and Kristine Höglund. 2019. "Violence in the City That Belongs to No One: Urban Distinctiveness and Interconnected Insecurities in Nairobi (Kenya)." *Conflict, Security, and Development* 19(4): 347–70.

Eppler, Mirko, Stella Gaetani, Francy Koellner, Jana Kuhnt, Charles Martin-Shields, Nyat Mebrahtu, Antonia Peters, and Carlotta Preiss. 2020. "Information and Communication Technology in the Lives of Forcibly Displaced Persons in Kenya." Bonn: German Development Institute.

Ermakoff, Ivan. 2019. "Causality and History: Modes of Causal Investigation in Historical Social Sciences." *Annual Review of Sociology* 45: 581–606.

European Union. 2022. "EU Emergency Trust Fund for Africa." https://trust-fund-for-africa.europa.eu/index_en.

Filomeno, Felipe Amin. 2017. "The Migration–Development Nexus in Local Immigration Policy: Baltimore City and the Hispanic Diaspora." *Urban Affairs Review* 53(1): 102–37.

Fintech News Malaysia. 2022. "Fintech Report 2022: Malaysia Charts a New Path for Fintech Growth." *FinTechNews* (blog). https://fintechnews.my/31945/malaysia/fintech-report-malaysia-2022.

Flinn, William. 1966. "Rural to Urban Migration: A Colombian Case." University of Wisconsin Land Tenure Center.

– 1968. "The Process of Migration to a Shantytown in Bogotá, Colombia." University of Wisconsin Land Tenure Center.

Fordham News. 2017. "Tracing the History of Jewish Immigrants and Their Impact on New York City." https://news.fordham.edu/inside-fordham/faculty-reads/tracing-history-jewish-immigrants-impact-new-york-city.

Foucault, Michel. 1977. *Discipline and Punish: The Birth of the Prison*. Translated by Alan Sheridan. New York: Vintage Books.

– 1980. *Power/Knowledge: Selected Interviews and Other Writings 1972–1977*. Translated by Colin Gordon, Leo Marshall, John Mepham, and Kate Soper. Edited by Colon Gordon. Vol. 5. New York: Pantheon Books.

Fuller, Theodore D., Peerasit Kamnuansilpa, and Paul Lightfoot. 1990. "Urban Ties of Rural Thais." *International Migration Review* 24 (3): 534–62.

Fuseini, Issahaka, and Jaco Kemp. 2015. "A Review of Spatial Planning in Ghana's Socio-Economic Development Trajectory: A Sustainable Development Perspective." *Land Use Policy* 47: 309–20.

Gara, Larry. 1961. *The Liberty Line: The Legend of the Underground Railroad*, vol. 1. Lexington: University Press of Kentucky.

Gatrell, Peter. 2013. *The Making of the Modern Refugee*. Oxford: Oxford University Press.

Gawlewicz, Anna, and Oren Yiftachel. 2022. "'Throwntogetherness' in Hostile Environments." *City* 26(2–3): 346–58.

Georgiou, Myria. 2013. "Diaspora in the Digital Era: Minorities and Media Representation." *Journal on Ethnopolitics and Minority Issues in Europe* 12(4): 80–99.

Georgiou, Myria, and Koen Leurs. 2022. "Smartphones as Personal Digital Archives? Recentring Migrant Authority as Curating and Storytelling Subjects." *Journalism* 23(3): 668–89.

Gerring, John, and Lee Cojocaru. 2016. "Selecting Cases for Intensive Analysis: A Diversity of Goals and Methods." *Sociological Methods and Research* 45(3): 392–423.

Gershon, Livia. 2016. "How 19th Century Cotton Mills Influenced Workplace Gender Roles." *JSTOR Daily*, 3 April 2016.

Gibson, Campbell, and Emily Lennon. 1999. *Historical Census Statistics on the Foreign-born Population of the United States: 1850–1990*. Washington, DC: US Census Bureau.

Glaeser, Edward. 2011. *Triumph of the City: How Our Greatest Invention Makes Us Richer, Smarter, Greener, Healthier, and Happier*. New York: Penguin.

Goh, Ai Tee. 2022. Town Planning in New Villages in Malaysia: Case Study on Cha'ah New Village. ICOMOS Open Archive. ICOMOS Malaysia New Village Working Group, Kuala Lumpur.

Goldfeld, Alex R. 2009. *The North End: A Brief History of Boston's Oldest Neighborhood*. Charleston: History Press.

Gonzalez, Daniel. 2017. "Socioeconomic Stratification as a Policy for Segregation in Bogotá, Colombia." https://www.arcgis.com/apps/Cascade/index.html?appid=6419926a9b484562b746b74ffeaa0c58.

Gotham Center for New York City History. n.d. "Garment Industry History Initiative." https://www.gothamcenter.org/garment-industry-history-project.

Grab. 2022. "Grab." https://www.grab.com/my.

Grabska, Katarzyna. 2006. "Marginalization in Urban Spaces of the Global South: Urban Refugees in Cairo." *Journal of Refugee Studies* 19(3): 287–307.

Graham, Mark. 2020. "Regulate, Replicate, and Resist – the Conjunctural Geographies of Platform Urbanism." *Urban Geography*. https://doi.org/10.1080/02723638.2020.1717028.

Graham, Stephen, and David Wood. 2003. "Digitizing Surveillance: Categorization, Space, Inequality." *Critical Social Policy* 23(2): 227–48.

Grant, Keneshia. 2020. *The Great Migration and the Democratic Party: Black Voters and the Realignment of American Politics in the 20th Century*. Philadelphia: Temple University Press.

Gregory, James N. 2005. *The Southern Diaspora: How the Great Migrations of Black and White Southerners Transformed America*. Chapel Hill: University of North Carolina Press.

Greiner, Clemens, and Patrick Sakdapolrak. 2013. "Translocality: Concepts, Applications, and Emerging Research." *Geography Compass* 7(5): 373–84.

Griffin, Emma. 2014. *Liberty's Dawn: A People's History of the Industrial Revolution*. New Haven: Yale University Press.

Griffin, Oliver. 2020. "Residents of Bogotá Slum Facing Eviction Despite Quarantine." *Reuters*, 16 May 2020.

Grimmelmann, James. 2015. "The Virtues of Moderation." *Yale Journal of Law and Technology* 17(1–2): 42–109.

Grossman, James R. 1989. *Land of Hope: Chicago, Black Southerners, and the Great Migration*. Chicago: University of Chicago Press.

Gullick, J.M. 1955. "Kuala Lumpur, 1880–1895." *Singapore: Journal of the Malayan Branch of the Royal Asiatic Society*, vol. 28.

Hackl, Andreas. 2021. "Digital Refugee Livelihoods and Decent Work: Towards Inclusion in a Fairer Digital Economy." Geneva: International Labour Organization.

Hahn, Barbara. 2020. *Technology in the Industrial Revolution*. Cambridge: Cambridge University Press.

Harris, John R., and Michael P. Todaro. 1970. "Migration, Unemployment and Development: A Two-Sector Analysis." *American Economic Review* 60(1): 126–42.

Hartley, Daniel A. 2013. "Urban Decline in Rust-Belt Cities." Cleveland: Federal Reserve Bank of Cleveland.

Hirschman, Charles, and Elizabeth Mogford. 2009. "Immigration and the American Industrial Revolution from 1880 to 1920." *Social Science Research* 38(4): 897–920.

History of New York City Project. 2020. "Garment District." https://blogs.shu.edu/nyc-history/2020/04/26/garment-district-3.

Hornak, Leo. 2017. "The Word 'Refugee' Has a Surprising Origin." *The World*. https://theworld.org/stories/2017-02-20/word-refugee-has-surprising-origin.

Huff, Gregg, and Luis Angeles. 2011. "Globalization, Industrialization and Urbanization in Pre-World War II Southeast Asia." *Explorations in Economic History* 48(1): 20–36.

Ibáñez, Ana María, and Carlos Eduardo Vélez. 2008. "Civil Conflict and Forced Migration: The Micro Determinants and Welfare Losses of Displacement in Colombia." *World Development* 36(4): 659–76.

Ikanda, Fred Nyongesa. 2020. "The Snake's Head? Mistrust of Somali Refugees and the Encampment Policy in Kenya." https://www.bpb.de/themen/migration-integration/laenderprofile/english-version-country-profiles/318374/the-snake-s-head-mistrust-of-somali-refugees-and-the-encampment-policy-in-kenya.

Irazábal, Clara, ed. 2008. *Ordinary Places, Extraordinary Events: Citizenship, Democracy, and Public Space in Latin America*. New York: Routledge.

ITC News. 2018. "Connecting Somali Refugees and Their Kenyan Hosts to Online Markets." *eTrade for all* (blog). https://etradeforall.org/news/itc-connecting-somali-refugees-and-their-kenyan-hosts-to-online-markets.

ITU. 2020. "World Telecommunication/ICT Indicators Database." ITU. https://www.itu.int/en/ITU-D/Statistics/Pages/publications/wtid.aspx.

Jack, William, and Tavneet Suri. 2010. "The Economics of M-PESA: An Update." Georgetown University, Washington, DC.

Jacobs, Jane. 1961. *The Death and Life of Great American Cities*. New York: Random House.

– 1970. *The Economy of Cities*. New York: Vintage Books.

– 1985. *Cities and the Wealth of Nations: Principles of Economic Life*. New York: Vintage Books.

Johari, Amina. 2015. "Kenya's Konza Techno City: Utopian vision meets social reality." SIT Graduate Institute, Brattleboro. https://digitalcollections.sit.edu/isp_collection/2024.

Johnstone, Michael. 1983. "Urban Squatting and Migration in Peninsular Malaysia." *International Migration Review* 17(2): 291–322.

Kabbar, Eltahir F., and Barbara J. Crump. 2007. "Recommendations for Promoting ICTs Uptake among the Refugee Immigrant Community in New Zealand." *IADIS International Journal on www/Internet* 5: 73–85.

Kanwal, Faria, and Mariam Rehman. 2017. "Factors Affecting E-Learning Adoption in Developing Countries – Empirical Evidence from Pakistan's Higher Education Sector." *IEEE Access* 5: 10968–10978.

Karl, Robert. 2017. *Forgotten Peace: Reform, Violence, and the Making of Contemporary Colombia*. Berkeley: University of California Press.

Kaurin, Dragana. 2020. "Space and Imagination: Rethinking Refugees' Digital Access." https://www.unhcr.org/innovation/wp-content/uploads/2020/04/Space-and-imagination-rethinking-refugees%E2%80%99-digital-access_WEB042020.pdf.

Kebaso, George. 2020. "Cost of Eastleigh Lockdown on Local, National Economy." *Peoples Daily*, 8 May 2020.

Keeling, Drew. 2013. "Oceanic Travel Conditions and American Immigration, 1890–1914." Munich Personal RePEc Archive. https://mpra.ub.uni-muenchen.de/47850/1/MPRA_paper_47850.pdf.

Kemper, Robert, and Anya Paterson Royce. 1979. "Mexican Urbanization Since 1821: A Macro-Historical Approach." *Urban Anthropology* 8(3/4): 267–89.

KeNIA. 2022. "The Kenya National Innovation Agency." https://www.innovationagency.go.ke/about-us.

Kilcullen, David. 2013. *Out of the Mountains: The Coming Age of the Urban Guerrilla*. New York: Oxford University Press.

Kirchoff, Andreas. 2006. "50 Years on in Germany, Eastern Europe's Displaced Still Remember UNHCR." https://www.unhcr.org/news/latest/

2006/1/43bd42cb4/50-years-germany-eastern-europes-displaced-still-remember-unhcr.html.

Klier, John. 1989. "German Antisemitism and Russian Judeophobia in the 1880s: Brothers and Strangers." *Jahrbücher für Geschichte Osteuropas* 37(4): 524–40.

Kofman, Ava. 2018. "Google's 'Smart City of Surveillance' Faces New Resistance in Toronto." *The Intercept*, 13 November.

Kohlenberger, Judith. 2022. *Das Fluchtparadox: Über unseren widersprüchlichen Umgang mit Vertreibung und Vertriebenen*. Vienna: Verlag Kremayr & Scheriau.

Konza Technopolis. 2023. https://konza.go.ke.

Kramer, Anna. 2021. "Refugees Are Buying Groceries with Iris Scans. What Could Go Wrong?" *Protocol* (blog). https://www.protocol.com/policy/refugees-iris-scan-privacy-jordan.

Lee, Chang Siew. 1990. "Kuala Lumpur – from a Sanitary Board to City Hall." *New Straits Times*, 13 May.

Lefebvre, Henri. 2003. *The Urban Revolution*. Translated by Robert Bononno. Minneapolis: University of Minnesota Press.

Leurs, Koen. 2014. "The Politics of Transnational Affective Capital: Digital Connectivity among Young Somalis Stranded in Ethiopia." *Crossings: Journal of Migration and Culture* 5(1): 87–104.

– 2017. "Communication Rights from the Margins: Politicising Young Refugees' Smartphone Pocket Archives." *International Communication Gazette* 79(6–7): 674–98.

Levitt, Sarah. 1986. "Manchester Mackintoshes: A History of the Rubberized Garment Trade in Manchester." *Textile History* 17(1): 51–69.

Levy, Jack S. 2008. "Case Studies: Types, Designs, and Logics of Inference." *Conflict Management and Peace Science* 25: 1–18.

Library of Congress. 2014. "The Germans in America." https://www.loc.gov/rr/european/imde/germchro.html.

–. n.d. "Irish-Catholic Immigration to America." https://www.loc.gov/classroom-materials/immigration/irish/irish-catholic-immigration-to-america.

Lind, Jeremy, Patrick Mutahi, and Marjoke Oosterom. 2017. "'Killing a mosquito with a hammer': Al-Shabaab Violence and State Security Responses in Kenya." *Peacebuilding* 5(2). https://doi.org/10.1080/21647259.2016.1277010.

Lloyd, Martin. 2003. *The Passport: The History of Man's Most Travelled Document*. Stroud: Sutton Publishing.

Lloyd-Jones, Roger, and M.J. Lewis. 1986. "The Economic Structure of 'Cottonopolis': Manchester in 1815." *Textile History* 17(1): 71–89.

– 1988. *Manchester and the Age of the Factory: The Business Structure of Cottonopolis in the Industrial Revolution*. Beckenham: Croom Helm.

Malkiel, Theresa Serber. 1910. *The Diary of a Shirtwaist Striker: A Story of the Shirtwaist Makers' Strike in New York*. New York: Co-Operative Press.

Mann, Barbra. 2020. "History of Hospitals." https://www.nursing.upenn.edu/nhhc/nurses-institutions-caring/history-of-hospitals.

Manske, Julia. 2015. "Innovations Out of Africa: The Emergence, Challenges, and Potential of the Kenyan Tech Ecosystem." Vodafone Institute for Society and Communications. https://www.vodafone-institut.de/wp-content/uploads/2015/09/VFI_InnovationsAfrica_EN.pdf.

Manson, Katrina. 2012. "Big Money in Little Mogadishu: Ethnic Somalis Run a Thriving Informal Economy in Nairobi's Eastleigh Neighbourhood." *Financial Times*, 29 July.

Map Kibera. 2022. https://www.mapkibera.org.

Martin, A.M., and P.M. Bezemer. 2020. "The Concept and Planning of Public Native Housing Estates in Nairobi/Kenya, 1918–1948." *Planning Perspectives* 35(4): 609–34.

Martin-Shields, Charles. 2020. "Digital Sidewalks: Using Urban Theory to Understand Technology Use among Migrants in Bogotá." *Transient Spaces and Societies* (blog). https://www.transient-spaces.org/blog-digital-sidewalks-using-urban-theory-to-understand-technology-use-among-migrants-in-Bogotá.

– 2021. "Digitalization in Displacement Contexts: Technology and the Implementation of the Global Compact on Refugees." Geneva: UNHCR. https://www.unhcr.org/people-forced-to-flee-book/wp-content/uploads/sites/137/2021/10/Charles-Martin-Shields_Digitalization-in-Displacement-Contexts-Technology-and-the-implementation-of-the-Global-Compact-on-Refugees.pdf.

Martin-Shields, Charles, Sonia Camacho, Rodrigo Taborda, and Constantin Ruhe. 2022. "Digitalization and e-Government in the Lives of Urban Migrants: Evidence from Bogotá." *Policy and Internet* 14(2): 450–67.

Martin-Shields, Charles, and Jana Kuhnt. 2022. "Smart Phones, Better Neighbors? Technology and Social Cohesion among Urban Refugees." International Studies Association, Nashville, Tennessee, 31 March.

Martin-Shields, Charles, and Katrina Munir-Asen. 2022. "Do Information Communication Technologies (ICTs) Support Self-Reliance among Urban Refugees? Evidence from Kuala Lumpur and Penang, Malaysia." *International Migration Review*. https://doi.org/10.1177/01979183221139277.

Martin-Shields, Charles, Benjamin Schraven, and Steffen Angenendt. 2017.

"More Development – More Migration? The 'Migration Hump' and Its Significance for Development Policy Cooperation with Sub-Saharan Africa." Bonn: Deutsches Institut für Entwicklungspolitik.

Mas, Ignacio, and Daniel Radcliffe. 2011. "Mobile Payments Go Viral: M-PESA in Kenya." *Capco Institute Journal of Financial Transformation* 32: 169–82.

Massey, Doreen. 2005. *For Space*. London: Sage.

Matsaganis, Matthew D., Vikki S. Katz, and Sandra J. Ball-Rokeach. 2011. *Understanding Ethnic Media: Producers, Consumers, and Societies*. Thousand Oaks: Sage.

Maw, Peter, Terry Wyke, and Alan Kidd. 2009. "Warehouses, Wharves, and Transport Infrastructure in Manchester during the Industrial Revolution: The Rochdale Canal Company's Piccadilly Basin, 1792–1856." *Industrial Archeology Review* 31(1): 20–33.

– 2012. "Canals, Rivers, and the Industrial City: Manchester's Industrial Waterfront, 1790–1850." *Economic History Review* 65(4): 1495–523.

McDowell, Christopher. 1996. *Understanding Impoverishment: The Consequences of Development-Induced Displacement*. New York: Berghahn Books.

McGregor, Shannon. 2018. "Personalization, Social Media, and Voting: Effects of Candidate Self-Personalization on Vote Intention." *New Media and Society* 20(3): 1139–60.

McKeown, Adam. 2004. "Global Migration, 1846–1940." *Journal of World History* 15(2): 155–89.

MCMC (Malaysian Communications and Multimedia Commission). 2021. "Hand Phone Users Survey 2021." Malaysian Communications and Multimedia Commission (Cyberjaya). https://www.mcmc.gov.my/skmm govmy/media/General/pdf2/FULL-REPORT-HPUS-2021.pdf.

– 2022. "Facts and Figures – Interactive Dashboard." https://www.mcmc.gov.my/en/resources/statistics/facts-and-figures-interactive-dashboard.

Messer, C.M. 2021. *The 1921 Tulsa Race Massacre: Crafting a Legacy*. Cham: Palgrave Macmillan.

Meyers, Christopher. 2006. "'Killing Them by the Wholesale': A Lynching Rampage in South Georgia." *Georgia Historical Quarterly* 90(2): 214–35.

Mixed Migration Centre. 2020. "Urban Mixed Migration – Kuala Lumpur Case Study." https://mixedmigration.org/wp-content/uploads/2020/11/149_urban_case_study_KualaLumpur.pdf.

MinTIC. 2020. "Live Digital." https://www.mintic.gov.co/portal/inicio/English-overview/Vive-Digital.

Monet, Dolores. 2022. "Ready-to-Wear: A Short History of the Garment Industry." https://bellatory.com/fashion-industry/Ready-to-Wear-A-Short-History-of-the-Garment-Industry.

MPI (Migration Policy Institute). 2013. "Major U.S. Immigration Laws, 1790–Present." https://www.migrationpolicy.org/sites/default/files/publications/CIR-1790Timeline.pdf.

Mundia, Charles. 2017. "Nairobi Metropolitan Area." In *Urban Development in Asia and Africa*. Urban Book Series, edited by Yuji Murayama, Courage Kamusoko, Akio Yamashita, and Ronald Estoque, 293–317. Singapore: Springer.

National Museum of American History. n.d.a. "Atlantic Crossings." https://americanhistory.si.edu/on-the-water/ocean-crossings/liners-america/atlantic-crossings.

— n.d.b. "History of Sweatshops: 1880–1940." https://americanhistory.si.edu/sweatshops/history-1880-1940.

Ng'weno, Amolo. 2010. "How Mobile Money Has Changed Lives in Kenya." Seattle: Bill and Melinda Gates Foundation. https://docs.gatesfoundation.org/documents/mobile-money.pdf.

Nitsche, Lena. 2019. "Finding Digital Solutions to Local Problems, Kenya's Innovation Scene Is No One-Hit Wonder." DW Akademie. https://p.dw.com/p/3BhtL.

Njanja, Annie. 2022. "Uber Wants Court to Nullify Kenya's New Ride-Hailing Law That Caps Service Fee at 18%." *TechCrunch* (blog). https://techcrunch.com/2022/09/08/uber-wants-court-to-nullify-kenyas-new-ride-hailing-law-that-caps-service-fee-at-18.

Njeri, Mary Anne. 2015. "Institutional Factors Influencing Inclusive Education for Urban Refugee Pupils in Public Primary Schools within Dagoretti Sub-County Nairobi Kenya." Faculty of Education, University of Nairobi. http://hdl.handle.net/11295/90859.

Norwegian Refugee Council. 2017. "Recognising Nairobi's Refugees: The Challenges and Significance of Documentation Proving Identity and Status." Last updated 1 November 2017. https://www.nrc.no/globalassets/pdf/reports/refugees-in-nairobi/recognising-nairobis-refugees.pdf.

Nwabuzo, Ojeaku, and Lisa Schaeder. 2017. "Racism and Discrimination in the Context of Migration in Europe." Brussels: European Network Against Racism. https://ec.europa.eu/migrant-integration/library-document/racism-and-discrimination-context-migration-europe_en.

Nyabola, Nanjala. 2017. "Nyayo House: Unravelling the Architecture and Aesthetics of Torture." *The Elephant* (blog). https://www.theelephant.info/ideas/2017/08/17/nyayo-house-unravelling-the-architecture-and-aesthetics-of-torture.

O'Byrne, Darren J. 2001. "On Passports and Border Controls." *Annals of Tourism Research* 28(2): 399–416.

OHCHR. 1966. "Protocol Relating to the Status of Refugees." https://www.ohchr.org/en/instruments-mechanisms/instruments/protocol-relating-status-refugees.

Ombok, Eric. 2022. "Kenyan Mobile Money Gets Boost in Shift to Seamless Payments." *Bloomberg*, 8 April.

Ooi, Keat Gin. 2004. "Kuala Lumpur." In *Southeast Asia: A Historical Encyclopedia, from Angkor Wat to East Timor*, edited by Keat Gin Ooi, 138–9. Santa Barbara: ABC-CLIO.

Otiso, Kefa M., and George Owusu. 2008. "Comparative Urbanization in Ghana and Kenya in Time and Space." *GeoJournal* 71: 143–57.

Owuor, Samuel, and Teresa Mbatia. 2008. "Post-Independence Development of Nairobi City, Kenya." Workshop on African Capital Cities, Dakar, Senegal, 22 September.

Painter, Nell. 1977. *Exodusters: Black Migration to Kansas after Reconstruction*. New York: A.A. Knopf.

Parnell, Susan, and Jenny Robinson. 2006. "Development and Urban Policy: Johannesburg's City Development Strategy." *Urban Studies* 43(2): 337–55.

Pascucci, Elisa. 2017. "Community Infrastructures: Shelter, Self-Reliance and Polymorphic Borders in Urban Refugee Governance." *Territory, Politics, Governance* 5(3): 332–45.

Patterson, Jeffrey, and Koen Leurs. 2019. "We Live Here, and We Are Queer! Young Gay Connected Migrants' Transnational Ties and Integration in the Netherlands." *Media and Communication* 7(1). https://doi.org/10.17645/mac.v7i1.1686.

Pavanello, Sara, Samir Elhawary, and Sara Pantuliano. 2010. "Hidden and Exposed: Urban Refugees in Nairobi, Kenya." HPG working paper. London: Overseas Development Institute.

Pickstone, John. 1985. *Medicine and Industrial Society: A History of Hospital Development in Manchester and Its Region, 1752–1946*. Manchester: Manchester University Press.

Pines, Giulia. 2017. "The Contentious History of the Passport." *National Geographic*, 16 May 2017.

Porrúa, Miguel A. 2013. "E-Government in Latin America: A Review of the Success in Colombia, Uruguay, and Panama." In *The Global Information Technology Report 2013: Growth and Jobs in a Hyperconnected World*, edited by Beñat Bilbao-Osorio, Soumitra Dutta, and Bruno Lanvin, 127–36. Geneva: World Economic Forum.

Qarssifi, Wael. 2022. "Refugees in Malaysia Worry Government Tracking System a 'Trap.'" *Al Jazeera*, 11 August 2022.

Rimmer, Peter, and Howard Dick. 2009. *The City in Southeast Asia: Patterns, Processes, and Policy*. Singapore: National University of Singapore Press.

Rose, Michael E. 1971. "The Doctor in the Industrial Revolution." *British Journal of Industrial Medicine* 28: 22–6.

Rotich, Juliana. 2017. "Ushahidi: Empowering Citizens through Crowdsourcing and Digital Data Collection." *Field Actions Science Reports* 16: 36–8.

Rueda-Garcia, Nicolás. 2003. "Understanding Slums: Case Studies for the Global Report 2003 – Bogotá, Colombia." UN-HABITAT. https://www.ucl.ac.uk/dpu-projects/Global_Report/cities/Bogotá.htm.

Rushworth, Philip, and Andreas Hackl. 2022. "Writing Code, Decoding Culture: Digital Skills and the Promise of a Fast Lane to Decent Work among Refugees and Migrants in Berlin." *Journal of Ethnic and Migration Studies* 48(11): 2642–58.

Sammarco, Anthony Mitchell. 2007. *Boston's North End*. Boston: Arcadia.

Sanchez, Chelsey. 2021. "A Century Later, Garment Workers Still Face the Unfair Labor Conditions That Sparked International Women's Day." *Harper's Bazaar*, 8 March.

Sassen, Saskia. 2001. *The Global City: New York, London, Tokyo*. Princeton: Princeton University Press.

Saunders, Doug. 2010. *Arrival City: How the Largest Migration in History Is Reshaping Our World*. London: William Heinemann.

Schlebecker, John T. 1977. "The Use of Objects in Historical Research." *Agricultural History* 51(1): 200–8.

Science and Industry Museum. 2019. "Richard Arkwright: Father of the Factory System." https://www.scienceandindustrymuseum.org.uk/objects-and-stories/richard-arkwright.

Science Museum Group. 2022. "Spinning Mule." https://collection.sciencemuseumgroup.org.uk/objects/co8405253/spinning-mule-spinning-mule.

Scott, James C. 1999. *Seeing Like a State: How Certain Schemes to Improve the Human Condition Have Failed*. New Haven: Yale University Press.

Seto, Karen C. 2011. "Exploring the Dynamics of Migration to Mega-Delta Cities in Asia and Africa: Contemporary Drivers and Future Scenarios." *Global Environmental Change* 21(1): 94–107.

Seuferling, Philipp, and Koen Leurs. 2021. "Histories of Humanitarian Technophilia: How Imaginaries of Media Technologies Have Shaped Migration Infrastructures." *Mobilities* 16(5): 670–87.

Shadle, Brett. 2019. "Reluctant Humanitarians: British Policy toward Refugees in Kenya during the Italo-Ethiopian War, 1935–1940." *Journal of Imperial and Commonwealth History* 47(1): 167–86.

Shapshak, Toby. 2016. "Kenya's iHub Enters a New Chapter." *Forbes*, 11 March 2016.

Shuib, Liyana, Elaheh Yadegaridehkordi, and Sulaiman Ainin. 2019. "Malaysian Urban Poor Adoption of e-Government Applications and Their Satisfaction." *Cogent Social Sciences* 5(1). https://doi.org/10.1080/23311886.2019.1565293.

Shultz, James M., Ángela Milena Gómez Ceballos, Zelde Espinel, Sofia Rios Oliveros, Maria Fernanda Fonseca, and Luis Jorge Hernendez Florez. 2014. "Internal Displacement in Colombia: Fifteen Distinguishing Features." *Disaster Health* 16(2). https://doi.org/10.4161/dish.27885.

Siddiquee, Asiya, and Carolyn Kagan. 2006. "The Internet, Empowerment, and Identity: An Exploration of Participation by Refugee Women in a Community Internet Project (CIP) in the United Kingdom (UK)." *Journal of Community and Applied Social Psychology* 16(3): 189–206.

Simmons, Joel. 2016. *The Politics of Technological Progress: Parties, Time Horizons, and Long-Term Economic Development*. Cambridge: Cambridge University Press.

Söderström, Ola, Till Paasche, and Francisco Klauser. 2014. "Smart Cities as Corporate Storytelling." *City* 18(3): 307–20.

Sperber, Amanda. 2020. "Uber Made Big Promises in Kenya. Drivers Say It's Ruined Their Lives." *NBC News*. https://www.nbcnews.com/news/world/uber-made-big-promises-kenya-drivers-say-it-s-ruined-n1247964.

Stamp, Jimmy. 2013. "The Many, Many Designs of the Sewing Machine." *Smithsonian Magazine*, 16 October.

Stark, Oded. 1982. "On Modelling the Informal Sector." *World Development* 10(5): 413–16.

Starr, Paul. 1977. "Medicine, Economy, and Society in Nineteenth-Century America." *Journal of Social History* 10(4): 588–607.

Steger, Manfred B., and Paul James. 2019. "Outlining an Engaged Theory of Globalization." In *Globalization Matters: Engaging the Global in Unsettled Times*, edited by Manfred B. Steger and Paul James, 106–36. Cambridge: Cambridge University Press.

Steinmayr, Andreas. 2021. "Contact versus Exposure: Refugee Presence and Voting for the Far Right." *Review of Economics and Statistics* 103(2): 310–27.

Suruga, Tsubasa. 2022. "From Grab to Sea, ASEAN Tech Confronts End of Golden Decade: Investors Taste First Market Downturn as Unicorn High Wears Off." *NikkeiAsia*, 28 October.

Terdiman, Daniel. 2009. "Bringing Tech Jobs to Third World Refugees." *CNET* (blog). https://www.cnet.com/culture/bringing-tech-jobs-to-third-world-refugees.

Thompson, James D., and Frederick L. Bates. 1957. "Technology, Organization, and Administration." *Administrative Science Quarterly* 2(3): 325–45.

Todaro, Michael. 1997. "Urbanization, Unemployment, and Migration in Africa: Theory and Policy." Policy Research Division Working Paper no. 104. New York: Population Council.

Todeschini, Fabio. 2013. "Reflections on Some Aspects of Town-Building during the 1800s at the Cape of Good Hope, South Africa, of Relevance to Today." In *Urban Planning in Sub-Saharan Africa: Colonial and Post-Colonial Planning Cultures*, edited by Carlos Nunes Silva, 245–65. New York: Routledge.

Tøndel, Gunhild, and Kjartan Sarheim Anthun. 2013. "Statistics as a Technology of Governance: The Norwegian Need for Numbers and Numbers for Need." *International Journal of Sociology and Social Policy* 33(7–8): 474–90.

Trompetero, Maria Gabriela. 2022. "The Colombian Temporary Protection Status for Migrants from Venezuela: Novelty and Room for Improvement." *Routed*, 17 September.

Turkewitz, Julia. 2022. "The 66-Mile Trek from Despair to Uncertainty." *New York Times*, 8 October.

Tyson, Timothy. 2017. *The Blood of Emmett Till*. New York: Simon and Schuster.

Uduku, Ola. 2016. "Review: Architecture of Independence: African Modernism." *Journal of the Society of Architectural Historians* 75(4): 512–14.

UN E-Government Knowledgebase. 2022. "City Data: Kuala Lumpur." https://publicadministration.un.org/egovkb/en-us/Data/City/id/48-Kuala-Lumpur/dataYear/2022.

UNESCAP. 2022. "Malaysia's E-Government through a gender lens: Introduction." https://egov4women.unescapsdd.org/country-overviews/malaysia/malaysia%E2%80%99s-e-government-through-a-gender-lens-introduction.

UNESCO. n.d. "Kioscos Vive Digital Project – Digital Culture Activity." https://en.unesco.org/creativity/policy-monitoring-platform/kioscos-vive-digital-project.

UNHCR. 2022. "Kenya." https://www.unhcr.org/kenya.html.

– 2023. "Colombia." https://www.unhcr.org/colombia.html.

UNHCR Malaysia. 2022. "Figures at a Glance in Malaysia." https://www.unhcr.org/my/what-we-do/figures-glance-malaysia.

USHMM. 2022. "Refugee." https://encyclopedia.ushmm.org/content/en/article/refugees?series=137.

Valverde, Marianna. 1988. "'Giving the Female a Domestic Turn': The Social, Legal, and Moral Regulation of Women's Work in British Cotton Mills, 1820–1850." *Journal of Social History* 21(4): 619–34.

Van den Broeck, Jan. 2017. "'We Are Analogue in a Digital World': An Anthropological Exploration of Ontologies and Uncertainties around the Proposed Konza Techno City near Nairobi, Kenya." *Critical African Studies* 9(2). https://doi.org/10.1080/21681392.2017.1323302.

van Lunteren, Frans. 2019. "Historical Explanation and Causality." *Isis* 110(2): 223–400.

Van Noorloos, Femke, Diky Avianto, and Romanus Otieno Opiyo. 2019. "New Master-Planned Cities and Local Land Rights: The Case of Konza Techno City, Kenya." *Built Environment* 44(4): 420–37.

van Stapele, Naomi. 2016. "'We Are Not Kenyans': Extra-Judicial Killings, Manhood, and Citizenship in Mathare, a Nairobi Ghetto." *Conflict, Security, and Development* 16(4): 301–25.

– 2019. "Police Killings and the Vicissitudes of Borders and Bounding Orders in Mathare, Nairobi." *Environment and Planning D: Society and Space* 38(3): 417–35.

Vega, Diego Molano. 2013. "Colombia's Digital Agenda: Successes and the Challenges Ahead." In *The Global Information Technology Report 2013: Growth and Jobs in a Hyperconnected World*, edited by Beñat Bilbao-Osorio, Soumitra Dutta, and Bruno Lanvin, 111–17. Geneva: World Economic Forum.

Ventresca, Marc J., and John W. Mohr. 2017. "Archival Research Methods." In *The Blackwell Companion to Organizations*, edited by Joel A.C. Baum, 805–28. Oxford: Blackwell.

Vu, Khuong, and Kris Hartley. 2018. "Promoting Smart Cities in Developing Countries: Policy Insights from Vietnam." *Telecommunications Policy* 42(10): 845–59.

Wagner, F.E., and John Ward. 1980. "Urbanization and Migration in Brazil." *American Journal of Economics and Sociology* 39(3): 249–59.

Wairuri, Kamau. 2022. "'Thieves Should Not Live amongst People': Under-Protection and Popular Support for Police Violence in Nairobi." *African Affairs* 121(482): 61–79.

Wallace, Claire, Kathryn Vincent, Cristian Luguzan, Leanne Townsend, and David Beel. 2017. "Information Technology and Social Cohesion: A Tale of Two Villages." *Journal of Rural Studies* 54 (August): 426–34.

Wambua-Soi, Catherine. 2012. "Rising Xenophobia against Somalis in Kenya." *Al Jazeera*, 20 November.

Warner, R. Stephen, and Judith Wittner, eds. 1998. *Gatherings in Diaspora: Religious Communities and the New Immigration*. Philadelphia: Temple University Press.

Webster, C. William R. 2012. "Surveillance as X-ray." *Information Polity* 17(3–4): 251–65.

Weisner, Thomas S. 1976. "The Structure of Sociability: Urban Migration and Urban–Rural Ties in Kenya." *Urban Anthropology* 5(2): 199–223.

WHO (World Health Organization). 2020. "Fighting Fake Immunization Travel Certificates with Frontier Technologies." https://www.afro.who.int/news/fighting-fake-immunization-travel-certificates-frontier-technologies.

Wilkerson, Isabel. 2010. *The Warmth of Other Suns: The Epic Story of America's Great Migration*. New York: Vintage.

Williams, Bill. 1985. *The Making of Manchester Jewry, 1740–1875*, vol. 1. Manchester: Manchester University Press.

Williamson, Jeffrey G. 1988a. "Migrant Selectivity, Urbanization, and Industrial Revolutions." *Population and Development Review* 1(2): 287–314.

– 1988b. "Migration and Urbanization." In *Handbook of Development Economics*, edited by Hollis Chenery and T.N. Srinivasan, 426–65. Amsterdam: North Holland.

– 1990. *Coping with City Growth during the British Industrial Revolution*. Cambridge: Cambridge University Press.

Winner, Langdon. 1980. "Do Artifacts Have Politics?" *Daedalus* 109(1): 121–36.

Wong, Andrew. 2009. "The Impact of Mobile Phones on the New Urban Poor: Leaving an Urban Footprint?" *Journal of Urban Technology* 15(3): 25–38.

Woudstra, Rixt. 2020. "Planning the 'Multiracial City': Architecture, Decolonization, and the Design of Stability in British Africa (1945–1957)." PhD diss., Department of Architecture, Massachusetts Institute of Technology, Cambridge, MA. https://hdl.handle.net/1721.1/138587.

Yap, Ching Seng, Rizal Ahmad, Farhana Tahmida Newaz, and Cordella Mason. 2020. "Continuous Use and Extended Use of E-Government Portals in Malaysia." *International Journal of Public Administration* 44(15): 1329–40.

Yap, Lorene. 1976. "Internal Migration and Economic Development in Brazil." *Quarterly Journal of Economics* 90(1): 119–37.

– 1977. "The Attraction of Cities: A Review of the Migration Literature." *Journal of Development Economics* 4(3): 239–64.

Yew, Elizabeth. 1980. "Medical Inspection of Immigrants at Ellis Island, 1891–1924." *Bulletin of the NY Academy of Medicine* 58(5): 488–510.

Zeiderman, Austin. 2016. *Endangered City: The Politics of Security and Risk in Bogotá*. Durham: Duke University Press.

Index

Alien Enemies Act 1798, 74
Alliance of Chin Refugees in Malaysia, 139, 65
Ampang (Kuala Lumpur), 122–6
Antebellum period, 59
Association of Southeast Asian Nations (ASEAN), 19
Austria-Hungary, 54
autoethnographic, 97

Bangladesh, 33, 41, 121
Bangsar, 120
biometric(s), 16, 66, 76–80
Birmingham, 47
B'nai Brith, 56
Bogotá, 89–91, 92–3, 99–119, 172–3
Bolton, 48
Bosa, 99, 102–4, 117–18
Bretton Woods, 22
British East Africa, 142
Brooklyn, 29, 54
Brunner, Karl, 102–3

Cartwright, Edmund, 12
Chin (Myanmar), 133–9, 165
Ciudad Bolívar, 102, 104, 117

Civil War: American, 55–62; Colombian, 100
community internet projects, 89
Confederacy, 58
Congo/lese, 95, 144
contractors (garment industry), 57
Cottonopolis (Manchester), 48, 53
COVID-19, 41, 73, 104

Dadaab, 144, 168
Darien Gap, 173
Democratic Party, 13, 60–1
demographics, 14, 58, 61, 76, 96
Derbyshire, 49

Eastleigh, 9, 144, 154, 169
e-government, 100–1, 107–8, 112–15, 129
Egypt, 33
Emergency Quota Act (1921), 74–5
Engaged Theory, 10, 23, 97
Enhanced Border Security and Visa Entry Reform Act 2002, 76
ethical review, 96
European Union, 184
EU Trust Fund for Africa (EUTF), 185
e-wallets, 129, 146

Exoduster Movement, 59

Facebook, 94, 113, 132, 153, 165
factories, 44, 50, 57, 81, 171
famine, 54, 55
Federated Malay States, 123
Feynman, Richard, 29
fintech, 128, 146
First Industrial Revolution, 3, 12, 42, 44

garment industry, 53–8
gig economy, 8, 26, 39
Gombak, Kuala Lumpur, 122–6
Google, 34, 135
Grab (ride sharing firm), 110, 121, 128–30
Graham, Mark, 172, 183
Grammar of Moderation, 152–3
Great Migration: Black Americans, 45, 58–63; European, 12

Harlem, 175
Harris–Todaro model, 45, 185
Haussmann, Georges-Eugène, 69, 72
historical causation, 46–7
Huguenots, 78

iHub, 150–1
Immigration Act (1864), 74
Immigration and Nationality Act (1952), 75
Inclosures Acts, 12
information communication technology for development (ICT4D), 88
Instagram, 175–6
internally displaced person (IDP), 14, 93, 113

International Certificate of Vaccination and Prophylaxis (ICVP), 73
International Committee of the Red Cross (ICRC), 77, 91
International Organization for Migration (IOM), 6, 22, 187
Italo-Ethiopian War, 144

Jews: Ashkenazi, 54–8; in Manchester, 52
Jim Crow South, 59
Jobless Panopticon, empirical scenario, 38

Kakuma, 79–80, 144, 168
Kennedy (Bogotá), 102–7, 112, 118
Kenya National Innovation Agency (KeNIA), 147
Kioskos Vive Digital (KVD), 108
Klang, 122–3, 125–6; River, 122
Konza Technopolis, 150–1
Ku Klux Klan (KKK), 62

Lancashire, 49, 167
League of Nations, 75
Lemlich, Clara, 57
Lonely Hustle, empirical scenario, 38
lynching, 62

Macintosh, 50
Magnussen Act, 75
Malayan Emergency, 124
Malkiel, Theresa Serber, 4, 30, 171
Manhattan, 54, 57
Map Kibera, 148
migration clubs, 13, 60–1
mixed migration, 10–11, 43

mobile banking, 128
M-Pesa, 149–51
Myanmar, 121

National Origins Quota Act (1924), 75
Naturalization Act (1790), 74
Newcastle, 47, 70
New Villages, 124–6
North End, Boston, 163; empirical scenario, 38
Nyati House, 143
Nyayo House, 143

Oldham, 48–9
OpenStreetMap, 148
Organisation for Economic Co-operation and Development (OECD), 6, 22

país letrada, 102
país politico, 102
Pan-Africanism, 22, 142
Paris, 15, 22, 43, 69–70
Peterloo Massacre (1819), 170
Plan Vive Digital, 107
Potato Blight (1845), 56
Protocol relating to the Status of Refugees 1967, 78

ready-made clothing, 53–5, 64
reflective practice, 86
Refugee Convention (1951), 78
Rochdale, 48–9
Rochdale Canal, 51
Rochester, NY, 59
Romania, 54
Russian Empire, 54, 56
Rust Belt, empirical scenario, 38

Samasource, 146, 172
Scott, James, 59, 65, 80
self-reliance, 121, 133–4, 150, 186–7
sewing machine, 64, 172
sexual and gender-based violence (SGBV), 132–3, 136
Shirtwaist Strike, 4, 30, 57
Sidewalk Labs, 34
Silicon Savannah, 26
Singleton, Pap, 59, 61
Smart City, 34–5
Southern Diaspora, 13, 63
spinning mule, 49
steamship, 55
Steel Belt, 45
strata (Bogotá), 107
Suba, 104–7
sweatshop, 57, 166
Swettenham, Frank, 123, 126

Tahrir Square, 33
Techfugees, 157
Temporary Protection Status (TPS), 173, 177, 179
tenements, 26, 66, 70
thrownapartness, 91
throwntogetherness, 33, 91
Till, Emmet, 62
translocal, 33
Tubman, Harriet, 61
Tulsa, 62
Tunisia, 33

Underground Railroad, 59
Urban Footprint model, 33, 116
urbanismo, 101–2
urban society (Lefebvre), 27–8
Ushahidi, 147–8
Usme, 102–12

US Public Health Service, 73

Venezuela, Venezuelans, 109, 118, 130, 173

Wards Corner (Tottenham, London), 33
water frame, 49–50

Wilmington, NC, 62
World Bank, 22, 184
World Food Programme (WFP), 77

xenophobia, 53, 66, 72

YouTube, 5, 34, 135, 136